R Markdown Cookbook

Chapman & Hall/CRC
The R Series

Recently Published Titles

R Markdown Cookbook

Yihui Xie

Christophe Dervieux

Emily Riederer

C&H/CRC Press

Boca Raton and London

First edition published 2021
by CRC Press
6000 Broken Sound Parkway NW, Suite 300, Boca Raton, FL 33487-2742

and by CRC Press
2 Park Square, Milton Park, Abingdon, Oxon, OX14 4RN

ISBN: 9780367563820 (hbk)
ISBN: 9780367563837 (pbk)
ISBN: 9781003097471 (ebk)

To the most amazing cooks in my life, Xie Shaobai and Si Zhinan.

—Yihui

To my supporting wife, Caroline, and our lovely newborn, Axel.

—Christophe

To my mom, who taught me the joy of life-long learning.

—Emily

Contents

List of Tables

List of Figures

Preface

R Markdown is a powerful tool for combining analysis and reporting into the same document. Since the birth of the **rmarkdown** package (Allaire et al., 2020b) in early 2014, R Markdown has grown substantially from a package that supports a few output formats, to an extensive and diverse ecosystem that supports the creation of books, blogs, scientific articles, websites, and even resumes.

There is a wealth of guidance that has been written over the past few years, and the book *R Markdown: The Definitive Guide*[1] (Xie et al., 2018) provides a detailed reference on the built-in R Markdown output formats of the **rmarkdown** package, as well as several other extension packages. However, we have received comments from our readers and publisher that it would be beneficial to provide more practical and relatively short examples to show the interesting and useful usage of R Markdown, because it can be daunting to find out how to achieve a certain task from the aforementioned reference book (put another way, that book is too dry to read). As a result, this cookbook was born.

Despite the existence of the official documentation, R Markdown users often seek help on Stack Overflow, a popular Q&A forum. At the time of writing, there are more than 6,000 questions with the r-markdown tag.[2] This huge number means that the use of the forum can be difficult if you do not have a specific problem to search for. Therefore, it may be hard for you to realize all possible things that you could do with R Markdown or how to do them. This book aims to draw together popular posts from Stack Overflow and other online resources (such as blog posts or tutorials) to provide up-to-date solutions for everyday queries that users commonly make. In fact, to help us make decisions on the potential topics to cover in this book, the second author of this book, Christophe, has built an R Markdown dashboard to scrape Stack Overflow daily for the most popular posts. Hopefully, our cookbook can become more useful by including recipes from these popular posts.

---

[1] https://bookdown.org/yihui/rmarkdown/
[2] https://stackoverflow.com/questions/tagged/r-markdown

This book is designed to provide a range of examples on how to extend the functionality of your R Markdown documents. As a cookbook, this guide is recommended to new and intermediate R Markdown users who desire to enhance the efficiency of using R Markdown and also explore the power of R Markdown.

How to read this book

It is recommended that readers have a basic understanding of R Markdown. Chapter 2[3] of *R Markdown: The Definitive Guide* (Xie et al., 2018) provides an overview of the basics of R Markdown and is recommended background reading for any new users of R Markdown. For example, we did not cover Markdown syntax in this book, and expect readers to learn Markdown elsewhere. In particular, we strongly recommend that you go through the full manual of Pandoc[4] at least once. The manual is quite lengthy, but it is also a gold mine. You do not have to remember everything, but it will be very helpful if you are aware of the possible features of Markdown. For countless times, I have seen[5] people fail to write verbatim code blocks that contain three backticks, or list items that contain child elements. Without fully reading the Markdown syntax in the manual, perhaps you will never know or understand the rule "N + 1 outer backticks for N inner backticks" or "indent properly to indicate child elements."

We do not intend to provide a full technical reference for R Markdown in this cookbook. This cookbook aims to supplement, instead of replace, the existing literature. Therefore, readers may explore the following books if they want to seek further information:

- *R Markdown: The Definitive Guide* (Xie et al., 2018), the technical reference for all R Markdown output formats in the **rmarkdown** package and several other extension packages.

- Part V ("Communicate") of *R for Data Science* (Wickham and Grolemund, 2016). This part is less technical than the above "Definitive Guide," and hence may be a gentler introduction to R Markdown.

---

[3] https://bookdown.org/yihui/rmarkdown/basics.html
[4] https://pandoc.org/MANUAL.html
[5] https://yihui.org/en/2018/11/hard-markdown/

- *Dynamic Documents with R and knitr* (Xie, 2015) provides a thorough introduction to the **knitr** package (Xie, 2020d) (note that R Markdown is only one of the document formats that **knitr** supports). If you want to read a shorter version, you may find Karl Broman's minimal tutorial "knitr in a knutshell"[6] helpful.

- *bookdown: Authoring Books and Technical Documents with R Markdown* (Xie, 2016) is a short book as the official documentation of the **bookdown** package (Xie, 2020c), which is designed to simplify the creation of long-format documents in R Markdown.

- *blogdown: Creating Websites with R Markdown* (Xie et al., 2017) introduces how to create websites in R Markdown with the **blogdown** package (Xie, 2020b).

Where relevant, this book provides references to these existing resources. By the way, the official R Markdown website also contains a lot of resources that you may find helpful: `https://rmarkdown.rstudio.com`.

You do not need to read this book in a particular order. Later chapters are not necessarily more challenging than previous chapters. The chapters and sections that we consider to be more advanced than others are marked with an asterisk (*) in their titles. It may be most efficient to read this book when you have some specific tasks in mind that you want to do with R Markdown, otherwise you can thumb through the table of contents and see if you are interested in any particular parts. We have tried to make each section and example as self-contained as possible, so you do not have to go back and forth among different parts of this book. In some cases, cross-referencing is unavoidable, and we will refer you to the background knowledge required to understand a certain example.

If you want to try the examples by yourself, the full source code of this book and examples are freely provided on GitHub at `https://github.com/yihui/rmarkdown-cookbook`. If you are reading the electronic version of this book, you may also just copy and paste the examples from the pages and run them in your favorite editor.

---

[6]`https://kbroman.org/knitr_knutshell/`

Structure of the book

The book is broken down into small "recipes" that aim to demonstrate a single concept at a time. Chapter 1 provides instructions on how to install the necessary software tools. Chapter 2 gives a conceptual overview of R Markdown. Chapter 3 introduces the basic components of R Markdown, and how to convert between R Markdown documents and R scripts. Chapter 4 tells you how to generate certain document elements, such as page breaks, bibliographies, numbered figures, animations, diagrams, etc. Chapter 5 shows how to format content, such as adjusting the figure size and alignment. Chapter 6 introduces tips and tricks for those who only want LaTeX/PDF output. Similarly, Chapter 7 is for HTML users, and Chapter 8 is for Word users. If you want to produce output documents in multiple output formats (which is often tricky), you may find Chapter 9 useful. Chapter 10 is, to be honest, my least favorite chapter, but I know a lot of users really want to learn how to produce tables. I'm not an expert on fancy tables, but hope you will at least find the list of packages there helpful. Chapter 11 shows some applications of **knitr**'s chunk options that you may not know. Chapter 12 and Chapter 13 are a little advanced, but should also be very useful because they show you the great power of being able to control **knitr**'s output and behavior with custom hook functions. Chapter 14 introduces a variety of **knitr** tricks. Chapter 15 shows examples of using other languages in R Markdown, so you know R Markdown is not only for R. It also teaches you how to make **knitr** work with a new language that has not been supported yet. Chapter 16 introduces tips on managing projects related to R Markdown. Chapter 17 presents some tips on enhancing your workflow.

The recipes in this book are usually independent of each other, so you can pick up any one to read if you do not have a specific goal in mind.

Software information and conventions

The basic R session information when compiling this book is as follows:

```
xfun::session_info(c(
  'bookdown', 'knitr', 'rmarkdown', 'xfun'
), dependencies = FALSE)
```

```
## R version 4.0.2 (2020-06-22)
## Platform: x86_64-apple-darwin17.0 (64-bit)
## Running under: macOS Catalina 10.15.5
##
## Locale: en_US.UTF-8 / en_US.UTF-8 / en_US.UTF-8 / C / en_US.UTF-
8 / en_US.UTF-8
##
## Package version:
##   bookdown_0.20.2 knitr_1.29.4    rmarkdown_2.3.2
##   xfun_0.16.1
##
## Pandoc version: 2.10.1
```

We do not add prompts (> and +) to R source code in this book, and we comment out the text output with two hashes `##` by default, as you can see from the R session information above. This is for your convenience when you want to copy and run the code (the text output will be ignored since it is commented out). Package names are in bold text (e.g., **rmarkdown**), and inline code and filenames are formatted in a typewriter font (e.g., `knitr::knit('foo.Rmd')`). Function names are followed by parentheses (e.g., `blogdown::serve_site()`). The double-colon operator `::` means accessing an object from a package.

"Rmd" is the filename extension of R Markdown files, and also an abbreviation of R Markdown in this book.

Acknowledgments

As usual, first I want to thank my employer RStudio for giving me the freedom to work on this book. Since I started working on it, my weekly meeting time with my manager, Tareef Kawaf, was first reduced from 15 minutes to 5 minutes, and then the meetings were just canceled. I have heard from several friends that they have too many unbearable meetings in their institutions, which waste a lot of their time. In terms of managing distractions, one of them recently lamented, "You may be able to mute Slack for five minutes, but can you possibly mute it for *a whole day?*" "Of course, I can!" I told her. I can probably mute it for a whole month if I like. Do not get me wrong—I do not mean Tareef or my colleagues are distractions. I only mean how much freedom they can offer me.

I came up with the idea of writing this cookbook after I published the *R Markdown Definitive Guide*, but ideas are often cheap. It is the execution that is hard and expensive. If it were not for Michael Harper's[7] initial pushing, I would never have started working on it seriously. Christophe Dervieux has always been around whenever I need help. He used his R and R Markdown skills to build a dashboard (with the **flexdashboard** package) to guide me to the potentially interesting and useful topics to write on. Meanwhile, he has also helped me in numerous other GitHub issues, so I could have more time for writing the book, instead of spending whole days on wrestling with bug reports that do not have minimal reproducible examples attached. Similarly, several people have been helping with answering R Markdown questions on Stack Overflow, including Martin Schmelzer, Marcel Schilling, and Ralf Stubner. Perhaps it was not their intention to save me time, but their effort did save me a lot of time. Recently, Johannes Friedrich also came to my attention on Stack Overflow, after a few times when I opened a new Stack Overflow question only to find it already answered by him.

David Keyes saved my life in Section 10.3, since he had written a wonderful blog post[8] to introduce several R packages to create tables, with which I was not very familiar. Other online materials that have helped me a lot include Holtz Yan's post on some R Markdown tips,[9] Nicholas Tierney's book [R Markdown for Scientists,(https://rmd4sci.njtierney.com) Maëlle Salmon's R Markdown course,[10] Jennifer Thompson's R Markdown course,[11] Emi Tanaka's R Markdown workshop,[12] Alison Hill's R Markdown workshop[13] (co-taught with me), and Alison Hill and Emi Tanaka's R Markdown workshop.[14]

---

[7]http://mikeyharper.uk

[8]https://rfortherestofus.com/2019/11/how-to-make-beautiful-tables-in-r/

[9]https://holtzy.github.io/Pimp-my-rmd/

[10]https://github.com/maelle/rmd_course_isglobal

[11]https://github.com/jenniferthompson/RepResearchRMarkdown

[12]https://github.com/emitanaka/combine2019

[13]https://arm.rbind.io

[14]https://ysc-rmarkdown.netlify.app

Many people have made contributions in the GitHub repository of this book by either sending pull requests or filing issues, including Maria Bekker-Nielsen Dunbar, Nathan Eastwood, Johannes Friedrich, Krishnakumar Gopalakrishnan, Xiangyun Huang, Florian Kohrt, Romain Lesur, Jiaxiang Li, Song Li, Ulrik Lyngs, Matt Small, Jake Stephen, Atsushi Yasumoto, Hao Zhu, and John Zobolas. The marvelous cover artwork of this book was designed by Allison Horst[15] and the full cover was finalized by Kevin Craig.

The original idea of this book was partially motivated from a remote talk that I delivered to the RaukR Summer School in 2018, in which I introduced some lesser known features of **knitr**. The audience seemed to like those short introductions of **knitr** features, which were like recipes. I'd like to thank the organizers of the summer school, including Marcin Kierczak and Sebastian Dilorenzo, for inviting me. I have given similar talks later at Genentech and DahShu.[16] I want to thank Michael Lawrence and Yuqing Zhang for the invitations, as well as the audience of these talks, for their feedback. Paul Johnson published a very helpful critique of our book *R Markdown: The Definitive Guide* in the journal *The American Statistician* in 2020. He complained that the book lacked in-depth examples, therefore the definitive guide was not definitive enough. I truly appreciate and agree with his comments. I hope this new (cook)book can fill the gap.

This is the fifth book that I have published with my editor John Kimmel. It has always been a pleasure to work with him and the team at Chapman & Hall/CRC. I'm excited every time John tells me the new success of **bookdown** as it is more widely adopted by other authors. I feel honored to hear from John that Suzanne Lassandro, the production editor of my previous books, still tried hard to help with this book even though she has many other responsibilities and rarely works directly with authors now. Suzanne and our proofreader (Rebecca Condit) managed to identify "only" 377 issues in the our first draft. Apparently, I was too optimistic when I wondered last time[17] if I would have less than 30 issues in my next book. The LaTeX expert Shashi Kumar helped us fix a thorny LaTeX issue, which was our last obstacle before the PDF could be printed.

John reached out to several reviewers for their feedback on the manuscript. Eventually we received nine great reviews. One of them was so great that we could not help inviting her to co-author this book! It was a lot of work to deal

---

[15] https://github.com/yihui/rmarkdown-cookbook/issues/180
[16] http://dahshu.org
[17] https://bookdown.org/yihui/rmarkdown/acknowledgments.html

with the nine reviews, but it was definitely worth the effort. I'd like to thank all these reviewers for their helpful feedback, including Carl Boettiger, John Blischak, Sharla Gelfand, Johannes Friedrich, Atsushi Yasumoto, and other anonymous reviewers.

I worked on the last part of this book in the vacant house (without Internet!) of my good old neighbors, Dong Guo and Qian Jia, after they moved to another city. I'm grateful to them for letting me use their house as my temporary office to finish up the book when I felt rather exhausted and needed a quiet environment. It was sad to say goodbye to them. To me, this book, finished in their house, will also be associated with some of my fond memories of this family, including their parents and lovely little daughter.

Lastly, I will definitely not miss this unique opportunity to thank my two little "super helpful co-workers" (5 and 3) at home during the COVID-19 pandemic, without whom I could have published this book five months earlier. Now I miss the teachers at their daycare center (Small Miracle) and feel daycare centers are perhaps not that expensive...

Yihui Xie
Elkhorn, Nebraska

About the Authors

Yihui typed out most of the words in this book, which is the only justification for him being the "first" author. Christophe has made substantial contribution to this book by helping Yihui organize all the GitHub issues and occasionally writing a few sections. Emily was originally a reviewer of this book. Since Yihui was not patient enough to deal with her lengthy comments, he invited her to become a co-author of this book (out of revenge) to feel his pain of having to deal with so many additional things when he thought he was pretty much done! Just kidding... No, he invited her out of full appreciation, because her comments were so helpful, yet Yihui lacked the time to do all the improvements that she suggested.

When you see the pronoun "I" in this book, it refers to Yihui. Using "I" instead of "We" does not mean the co-authors were forgotten, but Yihui wanted to express certain opinions completely on his own. He certainly wants to appear smart, but in case he is actually silly, he wants to be silly alone.

Yihui Xie

Yihui Xie (https://yihui.org) is a software engineer at RStudio (https://www.rstudio.com). He earned his PhD from the Department of Statistics, Iowa State University. He is interested in interactive statistical graphics and statistical computing. As an active R user, he has authored several R packages, such as **knitr**, **bookdown**, **blogdown**, **xaringan**, **tinytex**, **rolldown**, **animation**, **DT**, **tufte**, **formatR**, **fun**, **xfun**, **testit**, **mime**, **highr**, **servr**, and **Rd2roxygen**, among which the **animation** package won the 2009 John M. Chambers Statistical Software Award (ASA). He also co-authored a few other R packages, including **shiny**, **rmarkdown**, **pagedown**, and **leaflet**.

He has authored two books, *Dynamic Documents with knitr* (Xie, 2015), and *bookdown: Authoring Books and Technical Documents with R Markdown* (Xie,

2016), and co-authored two books, *blogdown: Creating Websites with R Markdown* (Xie et al., 2017), and *R Markdown: The Definitive Guide* (Xie et al., 2018).

In 2006, he founded the Capital of Statistics (`https://cosx.org`), which has grown into a large online community on statistics in China. He initiated the Chinese R conference in 2008, and has been involved in organizing R conferences in China since then. During his PhD training at Iowa State University, he won the Vince Sposito Statistical Computing Award (2011) and the Snedecor Award (2012) in the Department of Statistics.

He usually reads Twitter messages once a week (`https://twitter.com/xieyihui`), and most of the time you can find him on GitHub (`https://github.com/yihui`).

He has four hobbies: reading, writing (mostly blogging), cooking, and playing badminton. He is actually more interested in cooking than eating. There are not many types of food that he cannot resist eating, and spicy food is one of the few. Since cooking is more fun, he rarely goes to restaurants. When he does go and is asked "how spicy you want your food to be" in the restaurant, he usually answers "as spicy as your chef can make it to be."

Christophe Dervieux

Christophe Dervieux is an active member of the R community, currently living in France. With a master's degree in energy and economics, he started working with R as an analyst doing economic studies about market designs, before becoming a developer advocate and R admin, promoting R and supporting R users where he works.

He is interested in helping others get the most from R, and you can find him wandering in the RStudio Community as a sustainer, or on several GitHub issue boards for various R packages. In both places, you may better recognize him by his shorter handle "cderv."

As an R developer, he is a contributor to several R packages, such as **bookdown**, **rmarkdown**, and **knitr**. He has also co-authored the **crrri** package. His own projects can be found on GitHub (`https://github.com/cderv`), and sometimes he shares his ideas on Twitter (`https://twitter.com/chrisderv`).

He does not like spicy food, but he enjoys playing badminton every week.

Emily Riederer

Emily Riederer works in data science for the consumer finance industry where she leads a team to build analysis tools in R and cultivate an open science culture in industry. Previously, she studied mathematics and statistics at the University of North Carolina at Chapel Hill.

Emily frequently discusses R on Twitter (https://twitter.com/emilyriederer) and in her blog (https://emily.rbind.io) and shared projects, including her **projmgr** R package, on GitHub (https://github.com/emilyriederer). She has also served as a package reviewer for rOpenSci and a founding co-organizer of the annual satRday Chicago R conference.

Emily's other interests include reading and weightlifting. She thinks she likes spicy food, but since she has only ever lived in the United States, she has been told that she does not really know what that actually means.

1

Installation

To use R Markdown, you have to install R (R Core Team, 2020) and the R package **rmarkdown** (Allaire et al., 2020b).

```
# install the rmarkdown package from CRAN in R
install.packages("rmarkdown")

# or install from GitHub if you want to test the
# development version
if (!requireNamespace("remotes")) install.packages("remotes")
remotes::install_github("rstudio/rmarkdown")
```

Unless you have a favorite editor or IDE (Integrated Development Environment), we recommend that you also install the RStudio IDE (https://www.rstudio.com). RStudio is not required, but it will make it easier for an average user to work with R Markdown because of the strong editor support. If you choose not to use the RStudio IDE, you will need to install Pandoc (see Section 1.1), which is the tool used by **rmarkdown** to convert Markdown to other document formats.

If you need to create PDF output, you may need to install LaTeX (Section 1.2) and certain LaTeX packages (Section 1.3).

1.1 Use a Pandoc version not bundled with the RStudio IDE

The RStudio IDE has bundled a version of Pandoc, so you do not need to install Pandoc by yourself if you are using the RStudio IDE. However, the bundled version is often not the latest, or may not be the exact version that you want. You can choose to install a separate copy of Pandoc by yourself. Please keep in mind that the bundled version may be more thoroughly tested with R Markdown, because most RStudio users may just use the bundled version. If you want to go with a different version (especially a higher version), you might run into problems that have not been discovered by other R Markdown users or developers.

There are detailed instructions on how to install Pandoc on different platforms on the Pandoc website at https://pandoc.org/installing.html. If you have installed Pandoc by yourself and want to use that specific version, you may inform the **rmarkdown** package by calling the function rmarkdown::find_pandoc(), e.g.,

```
# to find a specific version
rmarkdown::find_pandoc(version = "2.9.1")

# to find Pandoc under a specific directory
rmarkdown::find_pandoc(dir = "~/Downloads/Pandoc")

# ignore the previously found Pandoc and search again
rmarkdown::find_pandoc(cache = FALSE)
```

As you can see in the above code chunk, there are several ways to find a version of Pandoc. By default, rmarkdown::find_pandoc() tries to find the highest version of Pandoc in your system. Once found, the version information is cached, and you can invalidate the cache with cache = FALSE. Please see the help page ?rmarkdown::find_pandoc for the potential directories under which the pandoc executable may be found.

This function can be called either inside or outside an Rmd document. If you want an Rmd document to be compiled by a specific version of Pandoc installed on your computer, you may call this function in any code chunk in the document, e.g., in a setup chunk:

```
```{r, setup, include=FALSE}
rmarkdown::find_pandoc(version = '2.9.1')
```
```

1.2   Install LaTeX (TinyTeX) for PDF reports

If you would like to create PDF documents from R Markdown, you will need to have a LaTeX distribution installed. Although there are several traditional options including MiKTeX, MacTeX, and TeX Live, we recommend that R Markdown users install TinyTeX.[1]

TinyTeX is a custom LaTeX distribution based on TeX Live that is relatively small in size, but functions well in most cases, especially for R users. Installing or running TinyTeX does not require sysadmin privileges.[2] You can install TinyTeX with the R package **tinytex** (Xie, 2020e):

```
tinytex::install_tinytex()
# to uninstall TinyTeX, run tinytex::uninstall_tinytex()
```

Please note that "**tinytex**" refers to the R package, and "TinyTeX" refers to the LaTeX distribution. There are two advantages of using TinyTeX:

1.   TinyTeX is lightweight (compared to other LaTeX distributions), cross-platform, and portable. For example, you can store a copy of TinyTeX on your USB drive or other portable devices, and use it on other computers with the same operating system.

2.   When R Markdown is converted to PDF, Pandoc converts Markdown to an intermediate LaTeX document first. The R package **tinytex** has provided helper functions to compile LaTeX documents to PDF (the main function is `tinytex::latexmk()`). If you use TinyTeX and certain LaTeX packages are required but not installed, **tinytex** will try to automatically install them for you. It will also try to compile the LaTeX file for a sufficient number of times to make sure all cross-references are resolved.

If you are interested in the technical details, you may check out the article Xie (2019b) and the FAQ page at `https://yihui.org/tinytex/faq/`.

---

[1] `https://yihui.org/tinytex/`

[2] Actually, we recommend that you **do not** use your root privilege (i.e., sudo) to install TinyTeX on Linux or macOS, if you are the only user of your system.

1.3   Install missing LaTeX packages

When you compile a document to PDF through LaTeX, you may run into errors like these:

```
! LaTeX Error: File `ocgbase.sty' not found.

!pdfTeX error: pdflatex (file 8r.enc):
  cannot open encoding file for reading

!pdfTeX error: /usr/local/bin/pdflatex (file tcrm0700):
  Font tcrm0700 at 600 not found
```

If you are using TinyTeX as introduced in Section 1.2, usually you do not need to deal with such errors, since **tinytex** (Xie, 2020e) will automatically deal with them, but if you run into such errors anyway, it is still easy to install the missing LaTeX package(s) via `tinytex::parse_install()`. This function takes the path of the LaTeX log file as the input, tries to figure out the missing packages automatically, and installs them if they are found on CTAN (the Comprehensive TEX Archive Network, `https://ctan.org`). The LaTeX log file typically has the same base name as your input document, and has an extension .log. If you cannot find this log file, you can pass the error message to the `text` argument of this function. Both ways should work:

```
# if the log file is filename.log
tinytex::parse_install("filename.log")

# or use the `text` argument
tinytex::parse_install(
  text = "! LaTeX Error: File `ocgbase.sty' not found."
)
# it will install the "ocgx2" package
```

If you do not use TinyTeX, the R package **tinytex** can still help you figure out the LaTeX package names from the error log—use the function `tinytex::parse_packages()`, e.g.,

```
# if the log file is filename.log
tinytex::parse_packages("filename.log")

# or use the `text` argument
tinytex::parse_packages(
  text = "! LaTeX Error: File `ocgbase.sty' not found."
)
# it should return "ocgx2"
```

Once you know the package names, you can install them with the package manager of your LaTeX distribution.

If you are using MiKTeX instead, it can also install missing packages automatically. During the installation of MiKTeX, be sure to check the setting "Always install missing packages on-the-fly." If you have already installed it without this setting, you can still change it in the MiKTeX Console.[3]

---

[3]https://github.com/rstudio/rmarkdown/issues/1285#issuecomment-374340175

2

Conceptual Overview

The goal of this text is to showcase many tips and tricks for getting the most value from R Markdown. The following chapters demonstrate techniques to write more efficient and succinct code and to customize your output. Before we begin, it may be helpful to learn just a bit more about how R Markdown works, to help you to understand, remember, apply, and "remix" these tricks. In this section, we provide a brief overview of the process of knitting a document and the "key levers to pull" to change the output. This material is not necessary to understand the subsequent chapters (so feel free to skip ahead!), but it may help you to build a richer mental model for how all the pieces fit together.

2.1 What happens when we render?

R Markdown combines several different processes together to create documents, and one of the main sources of confusion from R Markdown is how all the components work together.[1] Fortunately, as a user, it is not essential to understand all the inner workings of these processes to be able to create documents. However, as a user who may be seeking to alter the behavior of a document, it is important to understand which component is responsible for what. This makes it a lot easier to seek help as you can target your searches on the correct area.

The basic workflow structure for an R Markdown document is shown in Figure 2.1, highlighting the steps (arrows) and the intermediate files that are created before producing the output. The whole process is implemented via

---

[1] Allison Horst has created an amusing artwork that describes the R Markdown process as wizardry: https://github.com/allisonhorst/stats-illustrations/raw/master/rstats-artwork/rmarkdown_wizards.png. As a matter of fact, the cover image of this book was adapted from this artwork.

the function `rmarkdown::render()`. Each stage is explained in further detail below.

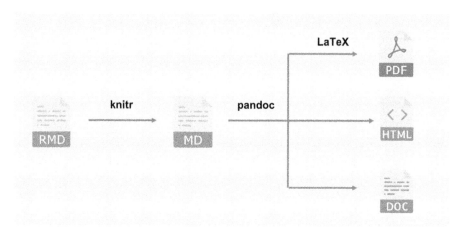

FIGURE 2.1: A diagram illustrating how an R Markdown document is converted to the final output document.

The `.Rmd` document is the original format of the document. It contains a combination of YAML (metadata), text (narratives), and code chunks.

First, the `knit()` function in **knitr** (Xie, 2020d) is used to execute all code embedded within the `.Rmd` file, and prepare the code output to be displayed within the output document. All these results are converted into the correct markup language to be contained within the temporary `.md` file.

Then the `.md` file is processed by Pandoc, a multipurpose tool designed to convert files from one markup language to another. It takes any parameters specified within the YAML frontmatter of the document (e.g., `title`, `author`, and `date`) to convert the document to the output format specified in the `output` parameter (such as `html_document` for HTML output).

If the output format is PDF, there is an additional layer of processing, as Pandoc will convert the intermediate `.md` file into an intermediate `.tex` file. This file is then processed by LaTeX to form the final PDF document. As we mentioned in Section 1.2, the **rmarkdown** package calls the `latexmk()` function in the **tinytex** package (Xie, 2020e), which in turn calls LaTeX to compile `.tex` to `.pdf`.

In short, `rmarkdown::render()` = `knitr::knit()` + Pandoc (+ LaTeX for PDF output only).

Robin Linacre has written a nice summary of the relationship between R Markdown, **knitr**, and Pandoc at `https://stackoverflow.com/q/40563479/559676`, which contains more technical details than the above overview.

Note that not all R Markdown documents are eventually compiled through Pandoc. The intermediate `.md` file could be compiled by other Markdown renderers. Below are two examples:

- The **xaringan** package (Xie, 2020f) passes the `.md` output to a JavaScript library, which renders the Markdown content in the web browser.

- The **blogdown** package (Xie, 2020b) supports the `.Rmarkdown` document format, which is knitted to `.markdown`, and this Markdown document is usually rendered to HTML by an external site generator.

2.2 R Markdown anatomy

We can dig one level deeper by considering the different components of an R Markdown. Specifically, let's look at when and how these are altered during the rendering workflow.

2.2.1 YAML metadata

The YAML metadata (also called the YAML header) is processed in many stages of the rendering process and can influence the final document in many different ways. It is read by each of Pandoc, **rmarkdown**, and **knitr**. Along the way, the information that it contains can affect the code, content, and the rendering process.

A typical YAML header looks like this, and contains basic metadata about the document and rendering instructions:

```
---
title: My R Markdown Report
author: Yihui Xie
output: html_document
---
```

In this case, the `title` and `author` fields are processed by Pandoc to set the values of template variables. With the default template, the title and author information will appear at the beginning of the resulting document. More details on how Pandoc uses information from the YAML header are included in the Pandoc manual's section on the YAML metadata block.[2]

In contrast, the `output` field is used by **rmarkdown** to apply the output format function `rmarkdown::html_document()` in the rendering process. We can further influence the rendering process by passing arguments to the output format that we are specifying in `output`. For example, writing:

```
output:
  html_document:
    toc: true
    toc_float: true
```

is the equivalent of telling `rmarkdown::render()` to apply the output format `rmarkdown::html_document(toc = TRUE, toc_float = TRUE)`. To find out what these options do, and to learn about other possible options, you may run `?rmarkdown::html_document` in your R console and read the help page. Note that `output:  html_document` is equivalent to `output: rmarkdown::html_document`. When an output format does not have a qualifier like `rmarkdown::`, it is assumed that it is from the **rmarkdown** package, otherwise it must be prefixed with the R package name, e.g., `bookdown::html_document2`.

The YAML header can also influence our content and code if we choose to use parameters in YAML, as described in Section 17.4. In short, we can include variables and R expressions in this header that can be referenced throughout our R Markdown document. For example, the following header defines `start_date` and `end_date` parameters, which will be reflected in a list called `params` later in the R Markdown document. Thus, if we want to use these values in our R code, we can access them via `params$start_date` and `params$end_date`.

```
---
title: My RMarkdown
author: Yihui Xie
output: html_document
params:
```

---

[2]https://pandoc.org/MANUAL.html#extension-yaml_metadata_block

```
start_date: '2020-01-01'
end_date: '2020-06-01'
---
```

2.2.2 Narrative

The narrative textual elements of R Markdown may be simpler to understand than the YAML metadata and code chunks. Typically, this will feel quite a bit like writing in a text editor. However, this Markdown content can be more powerful and interesting than simple text—both in how its content is made, and how the document structure is made from it.

While much of our narrative is human-written, many R Markdown documents will likely wish to reference the code and analysis being used. For this reason, Chapter 4 demonstrates the many ways that code can help generate parts of the text, such as combining words into a list (Section 4.11) or writing a bibliography (Section 4.5). This conversion is handled by **knitr** as we convert from .Rmd to .md.

Our Markdown text can also provide structure to the document. While we do not have enough space here to review the Markdown syntax,[3] one particularly relevant concept is section headers, which are denoted by one or more hashes (#) corresponding to different levels, e.g.,

```
# First-level header

## Second-level header

### Third-level header
```

These headers give structure to our entire document as **rmarkdown** converts the .md to our final output format. This structure is useful for referencing and formatting these sections by appending certain attributes to them. To create such references, Pandoc syntax allows us to provide a unique identifier by following the header notation with {#id}, or attach one or more classes to a section with {.class-name}, e.g.,

---

[3]Instead, for a review of the Markdown syntax, please see https://bookdown.org/yihui/bookdown/markdown-syntax.html.

```
## Second-level header {#introduction .important .large}
```

We can then access this section with many of the tools that you will learn, e.g., by referencing it with its ID or class. As examples, Section 4.7 demonstrates how to use the section ID to make cross-references throughout your document, and Section 7.6 introduces the .tabset class to help reorganize subsections.

The final interesting type of content that we might find in the textual part of our R Markdown is raw content written specifically for our desired output format, e.g., raw LaTeX code for LaTeX output (Section 6.11), raw HTML code for HTML output, and so on (Section 9.5). Raw content may help you achieve things that cannot be done with plain Markdown, but please keep in mind that it is usually ignored when the output format is a different format, e.g., raw LaTeX commands in Markdown will be ignored when the output format is HTML.

2.2.3   Code chunks

Code chunks are the beating heart of our R Markdown. The code in these chunks is run by **knitr**, and its output is translated to Markdown to dynamically keep our reports in sync with our current scripts and data. Each code chunk consists of a language engine (Chapter 15), an optional label, chunk options (Chapter 11), and code.

To understand some of the modifications that we can make to code chunks, it is worth understanding the **knitr** process in slightly more detail. For each chunk, a **knitr** language engine gets three pieces of input: the knitting environment (knitr::knit_global()), the code input, and a list of chunk options. It returns the formatted representations of the code as well as its output. As a side effect, the knitting environment may also be modified, e.g., new variables may have been created in this environment via the source code in the code chunk. This process is illustrated in Figure 2.2.

We can modify this process by:

• changing our language engine;

• modifying chunk options, which can be global, local, or engine-specific;

• and by using hooks (Chapter 12 and Chapter 13) to further process these inputs and outputs.

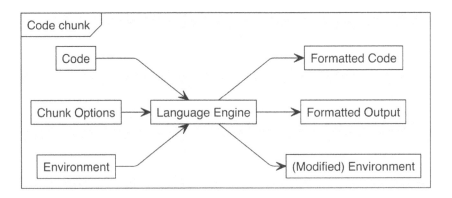

FIGURE 2.2: A flowchart of inputs and outputs to a language engine.

For example, in Section 12.1, you will learn how to add a hook to post-process the code output to redact certain lines in the source code.

Code chunks also have analogous concepts to the classes and unique identifiers that we explored for narratives in Section 2.2.2. A code chunk can specify an optional identifier (often called the "chunk label") immediately after its language engine. It can set classes for code and text output blocks in the output document via the chunk options `class.source` and `class.output`, respectively (see Section 7.3). For example, the chunk header ` ```{r summary-stats, class.output = 'large-text'} ` gives this chunk a label `summary-stats`, and the class `large-text` for the text output blocks. A chunk can have only one label, but can have multiple classes.

2.2.4 Document body

One important thing to understand when authoring and modifying a document is how code and narrative pieces create different sections, or containers within the document. For example, suppose we have a document that looks like this:

```
# Title

## Section X

This is my introduction.
```

```
```{r chunk-x}
x <- 1
print(x)
```
```

Subsection 1

Here are some details.

Subsection 2

These are more details.

Section Y

This is another section.

```
```{r chunk-y}
y <- 2
print(y)
```
```

When writing this document, we might think of each piece as linear with independent sections of text and code following in a sequence one after the other. However, what we are actually doing is creating a set of nested containers that conceptually[4] looks more like Figure 2.3.

Two key features of this diagram are (1) every section of text or code is its own discrete container, and (2) containers can be nested within one another. This nesting is particularly apparent if you are authoring your R Markdown document in the RStudio IDE and expand the document outline.

Note that in Figure 2.3, headers of the same level represent containers at the same level of nesting. Lower-level headers exist inside of the container of higher-level headers. In this case, it is common to call the higher-level sections the "parent" and the minor sections the "child." For example, a subsec-

---

[4]In reality, there are many more containers than shown. For example, for a knitted code chunk, the code and output exist in separate containers that share a common parent.

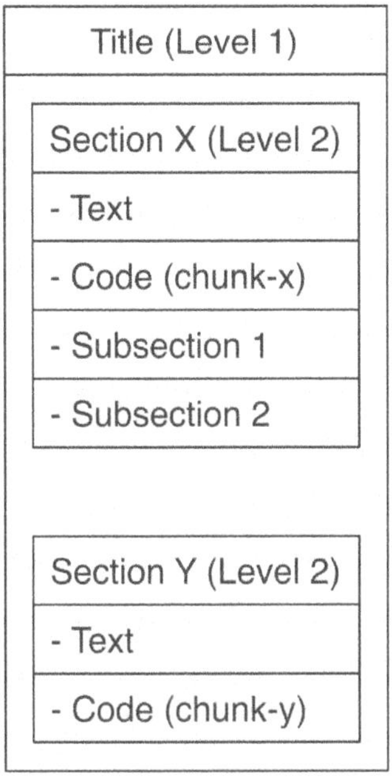

FIGURE 2.3: A simple R Markdown document illustrated as a set of nested containers.

tion is the child of a section. Besides headers, you can also create divisions in your text using : : :, as demonstrated in Section 5.8.

This structure has important implications as we attempt to apply some of the formatting and styling options that are described in this text. For example, we will see this nested structure when we learn about how Pandoc represents our document as an abstract syntax tree (Section 4.20), or when we use CSS selectors (Section 7.1, among others) to style our HTML output.

Formatting and styling can be applied to either containers of similar types (e.g., all code blocks), or all containers that exist inside of another container (e.g., everything under "Section Y"). Additionally, as explained in Section 2.2.2, we can apply the same classes to certain sections to designate them as being similar, and in this case, the common class names denote the common properties or intent of these sections.

As you read through this cookbook, it may be useful to quiz yourself and think about what sort of container the specific "recipe" is acting upon.

2.3   What can we change to change the results?

Let's summarize what we have seen so far and preview what is to come.

Rendering R Markdown documents with **rmarkdown** consists of converting .Rmd to .md with **knitr**, and then .md to our desired output with Pandoc (typically).

The .Rmd-to-.md step handles the execution and "translation" of all code within our report, so most changes to *content* involve editing the .Rmd with code for **knitr** to translate. Tools that we have control over these steps include **knitr** chunk options and hooks.

Our .md is a plain text file with no formatting. This is where Pandoc comes in to convert to the final output format such as HTML, PDF, or Word. Along the way, we add structure and style. A wide range of tools to help us in this process include style sheets (CSS), raw LaTeX or HTML code, Pandoc templates, and Lua filters. By understanding the nested structure of an R Markdown document, and by thoughtfully using identifiers and classes, we can apply some of these tools selectively to targeted parts of our output.

Finally, our YAML metadata may help us toggle any of these steps. Changing parameters can change how our code runs, changing metadata alters the text content, and changing output options provides the render() function with a different set of instructions.

Of course, these are all rough heuristics and should not be taken as absolute facts. Ultimately, there is not a completely clear division of labor. Throughout this book, you will see that there are often multiple valid paths to achieving many of the outcomes described in this book, and these may enter different stages of the pipeline. For example, for the simple task of inserting in image in your document, you may either use the R code knitr::include_graphics(), which would execute in the .Rmd to .md stage, or directly use Markdown syntax (). This may seem confusing, and sometimes different approaches will have different advantages. However, do not be concerned—if anything, this often means there are many valid ways to solve your problem, and you can follow whichever approach makes the most sense to you.

And that's that! In the rest of the book, you can now color in this rough sketch with many more concrete examples of ways to modify all of the components that we have discussed to get the most value out of R Markdown.

3

Basics

In this chapter, we present some key concepts about R Markdown. First, we introduce the basic components of an R Markdown document: the prose and code. Next, we show how to convert R Markdown documents to R scripts, and vice versa.

For those seeking lower-level basics, please read Chapter 2 of the *R Markdown Definitive Guide* (Xie et al., 2018).

3.1   Code chunks and inline R code

An R Markdown document consists of intermingled prose (narratives) and code. There are two types of code in an Rmd document: code chunks and inline R code. Below is a quick example:

```
```{r}
x <- 5  # radius of a circle
```


For a circle with the radius `r x`,
its area is `r pi * x^2`.
```

A code chunk usually starts with ```` ```{} ```` and ends with ```` ``` ````. You can write any number of lines of code in it. Inline R code is embedded in the narratives of the document using the syntax `r `. In the above example, we defined a variable x in a code chunk, which is the radius of a circle, and calculated its area in the next paragraph.

You can customize the behavior and output of code chunks through chunk options (provided inside the curly brackets {}). You will find several examples in Chapter 11. You may write code of other languages in code chunks, too (see Chapter 15).

3.2   Write Markdown in the RStudio visual editor

If you are not familiar with Markdown yet, or do not prefer writing Markdown code, RStudio v1.4 has included an experimental visual editor for Markdown documents, which feels similar to traditional WYSIWYG editors like Word, as shown in Figure 3.1. You can find the full documentation at `https://rstudio.github.io/visual-markdown-editing/`.

With the visual editor, you can visually edit almost any Markdown elements supported by Pandoc, such as section headers, figures, tables, footnotes, and so on. That means you do not have remember the syntax for all elements. In case you forget the syntax for a certain element, you may use the RStudio toolbar (see Figure 3.1) or a keyboard shortcut to add or edit it.

If you are already a Markdown expert, you can still write your document in the source mode by clicking the rightmost button on the toolbar, which allows you to switch between the source mode and the visual mode.

3.3   Render an R script to a report

Even if you are a long-time R Markdown user, you may have missed another possibility. Dean Attali called it "**knitr**'s best hidden gem".[1] That is, you can render a pure R script to a report directly. If you use the RStudio IDE, the keyboard shortcut to render R scripts is the same as when you knit Rmd documents (`Ctrl / Cmd + Shift + K`).

When rendering an R script to a report, the function `knitr::spin()` is called to convert the R script to an Rmd file first. This function is what Dean Attali called **knitr**'s best hidden gem. You will see all text and graphical output in the report.

---

[1] `https://deanattali.com/2015/03/24/knitrs-best-hidden-gem-spin/`

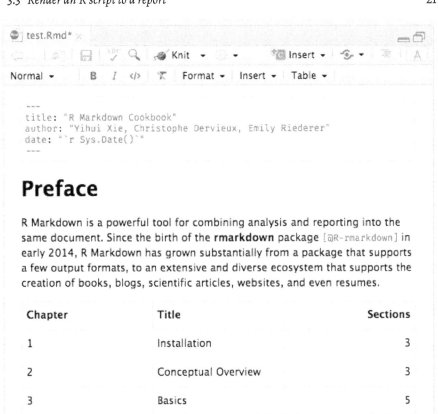

Preface

R Markdown is a powerful tool for combining analysis and reporting into the same document. Since the birth of the **rmarkdown** package [@R-rmarkdown] in early 2014, R Markdown has grown substantially from a package that supports a few output formats, to an extensive and diverse ecosystem that supports the creation of books, blogs, scientific articles, websites, and even resumes.

Chapter	Title	Sections
1	Installation	3
2	Conceptual Overview	3
3	Basics	5

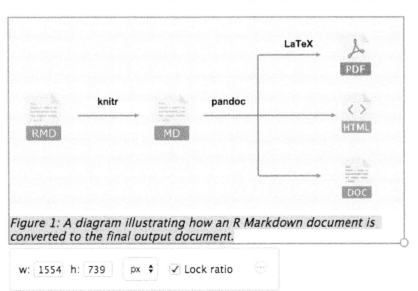

Figure 1: A diagram illustrating how an R Markdown document is converted to the final output document.

FIGURE 3.1: The visual Markdown editor in RStudio.

If you want granular control over the elements in the report, below are a few syntax rules to help you:

- Roxygen comments will be treated as normal text. A roxygen comment is an R comment that starts with #'. This can help you write narratives in your report. You can use any Markdown syntax in the comments.

- A comment starting with #+ is treated as the **knitr** chunk header. For example, knitr::spin() will translate the comment #+ label, fig.width=5 to the chunk header ```` ```{r label, fig.width=5} ```` in R Markdown.

- R code of the form {{ code }} is translated to an inline R expression in R Markdown. Please note that {{ code }} must be on its own line.

- The YAML frontmatter can be written in the beginning of the R script in roxygen comments, too. Please watch out for the indentation in YAML fields. It is very important. If you omit the indentation, the data structure expressed in your YAML will be different and incorrect. For example, the field keep_tex: true should be indented for two more spaces under pdf_document in the example below.

- Any text between /* and */ will be ignored (i.e., they are treated as true comments).

Below is a full example illustrating the above rules:

```
#' ---
#' title: "A report generated from a pure R script"
#' output:
#'   pdf_document:
#'     keep_tex: true
#' ---
#'
#' This is a report generated by `knitr::spin()`.
#'
#' Let's try some **knitr** options:

#+ echo=FALSE, fig.width=7
#   This is a normal R comment.
plot(cars)

#' Now write an inline value. We know the value of $\pi$ is
```

```
{{ pi }}
#' .
#'
#' Finally please note that all roxygen comments are
#' optional. You do not need chunk options, either,
#' unless you want more control over the output
#' elements such as the size of plots.

# /* Write comments between /* and */ like C comments:
Sys.sleep(60)
# */
```

When this script is rendered to a report, `knitr::spin()` will convert it to R Markdown:

```
---
title: "A report generated from a pure R script"
output:
  pdf_document:
    keep_tex: true
---

This is a report generated by `knitr::spin()`.

Let's try some **knitr** options:

```{r echo=FALSE, fig.width=7}
#   This is a normal R comment.
plot(cars)
```

Now write an inline value. We know the value of π is
`r  pi  `
.

Finally please note that all roxygen comments are
optional. You do not need chunk options, either,
unless you want more control over the output
elements such as the size of plots.
```

This method of generating reports can be particularly useful when you primarily work with R scripts and do not need a lot of narratives. If the proportion of text is substantial in your report, R Markdown may be a better choice, because you do not need to put all text in roxygen comments.

3.4   Convert R Markdown to R script

When you want to extract all R code from an R Markdown document, you can call the function `knitr::purl()`. Below is a simple Rmd example with the filename `purl.Rmd`:

```
---
title: Use `purl()` to extract R code
---


The function `knitr::purl()` extracts R code chunks from
a **knitr** document and save the code to an R script.

Below is a simple chunk:

```{r, simple, echo=TRUE}
1 + 1
```

Inline R expressions like `r 2 * pi` are ignored by default.

If you do not want certain code chunks to be extracted,
you can set the chunk option `purl = FALSE`, e.g.,

```{r, ignored, purl=FALSE}
x = rnorm(1000)
```
```

If we call `knitr::purl("purl.Rmd")`, it generates the following R script (with the filename `purl.R` by default):

```
## ---- simple, echo=TRUE--------------------------------
1 + 1
```

The above R script contains the chunk options in a comment. If you want pure R code, you may call `knitr::purl()` with the argument `documentation = 0`, which will generate the R script below:

```
1 + 1
```

If you want to retain all the text, you may use the argument `documentation = 2`, which generates the R script below:

```
#' ---
#' title: Use `purl()` to extract R code
#' ---
#'
#' The function `knitr::purl()` extracts R code chunks from
#' a **knitr** document and save the code to an R script.
#'
#' Below is a simple chunk:
#'
## ---- simple, echo=TRUE--------------------------------
1 + 1


#'
#' Inline R expressions like `r 2 * pi` are ignored by default.
#'
#' If you do not want certain code chunks to be extracted,
#' you can set the chunk option `purl = FALSE`, e.g.,
#'
```

Note that code chunks with the option `purl = FALSE` will be excluded in the R script.

Inline R expressions are ignored by default. If you want to include them in the R script, you need to set the global R option `options(knitr.purl.inline = TRUE)` before calling `knitr::purl()`.

3.5   R Markdown Notebooks

As mentioned in Section 2.2[2] of the *R Markdown Definitive Guide* (Xie et al., 2018), there are several ways to compile an Rmd document. One of them is to use R Markdown Notebooks, with the output format `html_notebook`, e.g.,

```
---
title: An R Markdown Notebook
output: html_notebook
---
```

When you use this output format in RStudio, the `Knit` button on the toolbar will become the `Preview` button.

The main advantage of using notebooks is that you can work on an Rmd document *iteratively in the same R session*. You can run one code chunk at a time by clicking the green arrow button on each chunk, and you will see the text or plot output in the editor. When you click the `Preview` button on the toolbar, it only renders the Rmd document to an HTML output document containing the output of all code chunks that you have already executed. The `Preview` button does not execute any code chunks. By comparison, when you use other output formats and hit the `Knit` button, RStudio launches a new R session to compile the whole document (hence all code chunks are executed at once), which usually takes more time.

If you do not like RStudio's default behavior of showing the output of code chunks inline when you run them individually, you can uncheck the option "Show output inline for all R Markdown documents" from the menu `Tools -> Global Options -> R Markdown`. After that, when you run a code chunk, the output will be shown in the R console instead of inside the source editor. You can also set this option for an individual Rmd document in its YAML metadata:

```
editor_options:
  chunk_output_type: console
```

---

[2]https://bookdown.org/yihui/rmarkdown/compile.html

4

Document Elements

In this chapter, we introduce some tips and tricks that can be used to customize or generate the document elements of R Markdown, including page breaks, the YAML metadata, section headings, citations, cross-references, equations, animations, interactive plots, diagrams, and comments.

4.1   Insert page breaks

When you want to break a page, you can insert the command \newpage in the document. It is a LaTeX command, but the **rmarkdown** package is able to recognize it for both LaTeX output formats and a few non-LaTeX output formats including HTML,[1] Word, and ODT. For example:

```
---
title: Breaking pages
output:
  pdf_document: default
  word_document: default
  html_document: default
  odt_document: default
---


# The first section

\newpage

# The second section
```

---

[1]For HTML output, page breaks only make sense when you print the HTML page, otherwise you will not see the page breaks, because an HTML page is just a single continuous page.

This feature is based on Pandoc's Lua filters (see Section 4.20). For those who are interested in the technology, you may view this package vignette:

```
vignette("lua-filters", package = "rmarkdown")
```

4.2   Set the document title dynamically

You can use inline R code (see Section 3.1) anywhere in an Rmd document, including the YAML metadata section. This means some YAML metadata can be dynamically generated with inline R code, such as the document title. For example:

```
---
title: "An analysis of `r nrow(mtcars)` cars"
---
```

If your title depends on an R variable created later in the document, you may add the title field in a later YAML section, e.g., the following:

```
---
author: "Smart Analyst"
output: pdf_document
---

I just tried really hard to calculate our market share:

```{r}
share <- runif(1)
```

---
title: "Our market share is `r round(100 * share, 2)`% now!"

I feel `r if(share > 0.8) "happy" else "sad"` about it.
```

In the example above, we added the document title after we created the variable `share`. The title works in this case because Pandoc can read any number of YAML sections in a document (and merge them).

You can also generate titles or any YAML fields dynamically from parameters in parameterized reports (see Section 17.4), e.g.,

```
---
title: "`r params$doc_title`"
author: "Smart Analyst"
params:
  doc_title: "The Default Title"
---
```

With the title being a dynamic parameter, you can easily generate a batch of reports with different titles.

We used the title as the example in this section, but the idea can be applied to any metadata fields in the YAML section.

4.3 Access the document metadata in R code

When an Rmd document is compiled, all of its metadata in the YAML section will be stored in the list object `rmarkdown::metadata`. For example, `rmark-down::metadata$title` gives you the title of the document. You can use this `metadata` object in your R code, so that you do not need to hard-code information that has been provided in the YAML metadata. For example, when you send an email with the **blastula** package (Iannone and Cheng, 2020) within an Rmd document, you may use the title of the document as the email subject, and get the sender information from the author field:

```
---
title: An important report
author: John Doe
email: john@example.com
---
```

```
We have done an important analysis, and want to email
the results.
```

```r
```{r}
library(rmarkdown)
library(blastula)
smtp_send(
  ...,
  from = setNames(metadata$email, metadata$author),
  subject = metadata$title
)
```
```

4.4   Unnumbered sections

Most output formats support an option `number_sections`, which can be used to enable numbering sections if set to `true`, e.g.,

```
output:
  html_document:
    number_sections: true
  pdf_document:
    number_sections: true
```

If you want a certain section to be unnumbered when the option `number_sections` is `true`, you may add `{-}` after the section heading, e.g.,

```
# This section is unnumbered {-}
```

Equivalently, you may also use `{.unnumbered}`. You can also add other attributes to the heading, e.g., `{.unnumbered #section-id}`. Please see `https://pandoc.org/MANUAL.html#extension-header_attributes` for more information.

Unnumbered sections are often used for providing extra information about the writing. For example, for this book, the chapters "Preface" and "About the Authors" are unnumbered, since they do not belong to the body of this book. As you may see in Figure 4.1, the actual body starts after the two unnumbered chapters, and the chapters in the book body are numbered.

FIGURE 4.1: A screenshot of the table of contents of this book to show numbered and unnumbered chapters.

Section numbers are incremental. If you insert an unnumbered section after a numbered section, and then start another numbered section, the section number will resume incrementing.

4.5   Bibliographies and citations

For an overview of including bibliographies in your output document, you may see Section 2.8[2] of Xie (2016). The basic usage requires us to specify a bibliography file using the `bibliography` metadata field in YAML. For example:

```
---
output: html_document
bibliography: references.bib
---
```

---

[2]https://bookdown.org/yihui/bookdown/citations.html

where the BibTeX database is a plain-text file with the `*.bib` extension that
consists of bibliography entries like this:

```
@Manual{R-base,
  title = {R: A Language and Environment for Statistical
          Computing},
  author = {{R Core Team}},
  organization = {R Foundation for Statistical Computing},
  address = {Vienna, Austria},
  year = {2019},
  url = {https://www.R-project.org},
}
```

Items can be cited directly within the documentation using the syntax `@key`
where `key` is the citation key in the first line of the entry, e.g., `@R-base`. To
put citations in parentheses, use `[@key]`. To cite multiple entries, separate
the keys by semicolons, e.g., `[@key-1; @key-2; @key-3]`. To suppress the
mention of the author, add a minus sign before `@`, e.g., `[-@R-base]`.

4.5.1 Changing citation style

By default, Pandoc will use a Chicago author-date format for citations and
references. To use another style, you will need to specify a CSL (Citation Style
Language) file in the `csl` metadata field, e.g.,

```
---
output: html_document
bibliography: references.bib
csl: biomed-central.csl
---
```

To find your required formats, we recommend using the Zotero Style Repository,[3] which makes it easy to search for and download your desired style.

CSL files can be tweaked to meet custom formatting requirements. For example, we can change the number of authors required before "et al." is used
to abbreviate them. This can be simplified through the use of visual editors
such as the one available at `https://editor.citationstyles.org`.

---

[3]`https://www.zotero.org/styles`

4.5.2   Add an item to a bibliography without using it

By default, the bibliography will only display items that are directly referenced in the document. If you want to include items in the bibliography without actually citing them in the body text, you can define a dummy `nocite`
metadata field and put the citations there.

```
---
nocite: |
  @item1, @item2
---
```

4.5.3   Add all items to the bibliography

If we do not wish to explicitly state all of the items within the bibliography
but would still like to show them in our references, we can use the following
syntax:

```
---
nocite: '@*'
---
```

This will force all items to be displayed in the bibliography.

4.5.4   Include appendix after bibliography (*)

By default, the bibliography appears at the very end of the document. However, there can be cases in which we want to place additional text after the references, most typically if we wish to include appendices in the document. We
can force the position of the references by using `<div id="refs"></div>`, as
shown below:

```
# References

<div id="refs"></div>

# Appendix
```

Although `<div>` is an HTML tag, this method also works for other output
formats such as PDF.

We can improve this further by using the **bookdown** package (Xie, 2020c), which allows you to insert a special header[4] `# (APPENDIX) Appendix {-}` before you start the appendix, e.g.,

```
# References

<div id="refs"></div>

# (APPENDIX) Appendix {-}

# More information

This will be Appendix A.

# One more thing

This will be Appendix B.
```

The numbering style of appendices will be automatically changed in La-TeX/PDF and HTML output (usually in the form A, A.1, A.2, B, B.1, and so on).

4.6   Generate R package citations

To cite an R package, you can use the function `citation()` from base R. If you want to generate a citation entry for BibTeX, you can pass the returned object of `citation()` to `toBibtex()`, e.g.,

```
toBibtex(citation("xaringan"))
```

```
Warning in citation("xaringan"): no date field in
DESCRIPTION file of package 'xaringan'
```

```
Warning in citation("xaringan"): could not determine
year for 'xaringan' from package DESCRIPTION file
```

---

[4]https://bookdown.org/yihui/bookdown/markdown-extensions-by-bookdown.html#special-headers

```
@Manual{,
  title = {xaringan: Presentation Ninja},
  author = {Yihui Xie},
  note = {R package version 0.16.1},
  url = {https://github.com/yihui/xaringan},
}
```

To use citation entries generated from `toBibtex()`, you have to copy the output to a `.bib` file, and add citation keys (e.g., change `@Manual{,` to `@Manual{R-xaringan,`). This can be automated via the function `knitr::write_bib()`, which generates citation entries to a file and adds keys automatically, e.g.,

```
knitr::write_bib(c(.packages(), "bookdown"), "packages.bib")
```

The first argument should be a character vector of package names, and the second argument is the path to the `.bib` file. In the above example, `.packages()` returns the names of all packages loaded in the current R session. This makes sure all packages being used will have their citation entries written to the `.bib` file. When any of these packages are updated (e.g., the author, title, year, or version of a package is changed), `write_bib()` can automatically update the `.bib` file.

There are two possible types of citation entries. One type is generated from the package's DESCRIPTION file, and the other type is generated from the package's CITATION file if provided. For the former type, the citation keys are of the form `R-pkgname`, where `pkgname` is the package name (e.g., `R-knitr`). For the latter type, the keys are created by concatenating the package name and the publication year (e.g., `knitr2015`). If there are multiple entries in the same year, a letter suffix will be added, e.g., `knitr2015a` and `knitr2015b`. The former type is often used to cite the package itself (i.e., the software), and the latter type often consists of publications related to the package, such as journal papers or books.

```
knitr::write_bib(c("knitr", "rmarkdown"), width = 60)
```

```
@Manual{R-knitr,
  title = {knitr: A General-Purpose Package for Dynamic Report
```

```
    Generation in R},
  author = {Yihui Xie},
  note = {R package version 1.29.4},
  url = {https://yihui.org/knitr/},
  year = {2020},
}

@Manual{R-rmarkdown,
  title = {rmarkdown: Dynamic Documents for R},
  author = {JJ Allaire and Yihui Xie and Jonathan McPherson
    and Javier Luraschi and Kevin Ushey and Aron Atkins and
    Hadley Wickham and Joe Cheng and Winston Chang and Richard
    Iannone},
  note = {R package version 2.3.2},
  url = {https://github.com/rstudio/rmarkdown},
  year = {2020},
}

@Book{knitr2015,
  title = {Dynamic Documents with {R} and knitr},
  author = {Yihui Xie},
  publisher = {Chapman and Hall/CRC},
  address = {Boca Raton, Florida},
  year = {2015},
  edition = {2nd},
  note = {ISBN 978-1498716963},
  url = {https://yihui.org/knitr/},
}

@InCollection{knitr2014,
  booktitle = {Implementing Reproducible Computational
    Research},
  editor = {Victoria Stodden and Friedrich Leisch and Roger D.
    Peng},
  title = {knitr: A Comprehensive Tool for Reproducible
    Research in {R}},
  author = {Yihui Xie},
  publisher = {Chapman and Hall/CRC},
```

```
  year = {2014},
  note = {ISBN 978-1466561595},
  url = {http://www.crcpress.com/product/isbn/9781466561595},
}

@Book{rmarkdown2018,
  title = {R Markdown: The Definitive Guide},
  author = {Yihui Xie and J.J. Allaire and Garrett Grolemund},
  publisher = {Chapman and Hall/CRC},
  address = {Boca Raton, Florida},
  year = {2018},
  note = {ISBN 9781138359338},
  url = {https://bookdown.org/yihui/rmarkdown},
}
```

Without the file path argument, `knitr::write_bib()` writes the citation entries to the R console, as you can see from the above example.

Note that `write_bib()` is designed to overwrite the existing bibliography file. If you want to manually add any other entries to the bibliography, it is recommended that you create a second `.bib` file and refer to it in the YAML field `bibliography`, e.g.,

```
---
bibliography: [packages.bib, references.bib]
---
```

```
```{r, include=FALSE}
knitr::write_bib(file = 'packages.bib')
```
```

In the above example, `packages.bib` is automatically generated, and you should not manually change it. All other citation entries can be manually written to `references.bib`.

We only introduced one way to generate R package citations above. To dynamically generate citations for other types of literature, you may check out the **knitcitations** package (Boettiger, 2019).

4.7   Cross-referencing within documents

Cross-referencing is a useful way of directing your readers through your document, and can be automatically done within R Markdown. While this has been explained in Chapter 2[5] from the **bookdown** book, we want to present a brief summary below.

To use cross-references, you will need:

- **A bookdown output format**: Cross-referencing is not provided directly within the base **rmarkdown** package, but is provided as an extension in **bookdown** (Xie, 2020c). We must therefore use an output format from **bookdown** (e.g., `html_document2`, `pdf_document2`, and `word_document2`, etc.) in the YAML `output` field.

- **A caption to your figure (or table)**: Figures without a caption will be included directly as images and will therefore not be a numbered figure.

- **A labeled code chunk**: This provides the identifier for referencing the figure generated by the chunk.

After these conditions are met, we can make cross-references within the text using the syntax `\@ref(type:label)`, where `label` is the chunk label and `type` is the environment being referenced (e.g. `tab`, `fig`, or `eqn`). An example is provided below:

```
---
title: Cross-referencing figures, tables, and equations
author: Generated by bookdown
output:
  bookdown::html_document2: default
  bookdown::pdf_document2: default
---

See Figure \@ref(fig:cars-plot).

```{r cars-plot, fig.cap="The cars data.", echo=FALSE}
par(mar = c(4, 4, .2, .1))
plot(cars)  # a scatterplot
```

---

[5]`https://bookdown.org/yihui/bookdown/components.html`
```

```
```

Also see Equation \@ref(eq:mean).

\begin{equation}
\bar{X} = \frac{\sum_{i=1}^n X_i}{n} (\#eq:mean)
\end{equation}

And see Table \@ref(tab:mtcars).

```{r mtcars, echo=FALSE}
knitr::kable(mtcars[1:5, 1:5], caption = "The mtcars data.")
```

The output of this document is shown in Figure 4.2.

You can also cross-reference equations, theorems, and section headers. These types of references are explained further in Section 2.2 and Section 2.6 of the **bookdown** book.

4.8   Update the date automatically

If you want the date on which the Rmd document is compiled to be reflected in the output report, you can add an inline R expression to the date field in YAML, and use the Sys.Date() or Sys.time() function to obtain the current date, e.g.,

```
date: "`r Sys.Date()`"
```

You may want to specify the desired date or date-time format to make it more human-readable, e.g.,

```
date: "`r format(Sys.time(), '%d %B, %Y')`"
```

This will generate the date dynamically each time you knit your document, e.g., 14 August, 2020. If you wish to customize the format of the dates, you

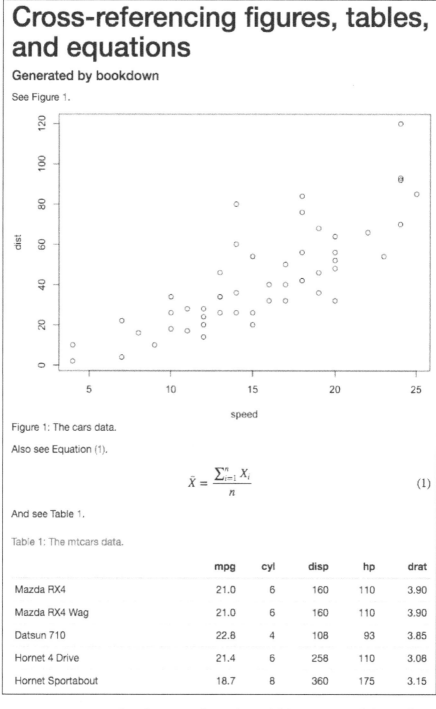

FIGURE 4.2: Example of cross-referencing within an R Markdown document.

TABLE 4.1: Date and time formats in R.

Code	Meaning	Code	Meaning
%a	Abbreviated weekday	%A	Full weekday
%b	Abbreviated month	%B	Full month
%c	Locale-specific date and time	%d	Decimal date
%H	Decimal hours (24 hour)	%I	Decimal hours (12 hour)
%j	Decimal day of the year	%m	Decimal month
%M	Decimal minute	%p	Locale-specific AM/PM
%S	Decimal second	%U	Decimal week of the year (starting on Sunday)
%w	Decimal Weekday (0=Sunday)	%W	Decimal week of the year (starting on Monday)
%x	Locale-specific Date	%X	Locale-specific Time
%y	2-digit year	%Y	4-digit year
%z	Offset from GMT	%Z	Time zone (character)

can alter the time format by providing your own format string. Here are some examples:

- %B %Y: August 2020
- %d/%m/%y: 14/08/20
- %a/%d/%b: Fri 14 Aug

A full table of POSIXct formats is shown in Table 4.1.

As a final note, you may also want to include some explanatory text along with the date. You can add any text such as "Last compiled on" before the R code as follows:

```
date: "Last compiled on `r format(Sys.time(), '%d %B, %Y')`"
```

4.9   Multiple authors in a document

We can add multiple authors to an R Markdown document within the YAML frontmatter in a number of ways. If we simply want to list them on the same line, we can provide a single string to the document, e.g.,

```
---
title: "Untitled"
author: "John Doe, Jane Doe"
---
```

Alternatively, if we wish each entry to be on its own line, we can provide a list of entries to the YAML field. This can be useful if you wish to include further information about each author such as an email address or institution, e.g.,

```
---
author:
  - John Doe, Institution One
  - Jane Doe, Institution Two
---
```

We can make use of the Markdown syntax ^[] to add additional information as a footnote to the document. This may be more useful if you have extended information that you wish to include for each author, such as providing a contact Email and address. The exact behavior will depend on the output format:

```
---
author:
  - John Doe^[Institution One, john@example.org]
  - Jane Doe^[Institution Two, jane@example.org]
---
```

Certain R Markdown templates will allow you to specify additional parameters directly within the YAML. For example, the Distill[6] output format allows url, affiliation, and affiliation_url to be specified. After you install the **distill** package (Allaire et al., 2020a):

---

[6]https://rstudio.github.io/distill/

```
install.packages("distill")
```

you can use the Distill format with detailed author information, e.g.,

```
---
title: "Distill for R Markdown"
author:
  - name: "JJ Allaire"
    url: https://github.com/jjallaire
    affiliation: RStudio
    affiliation_url: https://www.rstudio.com
output: distill::distill_article
---
```

4.10 Numbered figure captions

We can use **bookdown** (Xie, 2020c) output formats to add figure numbers to their captions. Below is an example:

```
---
output: bookdown::html_document2
---


```{r cars, fig.cap = "An amazing plot"}
plot(cars)
```


```{r mtcars, fig.cap = "Another amazing plot"}
plot(mpg ~ hp, mtcars)
```
```

Section 4.7 demonstrates how this works for other elements such as tables and equations, and how to cross-reference the numbered elements within the text. Besides html_document2, there are several other similar functions for other output formats, such as pdf_document2 and word_document2.

You can add this feature to R Markdown output formats outside **bookdown**, too. The key is to use those formats as the "base formats" of **bookdown** output formats. For example, to number and cross-reference figures in the rticles::jss_article format, you can use:

```
output:
  bookdown::pdf_book:
    base_format: rticles::jss_article
```

Please read the help pages of the **bookdown** output format functions to see if they have the base_format argument (e.g., ?bookdown::html_document2).

4.11   Combine words into a comma-separated phrase

When you want to output a character vector for humans to read (e.g., x <- c("apple", "banana", "cherry")), you probably do not want something like [1] "apple" "banana" "cherry", which is the normal way to print a vector in R. Instead, you may want a character string "apple, banana, and cherry". There is a base R function, paste(), that you can use to concatenate a character vector into a single string, e.g., paste(x, collapse = ', '), and the output will be "apple, banana, cherry". The problems are (1) the conjunction "and" is missing, and (2) when the vector only contains two elements, we should not use commas (e.g., the output should be "apple and banana" instead of "apple, banana").

The function knitr::combine_words() can be used to concatenate words into a phrase regardless of the length of the character vector. Basically, for a single word, it will just return this word; for two words A and B, it returns "A and B"; for three or more words, it returns "A, B, C, ..., Y, and Z". The function also has a few arguments that can customize the output. For example, if you want to output the words in pairs of backticks, you may use knitr::combine_words(x, before = '`'). Below are more examples with different arguments, and please see the help page ?knitr::combine_words if the meaning of any argument is not clear from the output here:

```
v <- c("apple", "banana", "cherry")
knitr::combine_words(v)
## apple, banana, and cherry
knitr::combine_words(v, before = "`", after = "'")
```

```
## `apple', `banana', and `cherry'
knitr::combine_words(v, and = "")
## apple, banana, cherry
knitr::combine_words(v, sep = " / ", and = "")
## apple / banana / cherry
knitr::combine_words(v[1])    # a single word
## apple
knitr::combine_words(v[1:2])    # two words
## apple and banana
knitr::combine_words(LETTERS[1:5])
## A, B, C, D, and E
```

This function can be particularly handy when it is used in an inline R expression, e.g.,

```
This morning we had `r knitr::combine_words(v)` for breakfast.
```

4.12 Preserve a large number of line breaks

Markdown users may be surprised to realize that whitespaces (including line breaks) are usually meaningless unless they are used in a verbatim environment (code blocks). Two or more spaces are the same as one space, and a line break is the same as a space. If you have used LaTeX or HTML before, you may not be surprised because the rule is the same in these languages.

In Markdown, we often use a blank line to separate elements such as paragraphs. To break a line without introducing a new paragraph, you have to use two trailing spaces. Sometimes you may want to break the lines many times, especially when you write or quote poems or lyrics. Adding two spaces after each line manually is a tedious task. The function blogdown:::quote_poem() can do this task automatically, e.g.,

```
blogdown:::quote_poem(c("This line", "should be", "broken."))
## [1] "> This line  \nshould be  \nbroken."
```

If you use the RStudio IDE and have installed the package **blogdown** (Xie,

2020b), you can select the text in which you want to preserve the line breaks, and click the RStudio addin "Quote Poem" in the drop-down menu "Addins" on the toolbar. For example, the text below (in a fenced code block) does not contain trailing spaces:

```
Like Barley Bending

Like barley bending
  In low fields by the sea,
Singing in hard wind
  Ceaselessly;

Like barley bending
  And rising again,
So would I, unbroken,
  Rise from pain;

So would I softly,
  Day long, night long,
Change my sorrow
  Into song.

--- Sara Teasdale
```

After we select the above poem and click the RStudio addin "Quote Poem," the output will be:

Like Barley Bending

Like barley bending
   In low fields by the sea,
Singing in hard wind
   Ceaselessly;

Like barley bending
   And rising again,
So would I, unbroken,
   Rise from pain;

So would I softly,

> Day long, night long,
> Change my sorrow
> Into song.

> — Sara Teasdale

Some users may ask, "Since the fenced code block preserves whitespaces, why not put poems in code blocks?" Code could be poetic, but poems are not code. Please do not be too addicted to coding...

4.13 Convert models to equations

The **equatiomatic** package (`https://github.com/datalorax/equatiomatic`) developed by Daniel Anderson et al. provides a convenient and automatic way to show the equations corresponding to models fitted in R. At the time of writing, this package is still very new on GitHub and its API may change significantly before its possible future CRAN release, so we only show a few brief examples below:

```
fit <- lm(mpg ~ cyl + disp, mtcars)
# show the theoretical model
equatiomatic::extract_eq(fit)
```

$$\text{mpg} = \alpha + \beta_1(\text{cyl}) + \beta_2(\text{disp}) + \epsilon$$

```
# display the actual coefficients
equatiomatic::extract_eq(fit, use_coefs = TRUE)
```

$$\text{mpg} = 34.66 - 1.59(\text{cyl}) - 0.02(\text{disp}) + \epsilon$$

To display the actual math equations, you need the chunk option `results = "asis"` (see Section 11.11 for the meaning of this option), otherwise the equations will be displayed as normal text output.

Please read the documentation and follow the development of this package on GitHub if you are interested in knowing more about it.

4.14   Create an animation from multiple R plots

When you generate a series of plots in a code chunk, you can combine them into an animation. It is easy to do so if the output format is HTML—you only need to install the **gifski** package (Ooms, 2018) and set the chunk option an-imation.hook = "gifski". Figure 4.3 shows a simple "Pac-man" animation created from the code chunk below:

```
```{r, animation.hook="gifski"}
for (i in 1:2) {
  pie(c(i %% 2, 6), col = c('red', 'yellow'), labels = NA)
}
```
```

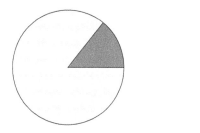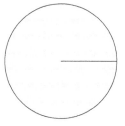

FIGURE 4.3: A Pac-man animation.

The image format of the animation is GIF, which works well for HTML output, but it is not straightforward to support GIF in LaTeX. That is why you only see two static image frames in Figure 4.3 if you are reading the PDF or printed version of this book. If you read the online version of this book, you will see the actual animation.

Animations can work in PDF, but there are two prerequisites. First, you have to load the LaTeX package **animate**[7] (see Section 6.4 for how). Second, you

---

[7]https://ctan.org/pkg/animate

can only use Acrobat Reader to view the animation. Then the chunk option `fig.show = "animate"` will use the **animate** package to create the animation. Below is an example:

```
---
title: Animations in PDF
output:
  pdf_document:
    extra_dependencies: animate
---

The animation below can only be viewed in Acrobat Reader.

```{r, fig.show='animate'}
for (i in 1:2) {
  pie(c(i %% 2, 6), col = c('red', 'yellow'), labels = NA)
}
```
```

The time interval between image frames in the animation can be set by the chunk option `interval`. By default, `interval = 1` (i.e., one second).

The R package **animation** (Xie, 2020a) contains several animation examples to illustrate methods and ideas in statistical computing. The **gganimate** package (Pedersen and Robinson, 2020) allows us to create smooth animations based on **ggplot2** (Wickham et al., 2020a). Both packages work with R Markdown.

4.15 Create diagrams

There are many separate programs (e.g., Graphviz) that can be used to produce diagrams and flowcharts, but it can be easier to manage them directly inside R code chunks in Rmd documents.

While there are several different packages available for R, we will only briefly introduce the package **DiagrammeR** (Iannone, 2020), and mention other packages at the end. You can find the full documentation of **DiagrammeR** at `https://rich-iannone.github.io/DiagrammeR/`. In this section, we will introduce the basic usages and also how to use R code in diagrams.

4.15.1   Basic diagrams

DiagrammeR provides methods to build graphs for a number of different graphing languages. We will present a Graphviz example in this section,[8] but you can also use pure R code to create graphs and diagrams with **DiagrammeR**.

The RStudio IDE provides native support for Graphviz (.gv) and mermaid (.mmd) files. Editing these types of files in RStudio has the advantage of syntax highlighting. RStudio also allows you to preview the diagrams by clicking the "Preview" button on the toolbar. Figure 4.4 is a simple flowchart example that has four rectangles representing four steps, generated by the code below:

```
DiagrammeR::grViz("digraph {
  graph [layout = dot, rankdir = TB]

  node [shape = rectangle]
  rec1 [label = 'Step 1. Wake up']
  rec2 [label = 'Step 2. Write code']
  rec3 [label =  'Step 3. ???']
  rec4 [label = 'Step 4. PROFIT']

  # edge definitions with the node IDs
  rec1 -> rec2 -> rec3 -> rec4
  }",
  height = 500)
```

There are extensive controls that can be used to define the shape of nodes, colors, line types, and add additional parameters.

4.15.2   Adding parameters to plots

Graphviz substitution allows for mixing R expressions into a Graphviz graph specification, without sacrificing readability. If you specify a substitution with @@, you must ensure there is a valid R expression for that substitution. The expressions are placed as footnotes and their evaluations must result in an R vector object. The @@ notation is immediately followed by a number, and that number should correspond to the number of the R expression foot-

---

[8] Depending on your background, this section may be a biased introduction to **DiagrammeR**. Please see its official documentation if you are interested in this package.

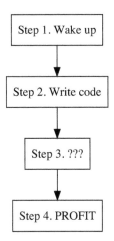

FIGURE 4.4: A diagram showing a programmer's daydream.

note. Figure 4.5 shows an example of embedding and evaluating R code in the diagram.

```
DiagrammeR::grViz("
  digraph graph2 {

  graph [layout = dot, rankdir = LR]

  # node definitions with substituted label text
  node [shape = oval]
  a [label = '@@1']
  b [label = '@@2']
  c [label = '@@3']
  d [label = '@@4']

  a -> b -> c -> d
  }

  [1]: names(iris)[1]
  [2]: names(iris)[2]
  [3]: names(iris)[3]
  [4]: names(iris)[4]
```

```
    ",
  height = 100)
```

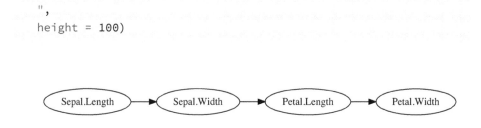

FIGURE 4.5: A diagram using parameters input from R.

4.15.3   Other packages for making diagrams

You may also check out these packages for creating diagrams: **nomnoml** (Luraschi et al., 2020), **diagram** (Soetaert, 2017), **dagitty** (Textor and van der Zander, 2016), **ggdag** (Barrett, 2020), and **plantuml** (https://github.com/rkrug/plantuml).

4.16   Escape special characters

Some characters have special meanings in the Markdown syntax. If you want these characters verbatim, you have to escape them. For example, a pair of underscores surrounding text usually makes the text italic. You need to escape the underscores if you want verbatim underscores instead of italic text. The way to escape a special character is to add a backslash before it, e.g., I do not want _italic text_ here. Similarly, if # does not indicate a section heading, you may write \# This is not a heading.

As mentioned in Section 4.12, a sequence of whitespaces will be rendered as a single regular space. If you want to render the sequence of spaces literally, you need to escape each of them, e.g., keep the social \ \ \ distance. When a space is escaped, it is converted to a "non-breaking space," which means the line will not be wrapped at this space, e.g., Mr.\ Dervieux.

4.17 Comment out text

It is useful to comment out text in the source document, which will not be displayed in the final output document. For this purpose, we can use the HTML syntax `<!-- your comment -->`. The comments will not be displayed in any output format.

Comments can span either a single line or multiple lines. This may be useful for you to write draft content.

If you use RStudio, you can use the keyboard shortcut `Ctrl + Shift + C` (`Command + Shift + C` on macOS) to comment out a line of text.

4.18 Omit a heading in the table of contents

If you do not want certain section headings to be included in the table of contents, you can add two classes to the heading: `unlisted` and `unnumbered`. For example:

```
# Section heading {.unlisted .unnumbered}
```

Note that this feature requires at least Pandoc 2.10. You may check your Pandoc version via `rmarkdown::pandoc_version()`. If the version is lower than 2.10, you may install a newer version (see Section 1.1).

4.19 Put together all code in the appendix (*)

Unless the target readers are highly interested in the computational details while they read a report, you may not want to show the source code blocks in the report. For this purpose, you can set the chunk option `echo = FALSE` to hide the source code instead, so readers will not be distracted by the program code for computing. However, the source code is still important for the sake of reproducible research. Sometimes readers may want to verify the computational correctness after they have finished reading the report. In this case, it can be a good idea to hold all code blocks in the body of the report, and display them at the end of a document (e.g., in an appendix).

There is a simple method of extracting all code chunks in a document and putting them together in a single code chunk using the chunk option `ref.label` and the function `knitr::all_labels()`, e.g.,

```
# Appendix: All code for this report

```{r ref.label=knitr::all_labels(), echo=TRUE, eval=FALSE}
```
```

Please read Section 14.1.3 if you are not familiar with the chunk option `ref.label`.

The function `knitr::all_labels()` returns a vector of all chunk labels in the document, so `ref.label` = `knitr::all_labels()` means retrieving all source code chunks to this code chunk. With the chunk options `echo` = `TRUE` (display the code) and `eval` = `FALSE` (do not evaluate this particular code chunk because all code has been executed before), you can show a copy of all your source code in one code chunk.

Since `ref.label` can be a character vector of arbitrary chunk labels, you can certainly filter the labels to decide a subset of code chunks to display in the code appendix. Below is an example (credits to Ariel Muldoon[9]) of excluding the labels `setup` and `get-labels`:

```
```{r get-labels, echo = FALSE}
labs = knitr::all_labels()
labs = setdiff(labs, c("setup", "get-labels"))
```

```{r all-code, ref.label=labs, eval=FALSE}
```
```

You can also filter code chunks using the arguments of `knitr::all_labels()`. For example, you may use `knitr::all_labels(engine == "Rcpp", echo == FALSE)` to obtain all your code chunks that use the Rcpp engine (`engine == "Rcpp"`) and are not displayed in the document (`echo = FALSE`). If you want precise control

---

[9]https://yihui.org/en/2018/09/code-appendix/

over which code chunks to display in the appendix, you may use a special chunk option `appendix = TRUE` on certain code chunks, and `ref.label = knitr::all_labels(appendix == TRUE)` to obtain the labels of these code chunks.

4.20 Manipulate Markdown via Pandoc Lua filters (*)

Technically, this section may be a little advanced, but once you learn how your Markdown content is translated into the Pandoc abstract syntax tree (AST), you will have the power of manipulating any Markdown elements with the programming language called Lua.

Basically, when Pandoc reads a Markdown file, the content will be parsed into an AST. Pandoc allows you to modify this AST with Lua scripts. We use the following simple Markdown file (named `ast.md`) to show what the AST means:

```
## Section One

Hello world!
```

This file contains a header and a paragraph. After Pandoc parses this content, it may be easier for R users to understand the resulting AST if we convert the file to the JSON format:

```
pandoc -f markdown -t json -o ast.json ast.md
```

Then read the JSON file into R, and print out the data structure.

When you do this, you will see that the Markdown content is represented in a recursive list. Its structure is printed below. The label t stands for "type," and c stands for "content." Take the header for example. Its type is "Header", and its content has three sub-elements: the header level (2), the attributes (e.g., the ID is `section-one`), and the text content.

```
xfun:::tree(
  jsonlite::fromJSON('ast.json', simplifyVector = FALSE)
)
```

```
List of 3
 |-blocks                  :List of 2
 |   |-:List of 2
 |   |   |-t: chr "Header"
 |   |   |-c:List of 3
 |   |       |-: int 2
 |   |       |-:List of 3
 |   |       |   |-: chr "section-one"
 |   |       |   |-: list()
 |   |       |   |-: list()
 |   |       |-:List of 3
 |   |           |-:List of 2
 |   |           |   |-t: chr "Str"
 |   |           |   |-c: chr "Section"
 |   |           |-:List of 1
 |   |           |   |-t: chr "Space"
 |   |           |-:List of 2
 |   |               |-t: chr "Str"
 |   |               |-c: chr "One"
 |   |-:List of 2
 |       |-t: chr "Para"
 |       |-c:List of 3
 |           |-:List of 2
 |           |   |-t: chr "Str"
 |           |   |-c: chr "Hello"
 |           |-:List of 1
 |           |   |-t: chr "Space"
 |           |-:List of 2
 |               |-t: chr "Str"
 |               |-c: chr "world!"
 |-pandoc-api-version:List of 2
 |   |-: int 1
 |   |-: int 21
 |-meta                    : Named list()
```

After you are aware of the AST, you can modify it with the Lua programming language. Pandoc has a built-in Lua interpreter, so you do not need to install additional tools. The Lua scripts are called "Lua filters" for Pandoc. Next we give a quick example of raising the levels of headers by one, e.g., convert level 3 headers to level 2 headers. This may be useful when the top-level headers of your document are level 2 headers, but you want to start with level 1 headers instead.

First, we create a Lua script file named `raise-header.lua`, which contains a function named `Header`, indicating that we want to modify elements of the type "Header" (in general, you can use the type name as the function name to process elements of a certain type):

```
function Header(el)
  -- The header level can be accessed via the attribute 'level'
  -- of the element. See the Pandoc documentation later.
  if (el.level <= 1) then
    error("I don't know how to raise the level of h1")
  end
  el.level = el.level - 1
  return el
end
```

Then we can pass this script to Pandoc via the argument `--lua-filter`, e.g.,

```
pandoc -t markdown --atx-headers \
  --lua-filter=raise-header.lua ast.md
```

```
# Section One
```

```
Hello world!
```

You can see that we have successfully converted `## Section One` to `# Section One`. You may feel this example is trivial, and wonder why not simply replace `##` with `#` with a regular expression like:

```
gsub("^##", "#", readLines("ast.md"))
```

Usually it is not robust to manipulate a structured document with regular expressions, because there are almost always exceptions, e.g., what if `##` means a comment in R code? The AST gives you the structured data, so you know for sure that you are modifying the expected elements.

Pandoc has extensive documentation on Lua filters at `https://pandoc.org/lua-filters.html`, where you can find a large number of examples. You can

also find some filters written by the community in the GitHub repository at
`https://github.com/pandoc/lua-filters`.

In the R Markdown world, below is an incomplete list of packages that have
made use of Lua filters (usually they are in the `inst/` directory):

- The **rmarkdown** package (`https://github.com/rstudio/rmarkdown`) contains filters that insert page breaks (see Section 4.1) and generate custom
  blocks (see Section 9.6).

- The **pagedown** package (Xie et al., 2020b) contains filters that help implement footnotes and the list of figures on HTML pages.

- The **govdown** package (Garmonsway, 2020) contains filters to convert Pandoc's fenced `Div`s to appropriate HTML tags.

You can also find an example in Section 5.1.2 in this book, which shows you
how to change the text color with a Lua filter.

For R Markdown users who do not want to create R packages to ship the Lua
filters (like the above packages), you may store these Lua scripts anywhere
on your computer, and apply them through the `pandoc_args` option of an R
Markdown output format, e.g.,

```
---
output:
  html_document:
    pandoc_args:
      - --lua-filter=raise-header.lua
---
```

5

Formatting

The greatest strength of the Markdown language is that its simplicity makes it very easy to read and write even to newcomers. This is its key design principle, as outlined by the creator of the original Markdown language:

> A Markdown-formatted document should be publishable as-is, as plain text, without looking like it's been marked up with tags or formatting instructions.
>
> — John Gruber[1]

However, this comes at a cost of customization. Many features of typical word processors are not directly available in Markdown, e.g.,

- changing the font size of a piece of text;
- changing the font color of certain words;
- specifying text alignment.

We leave it to you to decide whether such features are worth your effort. To some degree, Markdown reflects the philosophy of Stoicism: the "natural world" consists of plain text, and you should not be *controlled* by the desire for (visual) pleasure. Anyway, this chapter offers some tips on how you can customize the appearance and styling of elements in an R Markdown document.

If you need a reminder in the basics of the Markdown language, the R Markdown cheatsheet at `https://www.rstudio.com/resources/cheatsheets/` provides a good overview of the basic syntax.

---

[1]`http://daringfireball.net/projects/markdown/syntax#philosophy`

5.1 Font color

The Markdown syntax has no built-in method for changing text colors. We can use HTML and LaTeX syntax to change the formatting of words:

- For HTML, we can wrap the text in the `<span>` tag and set color with CSS, e.g., `<span style="color: red;">text</span>`.

- For PDF, we can use the LaTeX command `\textcolor{}{}`. This requires the LaTeX package **xcolor**, which is included in Pandoc's default LaTeX template.

As an example of changing the color in PDF text:

```
---
output: pdf_document
---
```

```
Roses are \textcolor{red}{red}, violets are \textcolor{blue}{blue}.
```

In the above example, the first set of curly braces contains the desired text color, and the second set of curly braces contains the text to which this color should be applied.

If you want to design an R Markdown document for multiple output formats, you should not embed raw HTML or LaTeX code in your document, because they will be ignored in the other output formats (e.g., LaTeX code will be ignored in HTML output, and HTML tags will be lost in LaTeX output). Next, we provide two possible methods to deal with this issue.

5.1.1 Using an R function to write raw HTML or LaTeX code

We can write a custom R function to insert the correct syntax depending on the output format using the `is_latex_output()` and `is_html_output()` functions in **knitr** as follows:

```
colorize <- function(x, color) {
  if (knitr::is_latex_output()) {
    sprintf("\\textcolor{%s}{%s}", color, x)
  } else if (knitr::is_html_output()) {
    sprintf("<span style='color: %s;'>%s</span>", color,
```

```
        x)
    } else x
}
```

We can then use the code in an inline R expression `` `r colorize("some words in red", "red")` ``, which will create some words in red (you will not see the red color if you are reading this book printed in black and white).

5.1.2   Using a Pandoc Lua filter (*)

This method may be a little advanced for R users because it involves another programming language, Lua, but it is extremely powerful—you can programmatically modify Markdown elements via Pandoc's Lua filters (see Section 4.20). Below is a full example:

```
---
title: "Color text with a Lua filter"
output:
  html_document:
    pandoc_args: ["--lua-filter=color-text.lua"]
  pdf_document:
    pandoc_args: ["--lua-filter=color-text.lua"]
    keep_tex: true
---
```

First, we define a Lua filter and write it to the file `color-text.lua`.

````
```{cat, engine.opts = list(file = "color-text.lua")}
Span = function(el)
  color = el.attributes['color']
  -- if no color attribute, return unchange
  if color == nil then return el end

  -- tranform to <span style="color: red;"></span>
  if FORMAT:match 'html' then
    -- remove color attributes
    el.attributes['color'] = nil
    -- use style attribute instead
````
````

```
      el.attributes['style'] = 'color: ' .. color .. ';'
      -- return full span element
      return el
    elseif FORMAT:match 'latex' then
      -- remove color attributes
      el.attributes['color'] = nil
      -- encapsulate in latex code
      table.insert(
        el.content, 1,
        pandoc.RawInline('latex', '\\textcolor{'..color..'}{')
      )
      table.insert(
        el.content,
        pandoc.RawInline('latex', '}')
      )
      -- returns only span content
      return el.content
    else
      -- for other format return unchanged
      return el
    end
  end
```

Now we can test the filter with some text in brackets with
the `color` attribute, e.g.,

```
> Roses are [red and **bold**]{color="red"} and
> violets are [blue]{color="blue"}.
```

In this example, we implicitly used a Pandoc Markdown extension named
bracketed_spans, which allows us to write text with attributes, e.g.,
[text]{.class attribute="value"}. The Lua filter defined in the cat code
chunk[2] puts text in if the output for-

---

[2]If you are not familiar with cat code chunks, please see Section 15.6. We used this engine
here to conveniently write out a chunk to a .lua file, so we do not have to manage the Lua
script in a separate file color-text.lua. If you do not want to use the cat engine, you can
definitely copy the Lua code and save it to a separate file, instead of embedding the Lua code
in a code chunk.

mat is HTML, and in `\textcolor{...}{}` if the output format is LaTeX. The Lua filter is written to a file `color-text.lua`, and enabled through the command-line option `--lua-filter` passed to Pandoc via the `pandoc_args` option of the output formats.

Compared to the previous method, the advantage of using the Lua filter is that you can still use Markdown syntax inside the brackets, whereas using the R function `colorize()` in the previous section does not allow Markdown syntax (e.g., `colorize('**bold**')` will not be bold).

5.2 Indent text

As mentioned in Section 4.12, whitespaces are often meaningless in Markdown. Markdown will also ignore spaces used for indentation by default. However, we may want to keep the indentation in certain cases, e.g., in verses and addresses. In these situations, we can use line blocks by starting the line with a vertical bar (|). The line breaks and any leading spaces will be preserved in the output. For example:[3]

```
| When dollars appear it's a sign
|    that your code does not quite align
| Ensure that your math
|    in xaringan hath
|    been placed on a single long line
```

The output is:

When dollars appear it's a sign
   that your code does not quite align
Ensure that your math
   in xaringan hath
   been placed on a single long line

---

[3]This is a limerick written by Claus Ekstrøm: `https://yihui.org/en/2018/06/xaringan-math-limerick/`.

The lines can be hard-wrapped in the Markdown source. If the continuation line begins with a space, the previous line break and the leading spaces on this line will be ignored as usual. For example:

```
| Hiring Manager
| School of Ninja,
  Hacker's University
| 404 Not Found Road,
  Undefined 0x1234, NA
```

The output is:

Hiring Manager
School of Ninja, Hacker's University
404 Not Found Road, Undefined 0x1234, NA

You can see that the line break after "School of Ninja" was ignored.

5.3   Control the width of text output

Sometimes the text output printed from R code may be too wide. If the output document has a fixed page width (e.g., PDF documents), the text output may exceed the page margins. See Figure 5.1 for an example.

The R global option `width` can be used to control the width of printed text output from some R functions, and you may try a smaller value if the default is too large. This option typically indicates a rough number of characters per line (except for East Asian languages). For example:

```
The output is too wide in this chunk:

```{r}
options(width = 300)
```
```

```
matrix(runif(100), ncol = 20)
```

The output of this chunk looks better:

```{r}
options(width = 60)
matrix(runif(100), ncol = 20)
```

Not all R functions respect the `width` option. If this option does not work, your only choice may be to wrap the long lines of text. This is actually the default behavior of the `html_document` output format. If the HTML output format that you are using does not wrap the long lines, you may apply the CSS code below (see Section 7.1 for instructions):

```
pre code {
  white-space: pre-wrap;
}
```

For PDF output, it is trickier to wrap the lines. One solution is to use the LaTeX package **listings**, which can be enabled via the Pandoc argument --listings. Then you have to set an option for this package, and the setup code can be included from an external LaTeX file (see Section 6.1 for how), e.g.,

```
---
output:
  pdf_document:
    pandoc_args: --listings
    includes:
      in_header: preamble.tex
---
```

In `preamble.tex`, we set an option of the **listings** package:

```
\lstset{
  breaklines=true
}
```

If you do not like the appearance of code blocks with **listings**, you can set up other **listings** options in \lstset{}, e.g., you may change the font family with basicstyle=\ttfamily. You can find more information about this package in its documentation: https://ctan.org/pkg/listings.

Figure 5.1 shows the default pdf_document output that contains wide text, which exceeds the page margin. Figure 5.2 shows the PDF output when we use the **listings** package to wrap the text.

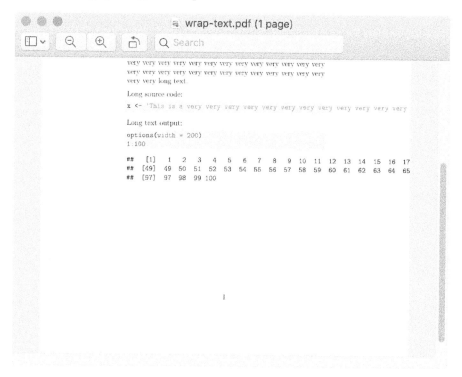

FIGURE 5.1: Normal text output that is too wide.

5.4   Control the size of plots/images

The size of plots made in R can be controlled by the chunk option fig.width and fig.height (in inches). Equivalently, you can use the fig.dim option to specify the width and height in a numeric vector of length 2, e.g., fig.dim = c(8, 6) means fig.width = 8 and fig.height = 6. These options set the physical size of plots, and you can choose to display a different size in the

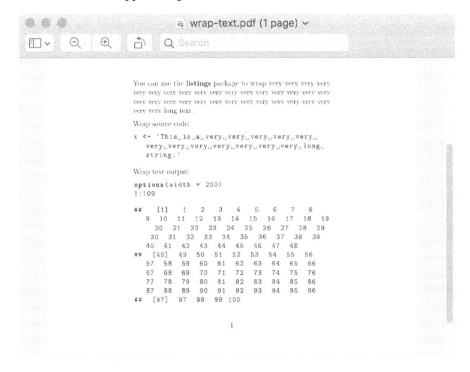

FIGURE 5.2: Text output wrapped with the listings package.

output using chunk options `out.width` and `out.height`, e.g., `out.width = "50%"`.

If a plot or an image is not generated from an R code chunk, you can include it in two ways:

- Use the Markdown syntax `![caption](path/to/image)`. In this case, you can set the size of the image using the `width` and/or `height` attributes, e.g.,

```
We include an image in the next paragraph:
```

```
![A nice image.](foo/bar.png){width=50%}
```

- Use the **knitr** function `knitr::include_graphics()` in a code chunk. You can use chunk options such as `out.width` and `out.height` for this chunk, e.g.,

```
We include an external image with the R function:

```{r, echo=FALSE, out.width="50%", fig.cap="A nice image."}
knitr::include_graphics("foo/bar.png")
```
```

We used the width 50% in the above examples, which means half of the width of the image container (if the image is directly contained by a page instead of a child element of the page, that means half of the page width). If you know that you only want to generate the image for a specific output format, you can use a specific unit. For example, you may use 300px if the output format is HTML.

5.5   Figure alignment

The chunk option `fig.align` specifies the alignment of figures. For example, you can center images with `fig.align = 'center'`, or right-align images with `fig.align = 'right'`. This option works for both HTML and LaTeX output, but may not work for other output formats (such as Word, unfortunately). It works for both plots drawn from R code chunks and external images included via `knitr::include_graphics()`.

5.6   Verbatim code chunks

Typically we write code chunks and inline expressions that we want to be parsed and evaluated by **knitr**. However, if you are trying to write a tutorial on using **knitr**, you may need to generate a verbatim code chunk or inline expression that is *not* parsed by **knitr**, and we want to display the content of the chunk header.

Unfortunately, we cannot wrap the code chunk in another layer of backticks, but instead we must make the code chunk invalid within the source code by inserting `` `r ''` `` in the chunk header. This will be evaluated as an inline expression to *an empty string* by **knitr**. For this example, the following "code chunk" in the source document:

````
```{r, eval=TRUE}`r ''`
1 + 1
```
````

will be rendered as:

````
```{r, eval=TRUE}
1 + 1
```
````

in the output. The inline expression is gone because it is substituted by an empty string. However, that is only the first step. To show something verbatim in the output, the syntax in Markdown is to wrap it in a code block (indent by four spaces or use backtick fences). This will be the actual source if you want to see the output above:

`````
````
```{r, eval=TRUE}`r ''`
1 + 1
```
````
`````

Why four backticks? That is because you have to use at least N+1 backticks to wrap up N backticks.

5.6.1 Show a verbatim inline expression

There are multiple ways to show a verbatim inline expression. The first way is to break the inline expression after `` `r ``, e.g.,

```
This will show a verbatim inline R expression `` `r
1+1` `` in the output.
```

In the output document, you should see:

This will show a verbatim inline R expression `` `r 1+1` `` in the output.

The trick works for two reasons: (1) a single line break is often the same as a space to Markdown parsers (by comparison, two consecutive line breaks means starting a new paragraph); (2) **knitr** requires a space after ` r to parse it; if the space is missing, it will not be treated as an inline expression.

Another way to show a verbatim inline R expression is to wrap the R code in `knitr::inline_expr()`, e.g.,

```
This will show a verbatim inline R expression
`` `r knitr::inline_expr("1+1")` `` in the output.
```

I'd recommend the second way, because the first way is more or less a hack taking advantage of the Markdown syntax and **knitr**'s parser.

5.7 Line numbers for code blocks (*)

You can add line numbers to either source code blocks, via the chunk option `attr.source = ".numberLines"`, or text output blocks, via `attr.output = ".numberLines"` (see Section 11.13 for more information on these options), e.g.,

```
```{r, attr.source='.numberLines'}
if (TRUE) {
  x <- 1:10
  x + 1
}
```
```

The output is:

```
1  if (TRUE) {
2    x <- 1:10
3    x + 1
4  }
```

Note that for HTML output, you have to choose a syntax highlighting theme provided by Pandoc, which means the `highlight` option of the output format should not be `default` or `textmate`. You can use other values for this option listed on the help page `?rmarkdown::html_document`, e.g.,

```
output:
  html_document:
    highlight: tango
```

For **bookdown**'s `gitbook` output format, you may need to adjust the CSS a little bit for the line numbers to be displayed properly on the left side of the code. Below is what we used for this book (if you find the line numbers too close to the left margin, increase the `left` value to, say, `-0.2em`):

```
pre.numberSource code > span > a:first-child::before {
  left: -0.3em;
}
```

For **revealjs**'s `revealjs_presentation` output format (El Hattab and Allaire, 2017), you may also need to adjust the CSS.

```
.reveal pre code {
  overflow: visible;
}
```

See Section 7.1 if you do not know how to apply custom CSS styles to HTML output.

You can also specify the starting number via the `startFrom` attribute, e.g.,

```
```{r, attr.source='.numberLines startFrom="5"'}
if (TRUE) {
  1:10
}
```
```

Line numbers are not supported for Word output at the moment.

5.8   Multi-column layout (*)

Pandoc's Markdown supports the multi-column layout for slides but not other types of documents. In this recipe, we show how to use the multi-

column layout in normal HTML documents and LaTeX documents. This
recipe was inspired by Atsushi Yasumoto's solutions to the **knitr** issue
`https://github.com/yihui/knitr/issues/1743`.

The recipe will be much simpler if you only need to consider HTML output,
because arranging HTML elements side by side is relatively simple via CSS.
It will be even simpler if you only need to arrange the text output of a code
chunk side by side. Below is the first example:

```
---

output: html_document

---
```

```
```{r attr.source="style='display:inline-block;'", collapse=TRUE}
1:10  # a sequence from 1 to 10
10:1  # in the reverse order
```
```

The CSS attribute `display: inline-block;` means the output code blocks
(i.e., the `<pre>` tags in HTML) should be displayed as inline elements. By
default, these blocks are displayed as block-level elements (i.e., `display:
block;`) and will occupy whole rows. The chunk option `collapse = TRUE`
means the text output will be merged into the R source code block, so both
the source and its text output will be placed in the same `<pre>` block.

If you want to arrange arbitrary content side by side in HTML output, you
can use Pandoc's fenced `Div`.[4] The name "Div" comes from the HTML tag
`<div>`, but you can interpret it as an arbitrary block or container. A `Div`
starts and ends with three or more colons (e.g., `:::`). A `Div` with more colons
can contain `Div`s with fewer colons. An important and useful feature of the
fenced `Div` is that you can attach attributes to it. For example, you can apply
the CSS attribute `display: flex;` to an outside container, so that the inside
containers will be placed side by side:

```
---

output: html_document

---
```

```
::::: {style="display: flex;"}
```

---

[4]`https://pandoc.org/MANUAL.html#divs-and-spans`

```
::: {}
Here is the **first** Div.

```{r}
str(iris)
```

:::

::: {}
And this block will be put on the right:

```{r}
plot(iris[, -5])
```

:::

::::
```

In the above example, the outside Div (::::) contains two Divs (:::). You can certainly add more Divs inside. To learn more about the very powerful CSS attribute display: flex; (CSS Flexbox), you may read the guide at https://css-tricks.com/snippets/css/a-guide-to-flexbox/. The CSS Grid (display: grid;) is also very powerful and can be used in the above example, too. If you want to try it, you may change display: flex; to display: grid; grid-template-columns: 1fr 1fr; grid-column-gap: 10px;. See the guide at https://css-tricks.com/snippets/css/complete-guide-grid/ if you want to learn more about the grid layout.

It is trickier if you want the layout to work for both HTML and LaTeX output. We show a full example below that works for HTML documents, LaTeX documents, and Beamer presentations:

```
---
output:
  html_document:
    css: columns.css
  pdf_document:
    keep_tex: true
    includes:
```

```
      in_header: columns.tex
  beamer_presentation:
    keep_tex: true
    includes:
      in_header: columns.tex
---
```

Two columns

Below is a Div containing three child Divs side by side. The Div
in the middle is empty, just to add more space between the left
and right Divs.

```
::::::: {.cols data-latex=""}

::: {.col data-latex="{0.55\textwidth}"}
```{r, echo=FALSE, fig.width=5, fig.height=4}
par(mar = c(4, 4, .2, .1))
plot(cars, pch = 19)
```
:::

::: {.col data-latex="{0.05\textwidth}"}
\
<!-- an empty Div (with a white space), serving as
a column separator -->
:::

::: {.col data-latex="{0.4\textwidth}"}
The figure on the left-hand side shows the `cars` data.
```

Lorem ipsum dolor sit amet, consectetur adipiscing elit, sed do
eiusmod tempor incididunt ut labore et dolore magna aliqua. Ut
enim ad minim veniam, quis nostrud exercitation ullamco laboris
nisi ut aliquip ex ea commodo consequat. Duis aute irure dolor
in reprehenderit in voluptate velit esse cillum dolore eu fugiat
nulla pariatur.

: : :

: : : : : :

Two columns

Below is a Div containing three child Divs side by side. The Div in the middle is empty, just to add more space between the left and right Divs.

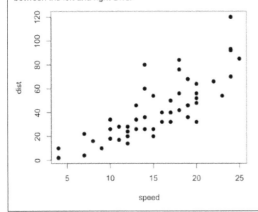

The figure on the left-hand side shows the `cars` data.

Lorem ipsum dolor sit amet, consectetur adipiscing elit, sed do eiusmod tempor incididunt ut labore et dolore magna aliqua. Ut enim ad minim veniam, quis nostrud exercitation ullamco laboris nisi ut aliquip ex ea commodo consequat. Duis aute irure dolor in reprehenderit in voluptate velit esse cillum dolore eu fugiat nulla pariatur.

FIGURE 5.3: A two-column layout that works for HTML, LaTeX, and Beamer output.

Figure 5.3 shows the output. In this example, we used an outside Div with the class .cols and three inside Divs with the class .col. For HTML output, we introduced an external CSS file columns.css, in which we applied the Flexbox layout to the outside Div so the inside Divs can be placed side by side:

```
.cols {display: flex; }
```

For LaTeX output (pdf_document), we have to introduce some dirty hacks stored in columns.tex to the LaTeX preamble to define the LaTeX environments cols and col:

```
\newenvironment{cols}[1][]{}{}
```

```
\newenvironment{col}[1]{\begin{minipage}{#1}\ignorespaces}{%
\end{minipage}
\ifhmode\unskip\fi
```

```
\aftergroup\useignorespacesandallpars}

\def\useignorespacesandallpars#1\ignorespaces\fi{%
#1\fi\ignorespacesandallpars}

\makeatletter
\def\ignorespacesandallpars{%
  \@ifnextchar\par
    {\expandafter\ignorespacesandallpars\@gobble}%
    {}%
}
\makeatother
```

The `col` environment is particularly complicated mainly because Pandoc starts a new paragraph for each `Div` in LaTeX output, and we have to remove these new paragraphs. Otherwise, the `Div`s cannot be placed side by side. The hacks were borrowed from https://tex.stackexchange.com/q/179016/9128.

For Beamer output, we apply the same hacks in `columns.tex`. Please note that Pandoc has provided some special `Div`'s for slide shows,[5] such as `:::` `{.columns}`, `:::` `{.column}`, and `:::` `{.incremental}`. Because they already have their special meanings, you must be careful *not* to use these types of `Div`'s if you intend to convert a `Div` to a LaTeX environment in the way mentioned in this section. That is why we did not use the `Div` types `columns` or `column`, but chose to use `cols` and `col` instead.

For more information about fenced `Div`'s, please refer to Section 9.6.

---

[5]https://pandoc.org/MANUAL.html#producing-slide-shows-with-pandoc

6

LaTeX Output

For many authors, the main output of their work will be the PDF report, in which case they can utilize the powerful styling of LaTeX. In this chapter, we discuss approaches that can be used to customize PDF reports, such as including LaTeX code or packages in the preamble, using custom LaTeX templates, adding headers and footers, generating sub-figures, and writing raw LaTeX code in the document body.

We want to offer a note of caution before we start, however. One benefit of R Markdown is the fact that a single source document can create documents with multiple formats. By tailoring your work to a single output format, you may improve the appearance and performance of a single output format, but at the expense of this transferability. This problem is not unique to LaTeX, but all other output formats as well.

6.1   Add LaTeX code to the preamble

The general structure of a LaTeX document is like this:

```
\documentclass{article}
% preamble
\begin{document}
% body
\end{document}
```

That is, you declare the document class in \documentclass{}, load certain LaTeX packages and set certain options if necessary in the preamble, and start writing the body of your document after \begin{document}. A Markdown document is mostly the body of the document.

If you want to add anything to the preamble, you have to use the `includes` option of `pdf_document`. This option has three sub-options: `in_header`, `be-fore_body`, and `after_body`. Each of them takes one or multiple file paths. The file(s) specified in `in_header` will be added to the preamble. The files specified in `before_body` and `after_body` are added before and after the document body, respectively.

For example, below is a trick that turns hyperlinks in text into footnotes. This trick is useful when the PDF output document is printed on paper, because readers will not be able to click the links (generated from `\href{URL}{text}`) on paper but can see the URLs in footnotes. This trick displays both the text and URL.

```
% you may want to save a copy of \href before redefining it
% \let\oldhref\href
\renewcommand{\href}[2]{#2\footnote{\url{#1}}}
```

You can save the above code in a file with an arbitrary filename, e.g., `pream-ble.tex`. Then include it in the preamble through:

```
output:
  pdf_document:
    includes:
      in_header: "preamble.tex"
```

For this particular trick, you do not really have to implement it by yourself, but can simply set the YAML option `links-as-notes` to `true` because it is a built-in feature of Pandoc's default LaTeX template (see Section 6.2).

Another way to add code to the preamble is to pass it directly to the `header-includes` field in the YAML frontmatter. We will show an example in Section 6.3. The advantage of using `header-includes` is that you can keep everything in one R Markdown document. However, if your report is to be generated in multiple output formats, we still recommend that you use the `includes` method, because the `header-includes` field is unconditional, and will be included in non-LaTeX output documents, too. By comparison, the `includes` option is only applied to the `pdf_document` format.

6.2 Pandoc options for LaTeX output

If you are using the default Pandoc template for LaTeX output, there are several options that you may set to adjust the appearance of the PDF output document. We list a few example options below, and you may see `https://pandoc.org/MANUAL.html#variables-for-latex` for a full list.

```
documentclass: book
classoption:
  - twocolumn
  - landscape
papersize: a5
linestretch: 1.5
fontsize: 12pt
links-as-notes: true
```

The meanings of these options should be clear if you have some knowledge about LaTeX. The `documentclass` option sets the document class, e.g., `article`, `book`, and `report`, etc. The `classoption` is a list of options to be passed to the document class, e.g., you can create a two-column document with the `twocolumn` option,[1] or the landscape layout with the `landscape` option (the default is the portrait layout). The `papersize` option sets the paper size, e.g., `a4`, `paper`, or `a5`. The `linestretch` option sets the line spacing. The `fontsize` option sets the font size, e.g., `10pt`, `11pt`, or `12pt`. The `links-as-notes` option turns links in text to footnotes, which is useful when the PDF is printed on paper, because readers will not be able to click the links on paper but can see the URLs in footnotes.

Changing fonts can be a little trickier. It depends on which LaTeX engine you are using. If you are using `pdflatex`, which is usually the default engine for most LaTeX-based output formats, you may use the `fontfamily` option to select a LaTeX font package to be loaded in your document to change the font, e.g.,

---

[1]This option changes the layout of the whole document, but if you want to switch back to the one-column mode from a certain point, you may insert a command \onecolumn at that point. If you want to continue the two-column mode, insert \twocolumn.

```
fontfamily: accanthis
output:
  pdf_document:
    latex_engine: pdflatex
```

Then the document will use the font Accanthis.[2] You may see `https://tug.org/FontCatalogue/` for a list of many other LaTeX font packages. If your LaTeX distribution is TinyTeX and the required font packages have not been installed, they should be automatically installed when the document is compiled (see Section 1.2).

If you use the LaTeX engine `xelatex` or `lualatex`, you will be able to select fonts that are available on your local computer, and do not have to install additional LaTeX packages. YAML options like `mainfont`, `sansfont`, and `monofont` can be used to specify the main font, sans serif font, and typewriter font, respectively, e.g.,

```
mainfont: Arial
output:
  pdf_document:
    latex_engine: xelatex
```

You can also use some of those LaTeX options when you generate Beamer slides, because a Beamer document is a LaTeX document, too. In addition, Pandoc has provided a few more options for Beamer slides, which can be found at `https://pandoc.org/MANUAL.html#variables-for-beamer-slides`. For example, you can specify the author affiliation via the `institute` option:

```
---
output: beamer_presentation
institute: "University of Hackers"
---
```

---

[2]`https://tug.org/FontCatalogue/accanthis/`

6.3 Add logo to title page

We can use the **titling** LaTeX package to alter our title block to include an image. Below is a full example that shows how to add the R logo (`logo.jpg`) to the title page. The image can be of any format that LaTeX supports (e.g., `jpg`, `png`, or `pdf`).

```
---
title: Adding a Logo to LaTeX Title
author: Michael Harper
date: December 7th, 2018
output: pdf_document
header-includes:
  - \usepackage{titling}
  - \pretitle{\begin{center}
    \includegraphics[width=2in,height=2in]{logo.jpg}\LARGE\\}
  - \posttitle{\end{center}}
---

<!-- Optionally include a page break. This will force the start
of the document to the second page -->

\newpage

This is your report.

```{r, include=FALSE}
# copy the R logo to the current directory
file.copy(file.path(R.home("doc"), "html", "logo.jpg"), '.')
```
```

An example output is shown in Figure 6.1.

An alternative method that does not require a special LaTeX package (**titling**) is to just insert the image in the `title` field using the Markdown syntax. For example:

FIGURE 6.1: A logo on a LaTeX title page.

```
title: |
  ![](logo.jpg){width=1in}
  Adding a Logo to LaTeX Title
```

In this case, you will not need the `header-includes` field in the YAML frontmatter in the first example. Please note that although you cannot see them, there are two trailing spaces after `![](logo.jpg){width=1in}`, which means a line break in Markdown (see Section 4.12). Without the line break, the image and the title would be on the same line, which may not be what you desire.

6.4   Include additional LaTeX packages

The use of additional LaTeX packages can allow for extensive customization of document styling. In addition, several packages such as **kableExtra** (Zhu, 2019) may have LaTeX dependencies for the R package to function. Much like R, we need to load packages within the R Markdown document before we are able to use their functions.

6.4.1   Loading LaTeX packages

We can load additional LaTeX packages using the `extra_dependencies` option within the `pdf_document` YAML settings. This allows us to provide a list of LaTeX packages to be loaded in the intermediate LaTeX output document, e.g.,

```
---
title: "Using more LaTeX packages"
output:
  pdf_document:
    extra_dependencies: ["bbm", "threeparttable"]
---
```

If you need to specify options when loading the package, you can add a second level to the list and provide the options as a list, e.g.,

```
output:
  pdf_document:
    extra_dependencies:
      caption: ["labelfont={bf}"]
      hyperref: ["unicode=true", "breaklinks=true"]
      lmodern: null
```

For those familiar with LaTeX, this is equivalent to the following LaTeX code:

```
\usepackage[labelfont={bf}]{caption}
\usepackage[unicode=true, breaklinks=true]{hyperref}
\userpackage{lmodern}
```

The advantage of using the `extra_dependencies` argument over the includes argument introduced in Section 6.1 is that you do not need to include an external file, so your Rmd document can be self-contained.

6.4.2   Example packages

There is an extensive community for LaTeX, and there are over 4,000 packages available through the Comprehensive TeX Archive Network[3] (CTAN). Here are some examples of LaTeX packages you could consider using within your report:

- pdfpages[4]: Include full PDF pages from an external PDF document within your document.
- caption[5]: Change the appearance of caption subtitles. For example, you can make the figure title italic or bold.
- fancyhdr[6]: Change the style of running headers of all pages.

6.5   Control the placement of figures

One common frustration with LaTeX is the placement of figures and tables. Unlike in a word processor like Microsoft Word, in which figures are placed directly where the user specifies, LaTeX will attempt to place a figure in a position that does not violate certain typographic rules. In doing so, figures may float away from where they are referenced in the text. This section will explain some background information on how floating environments (such as figures) work and provide several options for customizing their behavior.

6.5.1   Floating environments

By default, figures with captions are generated with the `figure` environment in LaTeX. For example, Pandoc will convert the following Markdown code that contains an image

```
![This is a figure.](images/cool.jpg)
```

to the LaTeX code:

---

[3] https://ctan.org
[4] https://ctan.org/pkg/pdfpages
[5] https://ctan.org/pkg/caption
[6] https://ctan.org/pkg/fancyhdr

```
\begin{figure}
  \includegraphics{images/cool.jpg}
  \caption{This is a figure.}
\end{figure}
```

The `figure` environment is a floating environment. You can read a detailed description of floats at `https://en.wikibooks.org/wiki/LaTeX/Floats, _Figures_and_Captions`. In summary, floats are used as containers for things that cannot be broken over a page, such as tables and figures. If the figure or table cannot be contained in the space left on the current page, La-TeX will try to place it at the top of the next page. If the figure is tall enough, it may occupy the whole next page, even if there is still space left for a few lines of text. The behavior can be controlled by different placement specifiers in square brackets after `\begin{figure}`, e.g., `\begin{figure}[b]`. Below is a list of possible specifiers:

- h: Place the float *here*, i.e., approximately at the same point it occurs in the source text.
- t: Position at the *top* of the page.
- b: Position at the *bottom* of the page.
- p: Put on a special *page* for floats only.
- !: Override internal parameters LaTeX uses for determining "good" float positions.
- H: Place the float at precisely the location in the LaTeX code. This requires the **float** package (`\usepackage{float}`).

These specifiers can be used in conjunction, e.g., `!b` forces LaTeX to place the figure at the bottom of a page. The default behavior is `tbp`. That is, LaTeX will try to position the figure at the top of the page, then at the bottom, and then on a separate page.

6.5.2 Prevent figures from floating

Many users will initially want to prevent figures from floating in their document, replicating the behavior of a traditional word processor. To do this, we must firstly load the LaTeX package **float**. This can be done by including the following line in the YAML:

```
output:
  pdf_document:
    extra_dependencies: ["float"]
```

We can use the chunk option `fig.pos` to control the float behavior. The option value `!H` will prevent any floating within the document. We can set the default behavior for the document so that all chunks have this setting by including the following line in the first code chunk in your R Markdown document:

```
knitr::opts_chunk$set(fig.pos = "!H", out.extra = "")
```

In general, we do not recommend that users force LaTeX to stop floating figures. This solution was included in this book by popular demand,[7] but there could be some serious side effects when LaTeX is unable to float figures.

6.5.3   Force floats forward

An alternative to forcing all floats to be held is to force floating forward in the text. This can remove a common issue, where a figure is shown at the top of the page before the relevant text comes. This can break the reading flow of a report. We can force the figure to always appear after the text by using the **flafter** LaTeX package as follows:

```
output:
  pdf_document:
    extra_dependencies: ["flafter"]
```

6.5.4   Adjust LaTeX placement rules (*)

LaTeX's own float placement parameters could prevent placements that seem entirely "reasonable" to you—they are notoriously rather conservative. These defaults are displayed in Table 6.1.

To encourage LaTeX not to move your figures, we can alter these default settings. We could include the following in our LaTeX preamble file, reducing

---

[7]The related Stack Overflow question has been viewed for over 45,000 times: https://stackoverflow.com/q/16626462/559676.

TABLE 6.1: Default LaTeX float settings.

Command	Description	Default
topfraction	max fraction of page for floats at top	0.7
bottomfraction	max fraction of page for floats at bottom	0.3
textfraction	min fraction of page for text	0.2
floatpagefraction	min fraction of page that should have floats	0.5
topnumber	max number of floats at top of page	2
bottomnumber	max number of floats at bottom of page	1
totalnumber	max number of floats on a page	3

the minimum amount of text required on a page and allow more room for floats:

```
\renewcommand{\topfraction}{.85}
\renewcommand{\bottomfraction}{.7}
\renewcommand{\textfraction}{.15}
\renewcommand{\floatpagefraction}{.66}
\setcounter{topnumber}{3}
\setcounter{bottomnumber}{3}
\setcounter{totalnumber}{4}
```

If we have added these lines to a .tex file, we could include this file in the preamble of the LaTeX document using the method introduced in Section 6.1.

6.6   LaTeX sub-figures

Sometimes you may want to include multiple images in a single figure environment. Sub-figures allow us to achieve this by arranging multiple images within a single environment and providing each with its own sub-caption.

Sub-figures require the LaTeX package **subfig**. We can load it via the extra_dependencies YAML option within the pdf_document output. For example:

```
---
output:
  pdf_document:
    extra_dependencies: "subfig"
---
```

To arrange all plots from a code chunk in sub-figures, you have to use the chunk options `fig.cap` (the caption for the whole figure environment) and `fig.subcap` (a character vector of the captions for sub-figures). For best output, you can also use the following options:

- `fig.ncol`: The number of columns of sub-figures. By default, all plots are arranged in a single row. You can break them into multiple rows.

- `out.width`: The output width of individual plots. You will normally set this to 100% divided by the number of columns. For example, if you have two plots, the `out.width` option should be equal to or less than 50%, otherwise the plots may exceed the page margin.

Below is an illustrative example:

```
---
output:
  pdf_document:
    extra_dependencies: "subfig"
---
```

```
```{r, fig.cap='Figure 1', fig.subcap=c('(a)', '(b)', '(c)')}
plot(1:10)
plot(cars, pch = 19)
boxplot(Sepal.Width ~ Species, data = iris)
```
```

The output is shown in Figure 6.2. For the sake of simplicity, we omitted a few chunk options in the chunk header of the above example, including `fig.ncol = 2`, `out.width = "50%"`, `fig.align = "center"`, and the actual long captions.

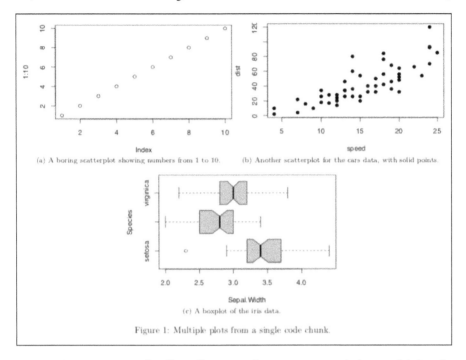

Figure 1: Multiple plots from a single code chunk.

FIGURE 6.2: An example of one figure environment containing multiple sub-figures.

6.7 Render documents containing Unicode characters

If you run into an error like this:

```
! Package inputenc Error:
  Unicode char \u8: not set up for use with LaTeX.
```

it probably means that you are using the default LaTeX engine, pdflatex, to render the (intermediate .tex) document to PDF, which was unable to process certain Unicode characters in your document. If that is the case, you may switch to xelatex or lualatex, e.g.,

```
output:
  pdf_document:
    latex_engine: xelatex
```

You may also change the LaTeX engine for other document output formats, especially those based on `pdf_document`, such as `bookdown::pdf_document2` and `tufte::tufte_handout`, e.g.,

```
output:
  bookdown::pdf_document2:
    latex_engine: lualatex
  tufte::tufte_handout:
    latex_engine: xelatex
```

6.8   Generate a LaTeX fragment

If you work primarily with pure LaTeX documents, you may still find R Markdown useful. Sometimes it may be more convenient to write in R Markdown and convert the document to a LaTeX fragment, which can be included in other LaTeX documents.

When you render an Rmd document to LaTeX, it generates a full LaTeX document that includes the `\documentclass{}`, `\begin{body}`, and `\end{body}`. A LaTeX fragment is basically the body of a full LaTeX document. To render a LaTeX fragment, you may use the `latex_fragment` output format, e.g.,

```
---
output: latex_fragment
---
```

This will render a `.tex` file, e.g., `foo.Rmd` will render `foo.tex`, and you can use `\input{foo.tex}` to include this fragment in another LaTeX document.

6.9   Add custom headers and footers (*)

The LaTeX package **fancyhdr** has provided several commands to customize the header and footer lines of your document. For a more complete guide, please refer to the full documentation at `https://ctan.org/pkg/fancyhdr`.

To begin with, we must load the package. Then we can change the header style, e.g.,

```
\usepackage{fancyhdr}
\pagestyle{fancy}
```

The package offers three different interfaces, but we will use the commands \fancyhead and \fancyfoot. The syntax for the formatting is \fancyhead[selectors]{output text}, whereby the selectors state the part of the header that we wish to customize. We can use the following selectors for the page locators:

- **E** for even pages
- **O** for odd pages
- **L** for the left side
- **C** for the center
- **R** for the right side

For example, \fancyhead[LE,RO]{Your Name} will print the text "Your Name" on the left side of the header for even pages, and the right side for odd pages. We can combine this with additional LaTeX commands to extract details from our document for each page:

- \thepage: the number of the current page.
- \thechapter: the number of the current chapter.
- \thesection: the number of the current section.
- \chaptername: the word "Chapter" in English, or its equivalent in the current language, or the text that the author specified by redefining this command.
- \leftmark: the name and number of the current top-level structure in uppercase letters.
- \rightmark: the name and number of the current next to top-level structure in uppercase letters.

Below is some example LaTeX code that you can add to the preamble using the methods introduced in Section 6.1:

```
\usepackage{fancyhdr}
\pagestyle{fancy}
% center of header
\fancyhead[CO,CE]{Your Document Header}
```

```
% center of footer
\fancyfoot[CO,CE]{And this is a fancy footer}
% page number on the left of even pages and right of odd pages
\fancyfoot[LE,RO]{\thepage}
```

By default, headers and footers will not be displayed on the first page of your PDF document. If we wish to show our footer on the front page, we must include an additional line `\fancypagestyle{plain}{\pagestyle{fancy}}`.

6.10   Use a custom Pandoc LaTeX template (*)

Pandoc converts Markdown to LaTeX through a template. The template is a LaTeX file containing Pandoc variables, and Pandoc will replace these variables with their values. Below is a simple template that only contains a single variable `$body$`:

```
\documentclass{article}
\begin{document}
$body$
\end{document}
```

The value of `$body$` is the LaTeX code generated from the body of the Markdown document. For example, if the body text is `Hello **world**!` in Markdown, the value of `$body$` will be `Hello \textbf{world}!`.

If the LaTeX customization methods in Sections 6.1, 6.2, and 6.4 are not enough for you, you may try to use a custom template instead. A template allows you to use arbitrary LaTeX code in it, and hence is much more flexible. To use a template, include the path of the template in the `template` option of `pdf_document`, e.g.,

```
output:
  pdf_document:
    template: my-template.tex
```

The default LaTeX template of Pandoc can be found at `https://github.com/jgm/pandoc/tree/master/data/templates` (named `default.latex`).

If you want to create your own template, you may want to start with this template.

For the full list of Pandoc variables and their meanings (such as $body$ and $title$), see Pandoc's manual at `https://pandoc.org/MANUAL.html#templates`. You can also use arbitrary custom variables, which are typically passed to the template from the YAML metadata. If you want to learn by examples, you may take a look at the **MonashEBSTemplates** package (`https://github.com/robjhyndman/MonashEBSTemplates`), which has provided several custom LaTeX templates. These templates are under the `inst/rmarkdown/templates/*/resources/` directories (here * denotes the template names). For example, the template for the output format `MonashEBSTemplates::memo` allows you to use a variable `branding` in the YAML metadata to control whether to include the brand logo of Monash University. This is achieved by an `if` statement in the template that looks like this:

```
$if(branding)$%
\includegraphics[height=1.5cm]{monash2}
\vspace*{-0.6cm}
$else$
\vspace*{-1cm}
$endif$
```

6.11 Write raw LaTeX code

By default, Pandoc will preserve raw LaTeX code in Markdown documents when converting the document to LaTeX, so you can use LaTeX commands or environments in Markdown. However, sometimes your LaTeX code might be too complex for Pandoc to parse, in which case Pandoc will treat the content as normal Markdown. The consequence is that special LaTeX characters may be escaped, e.g., Pandoc may convert a backslash \ to \textbackslash{}.

To make sure that Pandoc does not touch the raw LaTeX code in your Markdown document, you may wrap the code in a fenced code block with the attribute `=latex`, e.g.,

````
```{=latex}
\begin{tabular}{ll}
A & B \\
A & B \\
\end{tabular}
```
````

Do not forget the equal sign before `latex`, i.e., it is `=latex` instead of `latex`. This feature requires a Pandoc version higher than 2.0 (check `rmarkdown::pandoc_version()`).

6.12   For hardcore LaTeX users (*)

R Markdown is certainly not the best possible document format for authoring or typesetting documents. Simplicity is both its advantage and disadvantage. LaTeX is much more powerful than Markdown in terms of typesetting at the price of more commands to be typed. If typesetting is of much higher priority to you and you are comfortable with using all kinds of LaTeX commands and environments, you can just use pure LaTeX code instead of Markdown to write the whole document.

The **knitr** package supports a variety of source document formats, including but not limited to R Markdown. Below is an example of intermingling R code with pure LaTeX code:

```
\documentclass{article}
\usepackage[T1]{fontenc}

\begin{document}

Here is a code chunk.

<<foo, fig.height=4>>=
1 + 1
par(mar = c(4, 4, .2, .2))
plot(rnorm(100))
@
```

```
You can also write inline expressions, e.g. $\pi=\Sexpr{pi}$,
and \Sexpr{1.9910214e28} is a big number.
```

```
\end{document}
```

The filename usually has the extension .Rnw, e.g., the above file is latex.Rnw. The idea is the same but the syntax for writing R code chunks and inline R expressions is different. An R code chunk starts with <<>>= (with optional chunk options inside the angle brackets) and ends with @. An inline R expression is written in \Sexpr{}.

The function knitr::knit() can compile an Rnw document to a LaTeX (.tex) output file, which can be further compiled to PDF through your LaTeX tools such as pdflatex. You can also use knitr::knit2pdf() to compile Rnw to PDF in one step. If you use RStudio, you can hit the Compile PDF button on the toolbar. Please note that the default method to compile Rnw documents is through Sweave, and you may want to change it to **knitr** (see the post http://stackoverflow.com/q/27592837/559676 for how to do that).

An Rnw document gives you the full power of LaTeX. This could be your last resort if there are typesetting problems that are really difficult to solve in Markdown. However, before you drop Markdown, we would like to remind you of the fact that a custom Pandoc LaTeX template may also be helpful (see Section 6.10).

7

HTML Output

Compared to LaTeX, HTML may be a little weak in typesetting for paged output. However, it is much more powerful in presenting results, especially when combined with CSS and JavaScript. For example, you can embed interactive applications in HTML, and dynamically modify the appearance and even the content of an HTML page. Some useful yet simple CSS and JavaScript tricks for HTML output are very difficult (and often impossible) to reproduce in LaTeX output.

In this chapter, we introduce techniques to enhance your HTML output from R Markdown, including how to apply custom CSS rules, use custom HTML templates, style or fold code blocks, arrange content in tabs, and embed files on HTML pages.

7.1 Apply custom CSS

We strongly recommend that you learn some CSS and JavaScript if you wish to customize the appearance of HTML documents. Appendix B[1] of the **blogdown** book (Xie et al., 2017) contains short tutorials on HTML, CSS, and JavaScript.

For beginners, it is extremely important to understand selectors and precedence of rules in CSS, otherwise you may be confused why your custom CSS rules do not work as expected (they may not have enough precedence).

To include one or multiple custom stylesheets in an Rmd document, you can use the css option, e.g.,

```
output:
```

---

[1]https://bookdown.org/yihui/blogdown/website-basics.html

```
html_document:
  css: "style.css"
```

To include multiple stylesheets, you may list them in brackets, e.g.,

```
output:
  html_document:
    css: ["style-1.css", "style-2.css"]
```

Alternatively, you can use a css code chunk to embed the CSS rules directly in your Rmd document, e.g.,

```
We embed a `css` code chunk here.

```{css, echo=FALSE}
p {
  font-size: 32px;
}
```
```

The chunk option echo = FALSE means the CSS code will not be displayed verbatim in the output, but a <style> tag containing the CSS code will be generated to the HTML output file.

7.2   Center section headings

As an application of the methods mentioned in Section 7.1, we can use CSS to adjust the alignment of headings. For example, you may center section headings of level 1, 2, and 3 with the CSS code below:

```
h1, h2, h3 {
  text-align: center;
}
```

Please see Section 7.1 on how to apply the CSS to your Rmd document.

7.3 Style code blocks and text output

We can customize the style of code chunks and their text output using the chunk options `class.source` and `class.output`, respectively. These options take character vectors of class names (see Section 11.13 for more information). For example, when `class.source = "important"`, the HTML element containing the code chunk in the output will have a class `important`. Then you can define CSS rules for this class.[2] This can be useful when you want to highlight a certain code chunk or its text output.

By default, the HTML output of R Markdown includes the Bootstrap framework, which makes it easy for you to change the appearance of your code and output, because Bootstrap has predefined some CSS classes for backgrounds:[3] `"bg-primary"`, `"bg-success"`, `"bg-info"`, `"bg-warning"`, and `"bg-danger"`.

Below is an example using the chunk options `class.source = "bg-danger"` and `class.output = "bg-warning"`, and you can see its output in Figure 7.1.

```
---
title: Change the chunk style
output: html_document
---
```

```
When you subset a data frame, it does not necessarily return
a data frame. For example, if you subset two columns, you get
a data frame, but when you try to subset one column, you get
a vector:
```

````
```{r class.source="bg-danger", class.output="bg-warning"}
mtcars[1:5, "mpg"]
```
````

```
To make sure that we always get a data frame, we have to use
the argument `drop = FALSE`. Now we use the chunk option
`class.source = "bg-success"`.
```

---

[2] In this case, the rule would begin `.important` because in CSS, classes are prefixed with a period (.).

[3] https://getbootstrap.com/docs/3.4/css/#helper-classes

````
```{r df-drop-ok, class.source="bg-success"}
mtcars[1:5, "mpg", drop = FALSE]
```
````

When you subset a data frame, it does not necessarily return a data frame. For example, if you subset two columns, you get a data frame, but when you try to subset one column, you get a vector:

```
mtcars[1:5, "mpg"]
```

```
## [1] 21.0 21.0 22.8 21.4 18.7
```

To make sure that we always get a data frame, we have to use the argument `drop = FALSE`. Now we use the chunk option `class.source = "bg-success"`.

```
mtcars[1:5, "mpg", drop = FALSE]
```

```
##                      mpg
## Mazda RX4           21.0
## Mazda RX4 Wag       21.0
## Datsun 710          22.8
## Hornet 4 Drive      21.4
## Hornet Sportabout   18.7
```

FIGURE 7.1: A code chunk and its text output with background colors defined by Bootstrap.

You can also use arbitrary class names and define CSS rules accordingly. In this case, you will have to include your custom CSS rules using the methods mentioned in Section 7.1. Below is an example:

```
---
title: Assign custom classes to chunks
output: html_document
---
```

First we define some CSS rules for a class `watch-out`.

````
```{css, echo=FALSE}
.watch-out {
  background-color: lightpink;
  border: 3px solid red;
  font-weight: bold;
````
````

```
}
```

Then we assign a class `watch-out` to the code chunk via the chunk option `class.source`.

```
```{r class.source="watch-out"}
mtcars[1:5, "mpg"]
```
```

The output style is shown in Figure 7.2.

First we define some CSS rules for a class watch-out .

Then we assign a class watch-out to the code chunk via the chunk option class.source .

```
mtcars[1:5, "mpg"]
```

```
## [1] 21.0 21.0 22.8 21.4 18.7
```

FIGURE 7.2: A code chunk with a light pink background color and a thick red border.

If you want all code blocks in the document to use the custom style, you can set class.source in the global **knitr** options, e.g.,

```
knitr::opts_chunk$set(class.source = "watch-out")
```

You can apply multiple classes to the code blocks. For example, with class.source = c("important", "warning"), the code block will have two classes, "important" and "warning."

If you want to decorate individual elements in code blocks instead of the whole blocks, you may consider using the **flair** package (Bodwin and Glanz, 2020). With this package, you can highlight different parts of your code (such as fixed strings, function names, and arguments) with custom styles (e.g., color, font size, and/or font weight).

7.4 Scrollable code blocks (*)

When you have large amounts of code and/or verbatim text output to display on an HTML page, it may be desirable to limit their heights. Otherwise the page may look overwhelmingly lengthy, and it will be difficult for those who do not want to read the details in the code or its text output to skip these parts. There are multiple ways to solve this problem. One solution is to use the `code_fold` option in the `html_document` format. This option will fold code blocks in the output and readers can unfold them by clicking a button (see Section 7.5 for more details).

The other possible solution is to make the code blocks scrollable within a fixed height when they are too long. This can be achieved by the CSS properties `max-height` and `overflow-y`. Below is a full example with the output in Figure 7.3:

```
---
title: Scrollable code blocks
output: html_document
---

```{css, echo=FALSE}
pre {
  max-height: 300px;
  overflow-y: auto;
}

pre[class] {
  max-height: 100px;
}
```

We have defined some CSS rules to limit the height of
code blocks. Now we can test if these rules work on code
blocks and text output:

```{r}
# pretend that we have a lot of code in this chunk
```
```

```
if (1 + 1 == 2) {
  # of course that is true
  print(mtcars)
  # we just printed a lengthy data set
}
```

Next we add rules for a new class `scroll-100` to limit
the height to 100px, and add the class to the output of
a code chunk via the chunk option `class.output`:

````
```{css, echo=FALSE}
.scroll-100 {
  max-height: 100px;
  overflow-y: auto;
  background-color: inherit;
}
```
````

````
```{r, class.output="scroll-100"}
print(mtcars)
```
````

In the above example, we defined a global maximum height of 300px for all code blocks. Remember that code blocks are placed in <pre> tags in the HTML output. Then we limited the height of <pre> blocks to 100px with class attributes. That is what the CSS selector pre[class] means. By default, text output will be contained in <pre> </pre>, and R code blocks are contained in <pre class="r"> </pre> (note that the <pre> tag has a class attribute here).

The height of the text output from the second R code chunk is also 100px. That is because we assigned a custom class name scroll-100 to the output, and defined the maximum height to be 100px.

If you want to specify different maximum heights for individual code blocks, you may see the example in Section 12.3.

We have defined some CSS rules to limit the height of code blocks. Now we can test if these rules work on code blocks and text output:

```r
# pretend that we have a lot of code in this chunk
if (1 + 1 == 2) {
    # of course that is true
    print(mtcars)
    # we just printed a lengthy data set
```

```
##                      mpg cyl  disp  hp drat    wt  qsec vs am gear carb
## Mazda RX4           21.0   6 160.0 110 3.90 2.620 16.46  0  1    4    4
## Mazda RX4 Wag       21.0   6 160.0 110 3.90 2.875 17.02  0  1    4    4
## Datsun 710          22.8   4 108.0  93 3.85 2.320 18.61  1  1    4    1
## Hornet 4 Drive      21.4   6 258.0 110 3.08 3.215 19.44  1  0    3    1
## Hornet Sportabout   18.7   8 360.0 175 3.15 3.440 17.02  0  0    3    2
## Valiant             18.1   6 225.0 105 2.76 3.460 20.22  1  0    3    1
## Duster 360          14.3   8 360.0 245 3.21 3.570 15.84  0  0    3    4
## Merc 240D           24.4   4 146.7  62 3.69 3.190 20.00  1  0    4    2
## Merc 230            22.8   4 140.8  95 3.92 3.150 22.90  1  0    4    2
## Merc 280            19.2   6 167.6 123 3.92 3.440 18.30  1  0    4    4
## Merc 280C           17.8   6 167.6 123 3.92 3.440 18.90  1  0    4    4
## Merc 450SE          16.4   8 275.8 180 3.07 4.070 17.40  0  0    3    3
## Merc 450SL          17.3   8 275.8 180 3.07 3.730 17.60  0  0    3    3
## Merc 450SLC         15.2   8 275.8 180 3.07 3.780 18.00  0  0    3    3
## Cadillac Fleetwood  10.4   8 472.0 205 2.93 5.250 17.98  0  0    3    4
```

Next we add rules for a new class `scroll-100` to limit the height to 100px, and add the class to the output of a code chunk via the chunk option `class.output`:

```r
print(mtcars)
```

```
##                 mpg cyl  disp  hp drat    wt  qsec vs am gear carb
## Mazda RX4      21.0   6 160.0 110 3.90 2.620 16.46  0  1    4    4
## Mazda RX4 Wag  21.0   6 160.0 110 3.90 2.875 17.02  0  1    4    4
## Datsun 710     22.8   4 108.0  93 3.85 2.320 18.61  1  1    4    1
## Hornet 4 Drive 21.4   6 258.0 110 3.08 3.215 19.44  1  0    3    1
```

FIGURE 7.3: Scrollable code blocks using custom CSS.

7.5 Fold all code blocks but show some initially

If code blocks in the output document are potentially distracting to readers, you may choose to fold them initially. Readers can then choose to display them by clicking the fold buttons:

```yaml
output:
  html_document:
    code_fold: hide
```

You can also choose to unfold all code blocks initially (so readers can choose to fold them later):

```
output:
  html_document:
    code_fold: show
```

If you fold all code blocks initially, you can specify certain blocks to be un-folded initially with the chunk option `class.source = "fold-show"`, e.g.,

```
---
title: Hide all code blocks and show some initially
output:
  html_document:
    code_folding: hide
---
```

````
```{r}
1  # code is hidden initially
```
````

````
```{r class.source = 'fold-show'}
2  # code is shown initially
```
````

````
```{r}
3  # also hidden
```
````

You can also do it the other way around, i.e., show all code blocks but hide some of them initially. For example:

```
---
output:
  html_document:
    code_folding: show
---
```

````
```{r}
1  # code is shown initially
```
````

```
```
```{r class.source = 'fold-hide'}
2  # code is hidden initially
```
```

---

## 7.6   Put content in tabs

One natural way of organizing parallel sections in an HTML report is to use
tabsets. This allows readers to view the content of different sections by click-
ing the tab titles instead of scrolling back and forth on the page.

To turn sections into tabs, you can add a class attribute .tabset to the sec-
tion header that is one level higher than the headers to be converted to tabs,
e.g., adding the .tabset attribute to a level-2 header will convert all subse-
quent level-3 headers to tabs. Below is a full example:

```
---
title: Use tabs to organize content
output: html_document

You can turn parallel sections to tabs in `html_document` output.

Results {.tabset}

Plots

We show a scatter plot in this section.

```{r, fig.dim=c(5, 3)}
par(mar = c(4, 4, .5, .1))
plot(mpg ~ hp, data = mtcars, pch = 19)
```


Tables
```
```

```
We show the data in this tab.

```{r}
head(mtcars)
```
```

The output is shown in Figure 7.4. Note that you can only see one tab at a time in reality. In this figure, we actually concatenated two screenshots for you to see both tabs.

You can add another attribute `.tabset-pills` to the upper-level section header to add a "pill" effect to the tab, and the tab will have a dark blue background.

```
## Results {.tabset .tabset-pills}
```

By default, the first tab is active (i.e., displayed). If you want a different tab to be displayed initially, you may add the attribute `.active` to it.

To end the tabset, you need to start a new section header of the upper level. The new section header can be empty, e.g.,

```
## Results {.tabset}

### Tab One

### Tab Two

## {-}
```

```
With the above unnumbered (`{-}`) and empty section header,
we can end the tabset and continue to write more paragraphs.
```

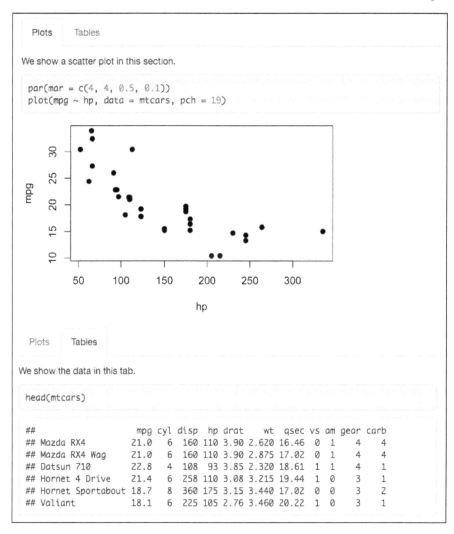

FIGURE 7.4: Turn sections into tabs.

7.7 Embed the Rmd source file in the HTML output file

When you share an HTML output page with others, they may want the Rmd source file, too. For example, they may want to change the Rmd source and compile the report by themselves. You can use the option `code_download` to embed a copy of the Rmd source file in the HTML output file:

```
output:
  html_document:
    code_download: true
```

After the option is turned on, the HTML output page will contain a download button, and readers of the page can hit the button to download the Rmd source file.

7.8 Embed arbitrary files in the HTML output file

As mentioned in Section 7.7, we can embed a copy of the Rmd source document in the HTML output file. Sometimes the Rmd source file alone may not be enough to reproduce the report. For example, the report may need an external data file. There is a series of functions in the **xfun** package (Xie, 2020g) that enable you to embed arbitrary files in the HTML output file. To use these functions, make sure you have the following R packages available:

```
xfun::pkg_load2(c("htmltools", "mime"))
```

Then you can use one of the functions `xfun::embed_file()`, `xfun::embed_files()`, or `xfun::embed_dir()` in an R code chunk to embed one or multiple files or an entire directory in the HTML output, e.g.,

````
```{r echo=FALSE}
# a single file
xfun::embed_file('source.Rmd')

# multiple files
xfun::embed_files(c('source.Rmd', 'data.csv'))

# a directory
xfun::embed_dir('data/', text = 'Download full data')
```
````

You can also provide the list of files programmatically, e.g.,

```
# embed all Rmd and csv files
xfun::embed_files(list.files(".", "[.](Rmd|csv)$"))
```

For multiple files, they are first compressed to a zip file, and the zip file will be embedded. These functions return a link, on which a reader can click on the HTML page to download the embedded file.

You can learn more technical details behind these functions from the help page `?xfun::embed_file` or the blog post at https://yihui.org/en/2018/07/embed-file/. Based on the same idea, the **downloadthis** package (Mattioni Maturana, 2020) has implemented download buttons, so that users can click buttons to download files instead of links. If you prefer using buttons, you may consider using this package.

7.9   Use a custom HTML template (*)

We mentioned LaTeX templates in Section 6.10. You can also specify a custom HTML template for Pandoc to convert Markdown to HTML. Below is a brief example template:

```
<html>
  <head>
    <title>$title$</title>
    $for(css)$
    <link rel="stylesheet" href="$css$" type="text/css" />
    $endfor$
  </head>
  <body>
  $body$
  </body>
</html>
```

You can see that the template contains a few variables such as $title$ and $body$. You can find the full list of Pandoc variables and their meanings at https://pandoc.org/MANUAL.html#templates.

The template gives you the ultimate power to customize the HTML output.

For example, you can include arbitrary CSS stylesheets or JavaScript code or libraries in the `<head>` area. For example, we could use a Boolean variable `draft` to indicate whether the document is a draft or a final version:

```
<head>
<style type="text/css">
.logo {
  float: right;
}
</style>
</head>

<body>
<div class="logo">
$if(draft)$
<!-- use draft.png to show that this is a draft -->
<img src="images/draft.png" alt="Draft mode" />
$else$
<!-- insert the formal logo if this is final -->
<img src="images/logo.png" alt="Final version" />
$endif$
</div>

$body$
</body>
```

Then we can set the variable `draft` to `true` or `false` in the YAML metadata of the Rmd document, e.g.,

```
---
title: "An Important Report"
draft: true
---
```

To apply a template to an Rmd document, you can save the template to a file, and pass the file path to the `template` option of `html_document`, e.g.,

```
output:
  html_output:
    template: my-template.html
```

The **rmarkdown** package uses a custom HTML template shipped with the package, which is different from Pandoc's default template. To use the latter, you can specify `template: null`.

7.10 Include the content of an existing HTML file (*)

With the `includes` option of the `html_document` format (or any other formats that support this option), you can include the content of an existing HTML file in the HTML output document in three possible places: the `<head>` area, the beginning of `<body>`, and the end of `</body>`.

```
output:
  html_document:
    includes:
      in_header: header.html
      before_body: before.html
      after_body: after.html
```

If you are not familiar with HTML, Section 7.9 may help you better understand these options.

With the `in_header` option, you can inject CSS and JavaScript code into the `<head>` tag. With `before_body`, you may include a header that shows a banner or logo. With `after_body`, you can include a footer, e.g.,

```
<div class="footer">Copyright &copy; John Doe 2020</div>
```

Sometimes you may want to include the content of an external HTML file in an arbitrary place of the body, which can be done with `html-tools::includeHTML()`. You pass the path of the HTML file to this function. It will read the file, and write its content to the output document. You may also use the technique in Section 9.5, e.g.,

```
````{=html}
```{r, echo=FALSE, results='asis'}
xfun::file_string('file.html')
```
````
```

Please note that you must not include the content of a full HTML file in another HTML file, but can only include an HTML fragment. A full HTML file contains the `<html>` tag, which cannot be embedded in another `<html>` tag. Below is an invalid HTML document when a full HTML document is included in another HTML document:

```html
<html>
  <head>  </head>

  <body>
  Parent HTML file.

  <!-- htmltools::includeHTML() below -->
    <html>
      <head>  </head>
      <body>
      Child HTML file.
      </body>
    </html>
  <!-- included above -->

  </body>
</html>
```

If you run into problems when including an HTML file in an HTML output document, you may check if the HTML file contains the `<html>` tag.

There is an output format `html_fragment` in the **rmarkdown** package, which generates an HTML fragment instead of a full HTML document. If you want to include the compiled results of an Rmd document in another Rmd document, the former Rmd document may use the `html_fragment` format instead of the usual `html_document`.

If you want to include an Rmd or Markdown document instead of an HTML file, you may use child documents introduced in Section 16.4.

## 7.11    Add a custom browser icon

Section 7.10 demonstrates that we can inject additional code into the HTML head, body, or footer with the `includes` option of the `html_document` format. This technique can be used to add a custom browser icon, called a favicon, to your HTML output.

Favicons are the website logos that are displayed in your browser's address bar, tab title, history, and bookmarks. For example, if you visit the CRAN website (`https://cran.r-project.org`) in Google Chrome, and look at the browser tab, you will see a small R logo. On mobile devices, favicons are also used in place of an App icon for websites that are pinned to the home screen.

To add a favicon to your HTML document, add the following line of code to a custom header file (such as the file `header.html` mentioned in Section 7.10):

```
<link rel="shortcut icon" href="{path to favicon file}" />
```

Recall that this file can be injected into the document `<head>` area using the YAML metadata:

```
output:
  html_document:
    includes:
      in_header: header.html
```

The path you provide to the `href` attribute in `<link>` should assume the same relative path structure as you would use to reference any other asset (e.g., an image or dataset). For the image itself, most small, square PNG files will work reasonably well. Bear in mind that a typical web browser will often display the image in a 16 x 16 pixel box, so simple designs are better.

If you want to ensure that each browser or platform on which your document is viewed uses a version of your icon with optimal resolution for its specific layout, you may use a service such as `https://realfavicongenerator.net` to generate a set of favicons and a slightly more complex version of the header HTML code. This service is currently used by the **pkgdown** package's `pkgdown::build_favicon()` function (Wickham and Hesselberth, 2020) to make a set of favicons out of R package logos.

## 7.12 Use the <details> disclosure element

As mentioned in Section 7.4, we can fold source code chunks via the option
code_fold: true in the html_document format. Currently it is not possible
to fold output blocks, but we can use some JavaScript tricks to make output
foldable, too. This can be useful especially when the output is relatively long
but not very important. We can fold it initially, and, if the reader is interested, they can unfold it to view the content. Figure 7.5 shows an example:
you may click on the "Details" button to unfold the output.

```
1:100
```

▶ Details

```
1:100
```

▼ Details

```
##    [1]   1   2   3   4   5   6   7   8   9  10  11  12  13
##   [14]  14  15  16  17  18  19  20  21  22  23  24  25  26
##   [27]  27  28  29  30  31  32  33  34  35  36  37  38  39
##   [40]  40  41  42  43  44  45  46  47  48  49  50  51  52
##   [53]  53  54  55  56  57  58  59  60  61  62  63  64  65
##   [66]  66  67  68  69  70  71  72  73  74  75  76  77  78
##   [79]  79  80  81  82  83  84  85  86  87  88  89  90  91
##   [92]  92  93  94  95  96  97  98  99 100
```

**FIGURE 7.5:** Wrap text output in the details element.

If you are viewing the HTML version of this book, you can actually see it in
action below. If you are reading the PDF or printed version, such an interac-
tion (clicking the "Details" button) is certainly not possible.

```
1:100
```

```
##    [1]   1   2   3   4   5   6   7   8   9  10  11  12
##   [13]  13  14  15  16  17  18  19  20  21  22  23  24
##   [25]  25  26  27  28  29  30  31  32  33  34  35  36
##   [37]  37  38  39  40  41  42  43  44  45  46  47  48
```

```
## [49]  49  50  51  52  53  54  55  56  57  58  59  60
## [61]  61  62  63  64  65  66  67  68  69  70  71  72
## [73]  73  74  75  76  77  78  79  80  81  82  83  84
## [85]  85  86  87  88  89  90  91  92  93  94  95  96
## [97]  97  98  99 100
```

Below is the full source Rmd document that includes the JavaScript code to find output blocks, and wrap them into the <details> tags.

```
---
title: Use the `<details>` disclosure element
output: html_document
---


We show text output inside the `<details>` tags in this
example. We used JavaScript to wrap text output blocks
in `<details></details>`. The JavaScript code needs to
be executed at the end of this document, so it is placed
at the end. Below is a testing code chunk:

```{r}
1:100
```

The actual JavaScript code is below.

```{js, echo=FALSE}
(function() {
  var codes = document.querySelectorAll('pre:not([class])');
  var code, i, d, s, p;
  for (i = 0; i < codes.length; i++) {
    code = codes[i];
    p = code.parentNode;
    d = document.createElement('details');
    s = document.createElement('summary');
    s.innerText = 'Details';
    // <details><summary>Details</summary></details>
    d.appendChild(s);
    // move the code into <details>
    p.replaceChild(d, code);
```
```

```
    d.appendChild(code);
  }
})();
```

You may try to adapt the JavaScript code above to your own need. The key is to find out the elements to be wrapped into `<details>`:

```
document.querySelectorAll('pre:not([class])');
```

The CSS selector `pre:not([class])` means all `<pre>` elements without the `class` attribute. You can also select other types of elements. For more about CSS selectors, see `https://www.w3schools.com/css/css_selectors.asp`. For more about the HTML tags `<details>` and `<summary>`, see `https://www.w3schools.com/tags/tag_details.asp`.

## 7.13 Sharing HTML output on the web

One appealing aspect of rendering R Markdown to HTML files is that it is very easy to host these files on the Internet and share them just as one shares any other website. This section briefly summarizes numerous options for sharing the HTML documents that you have created.

### 7.13.1 R-specific services

RStudio offers a number of services for publishing various types of content created in R Markdown to the Internet. These services make it particularly easy to publish content by using the RStudio IDE or the **rsconnect** package (Allaire, 2019).

- **RPubs**[4] enables free hosting of static single-file R Markdown content. It is easy to publish via the `Publish` button in the RStudio IDE or the `rsconnect::rpubsUpload()` function. Please see the "Getting Started" page (`https://rpubs.com/about/getting-started`) for more details.

---

[4]`https://rpubs.com`

- **ShinyApps.io**[5] allows for hosting dynamic content that requires a server to run R. For example, one can host interactive R Markdown documents that include Shiny components.[6] ShinyApps.io is an analog to RPubs for Shiny applications. Apps and interactive R Markdown documents can be published using the push-button in the RStudio IDE or the `rsconnect::deployApp()` function. See the user guide (`https://docs.rstudio.com/shinyapps.io/`) for more details.

- **bookdown.org**[7] offers free hosting specifically for books written with the **bookdown** package. You may easily publish static output files of your book using the `bookdown::publish_book()` function.

- **RStudio Connect**[8] is an enterprise product that organizations may run on their own servers. It can host a wide variety of content created in R (such as R Markdown documents, Shiny apps, and APIs) in a secured environment with document-level access controls, viewership history, and more. Content can be published to RStudio Connect using manual upload, the **rsconnect** package, or with GIT-based deployment.

### 7.13.2   Static website services

In a few words, a simple static website is composed of any number of HTML files (typically containing an `index.html`, which is the homepage), JavaScript, CSS files, and additional content such as images. This collection of files can be hosted as-is on a web server and rendered in a web browser.

When R Markdown is rendered to the HTML output format, the result may be treated as a static website. Websites can range in complexity from a single, standalone HTML file (which is what we get when we use the default `self_contained: true` option), a set of files, or a sophisticated project like a website based on **blogdown** (which relies upon a static website generator). For more details, see Section 2.1 on Static Sites[9] of the **blogdown** book (Xie et al., 2017).

---

[5] `https://www.shinyapps.io`

[6] You may include Shiny components in an R Markdown document by setting the option `runtime: shiny` or `runtime: shiny_prerendered` in the YAML metadata. You will no longer be able to render your document to an HTML document as before; instead, you run your document with `rmarkdown::run()`. To learn more, please refer to Xie et al. (2018) (Chapter 19: `https://bookdown.org/yihui/rmarkdown/shiny-documents.html`).

[7] `https://bookdown.org/home/about/`

[8] `https://rstudio.com/products/connect/`

[9] `https://bookdown.org/yihui/blogdown/static-sites.html`

As a result, in addition to R-specific services, you may host your HTML document on many freely available static website hosting services. Commonly used options in the R community are:

- **GitHub Pages**[10] makes it particularly easy to publish Markdown and HTML content straight from a GitHub repository. You may specify whether to host content from either the main branch's root, a `docs/` directory on the main branch, or a specific `gh-pages` branch. Publishing new content can be as simple as pushing new HTML files to your repository via GIT.

- **GitLab Pages**[11] offers similar functionality to GitHub Pages for GitLab repositories. GitLab deploys content stores in the `public/` directory of a repository. To build and publish content, you must provide a YAML file, `.gitlab-ci.yml` with instructions, but GitLab provides many helpful templates. For an example of hosting rendered HTML content, please see `https://gitlab.com/pages/plain-html/-/tree/master`.

- **Netlify**[12] is a platform to build and deploy static website content. It is a popular choice for web content created by the **blogdown** and **pkgdown** packages, but it can host all kinds of HTML files. There are many different publishing options including drag-and-drop, command line, or automated publishing from GitHub and GitLab repositories. Additionally, Netlify offers many helpful features such as website previews in pull requests. See the Netlify documentation (`https://docs.netlify.com`) or the RStudio webinar "Sharing on Short Notice"[13] for more details.

---

## 7.14 Improve accessibility of HTML pages

It is important to make your HTML output documents accessible to readers who are visually impaired or blind. These readers often have to use special tools, such as screen readers, to *hear* instead of visually reading your documents. Usually, screen readers can only read out text, but not (raster) images. This means you need to provide enough text hints to screen readers. The good news is that with some small efforts, you can actually greatly enhance

---

[10]`https://pages.github.com`
[11]`https://docs.gitlab.com/ce/user/project/pages/`
[12]`https://www.netlify.com`
[13]`https://rstudio.com/resources/webinars/sharing-on-short-notice-how-to-get-your-materials-online-with-r-markdown/`

the accessibility of your documents. Jonathan Godfrey has provided some tips in the article at `https://r-resources.massey.ac.nz/rmarkdown/` on making accessible R Markdown documents.[14] Based on this article, we highlight some tips below for the convenience of the readers of this book:

- HTML documents are often more accessible than PDF.

- Try to provide the Rmd source document along with the HTML output document if possible (e.g., Section 7.7 demonstrates one way to do this). In case anything in the HTML document is not accessible, the blind reader may be able to figure it out from the Rmd source, or fix it in the source.

- Provide informative text tags to your graphics. At the useR! conference in 2014, Jonathan explained this issue to me in person. It was the first time that I had learned about the importance of the `alt` attribute of images on web pages.

To understand this problem, first you have to know that images on web pages are generated by the HTML tag `<img  />`. This tag has an `src` attribute, which points to the source of the image, e.g., `<img src="foo_figures/image.png" />`. Sighted readers can see the image, but it is hard for blind users to know anything about the image, because usually screen readers cannot read it, especially when it is a raster image (vector graphics can be better, such as SVG). In this case, it is helpful to provide a text hint, which screen readers can read out to the blind reader. This text hint can be provided in the `alt` attribute of the image, which stands for "alternate text."

For images generated from code chunks in R Markdown, the `alt` attribute will be generated if you provide the chunk option `fig.cap` (i.e., figure caption). Alternatively, you can insert an image using the Markdown syntax `![]()`. You input the image path in parentheses, and the `alt` text in square brackets, e.g., `![an informative text](path/to/image.png)`.

The `alt` text is not displayed to sighted readers on an HTML page. However, when you provide the figure caption or alternate text to an image, the `rmarkdown::html_document` format will render a visible figure caption element by default. If you do not want the real figure captions, you can turn off the `fig_caption` option, e.g.,

---

[14]JooYoung Seo has also published a post about a few R packages to help visually impaired users at `https://jooyoungseo.com/post/ds4blind/`. It is not directly related to R Markdown, but it can be helpful for you to learn how blind users read graphs.

```
output:
  html_document:
    fig_caption: false
```

In this case, the `alt` attributes will still be generated, but are no longer visible.

- Write mathematical content using the LaTeX syntax (e.g., $ $ or $$ $$) instead of images. By default, R Markdown uses the MathJax library to render math content, and the result is readable to screen readers.

- Get rid of the leading hashes (`##`) in the text output of code chunks by setting the chunk option `comment = ""` (see Section 11.12).

We are not experts on accessibility, so we recommend that you read the original article to learn more details.

## 7.15 For hardcore HTML users (*)

In Section 6.12, we mentioned that if you feel the constraint of Markdown (due to its simplicity) is too strong, you can embed code chunks in a pure LaTeX document instead of Markdown. Similarly, if you are familiar and comfortable with writing raw HTML code, you can intermingle code chunks with HTML, too. Such documents have the conventional filename extension `.Rhtml`.

In an `Rhtml` document, code chunks are embedded between `<!--begin.rcode` and `end.rcode-->`, and inline R expressions are embedded in `<!--rinline -->`. Below is a full `Rhtml` example. You can save it to a file named `test.Rhtml`, and use `knitr::knit("test.Rhtml")` to compile it. The output will be an HTML (`.html`) file. In RStudio, you can also hit the `Knit` button on the toolbar to compile the document.

```html
<!DOCTYPE html>
<html>
<head>
  <title>A minimal knitr example in HTML</title>
</head>
```

```
<body>
<!--begin.rcode
  knitr::opts_chunk$set(fig.width=5, fig.height=5)
  end.rcode-->

  <p>This is a minimal example that shows
  how <strong>knitr</strong> works with pure HTML
  pages.</p>

  <p>Boring stuff as usual:</p>

<!--begin.rcode
    # a simple calculator
    1 + 1
    # boring random numbers
    set.seed(123)
    rnorm(5)
    end.rcode-->

  <p>We can also produce plots (centered by the
  option <code>fig.align='center'</code>):</p>

<!--begin.rcode cars-scatter, fig.align='center'
    plot(mpg ~ hp, data = mtcars)
    end.rcode-->

  <p>Errors, messages and warnings can be put into
  <code>div</code>s with different <code>class</code>es:</p>

<!--begin.rcode
    sqrt(-1)  # warning
    message('knitr says hello to HTML!')
    1 + 'a'  # mission impossible
    end.rcode-->

  <p>Well, everything seems to be working. Let's ask R what is
  the value of &pi;? Of course it is <!--rinline pi -->.</p>
```

```
</body>
</html>
```

# 8

## *Word*

To generate a Word document from R Markdown, you can use the output format `word_document`. If you want to include cross-references in the document, you may consider the output format `bookdown::word_document2`, as mentioned in Section 4.7.

```
---
output:
  word_document: default
  bookdown::word_document2: default  # for cross-references
---
```

From our experience, the most frequently asked questions about Word output are:

1. How can I apply a custom Word template to the document?

2. How can I incorporate changes made in Word in the original R Markdown document?

3. How can I style individual document elements?

We will address these questions in this chapter.

## 8.1 Custom Word templates

You can apply the styles defined in a Word template document to new Word documents generated from R Markdown. Such a template document is also called a "style reference document." The key is that you have to create this template document from Pandoc first, and change the style definitions in it later. Then pass the path of this template to the `reference_docx` option of `word_document`, e.g.,

```
---
output:
  word_document:
    reference_docx: "template.docx"
---
```

As we just mentioned, the document `template.docx` has to be generated from Pandoc. You can create this template from an arbitrary R Markdown document with the `word_document` output format (the actual content of this document does not matter, but it should contain the type of elements of which you want to style). Then open the `.docx` file, and edit the styles.

Figure 8.1 shows that you can open the "Styles" window from the "HOME" tab in Word. When you move the cursor to a specific element in the document, an item in the styles list will be highlighted. If you want to modify the style of any type of element, you can click the drop-down menu on the highlighted item, and you will see a dialog box like Figure 8.2.

After you finish modifying the styles, you can save the document (with a file-name that will not be accidentally overwritten), and use it as the template for future Word documents. When Pandoc renders a new Word document with a reference document (template), it will read the styles in the template and apply them to the new document.

You may watch a short video at https://vimeo.com/110804387, or read the article at https://rmarkdown.rstudio.com/articles_docx.html for more detailed instructions on how to create a Word template with custom styles.

Sometimes it may not be straightforward to find the style name for an element. There may be multiple styles applied to the same element, and you will only see one of them highlighted in the list of styles. It may require some guesswork and online searching to figure out the actual style that you want to modify. For example, you have to click the "Manage Styles" button (the third button from left to right at the bottom of the style list in Figure 8.1), and scroll through a large number of style names before you find the "Table" style (see Figure 8.3). Then you can modify this style for your tables (e.g., add borders).

**FIGURE 8.1:** Find the styles of a specific document element.

## 8.2 The two-way workflow between R Markdown and Word

While it is easy to generate a Word document from R Markdown, things can be particularly painful when someone else edits the Word document and you have to manually port the changes back to the original R Markdown document. Luckily, Noam Ross has provided a promising solution to this problem. The **redoc** package (`https://github.com/noamross/redoc`) allows you to generate a Word document, revise the Word document, and convert the

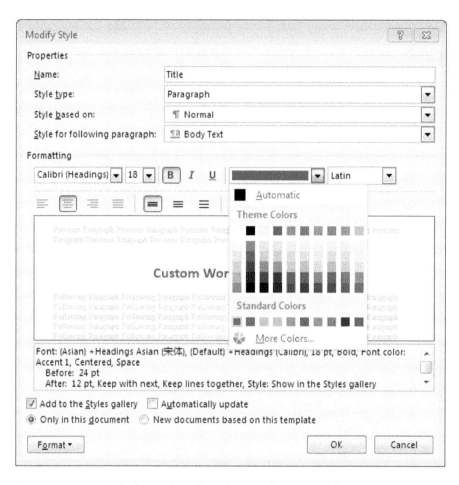

**FIGURE 8.2:** Modify the styles of an element in a Word document.

revised Word document back to R Markdown. Please note that as of this writing (June 2020), the **redoc** package is still experimental, and more unfortunately, its author has suspended the development. Anyway, if you want to try it out, you can install the package from GitHub:

```
remotes::install_github("noamross/redoc")
```

Once the package is installed, you may use the output format redoc::redoc:

```
---
```

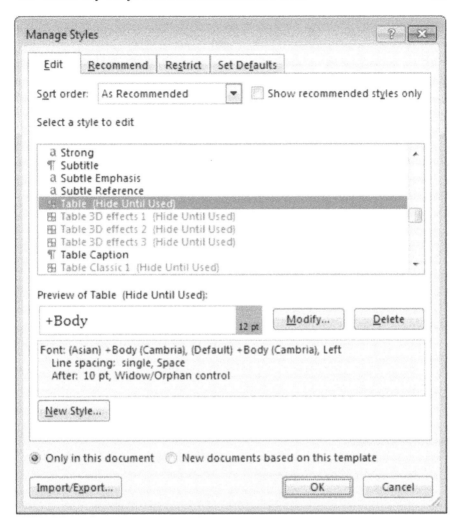

**FIGURE 8.3:** Modify the styles of tables in a Word document.

```
output: redoc::redoc
---
```

This output format generates a Word document that actually stores the original Rmd document, so the Word document can be converted back to Rmd. Tracked changes in Word will be converted to text written with the Critic-Markup syntax (http://criticmarkup.com). For example, {++ important ++} represents the insertion of the word "important" in the text.

You can convert the Word document generated by `redoc::redoc` to Rmd via the function `redoc::dedoc()`, e.g., `redoc::dedoc("file.docx")` will generate `file.Rmd`. In this process, you can decide how to deal with tracked changes in Word via the `track_changes` argument, e.g., you may accept or reject changes, or convert tracked changes to CriticMarkup. We recommend that you use `track_changes = 'criticmarkup'` to avoid the permanent loss of tracked changes.

When editing the Word document, you are expected to edit the parts that are *not* automatically generated by code chunks or inline R expressions in R Markdown. For example, you must not edit a table if it is automatically generated by `knitr::kable()` in a code chunk, because such changes will be lost when you convert Word to Rmd via `dedoc()`. To avoid accidentally editing the automatic results from code chunks, you may set the option `highlight_outputs` to `true` in the `redoc::redoc` format, which means the automatic output will be highlighted in Word (with a background color). You should tell your collaborator that they should not touch these highlighted parts in the Word document.

Again, the **redoc** package is still experimental and its future is unclear at the moment, so the introduction here is intentionally brief. When in doubt, we recommend that you read its documentation on GitHub.

---

## 8.3   Style individual elements

Due to the simplicity of Markdown, you can apply some global styles to the Word document (see Section 8.1), but it is not straightforward to style individual elements, such as changing the color of a word, or centering a paragraph.

Continuing his effort to make it easier to work with Office documents in R, David Gohel started to develop the **officedown** package (Gohel and Ross, 2020) in 2018, which aims to bring some **officer** (Gohel, 2020b) features into R Markdown. As of this writing, this package is still experimental, although its initial version has been published on CRAN. You may either install it from CRAN or GitHub:

```r
# install from CRAN
install.packages("officedown")

# or GitHub
remotes::install_github("davidgohel/officedown")
```

After the package is installed, you need to load it in your R Markdown document, e.g.,

````
```{r, setup, include=FALSE}
library(officedown)
```
````

There is an output format `rdocx_document` in the **officedown** package, which is based on `rmarkdown::word_document` by default, and has several other features such as styling tables and plots.

The **officedown** package allows you to style specific Word elements via the **officer** package. For example, you can create a style via the function `officer::fp_text()`, and apply the style to a piece of text via `ftext()` an inline R expression:

```
---
title: Style text with officedown
output:
  officedown::rdocx_document: default
---
```

````
```{r}
library(officedown)
library(officer)
ft <- fp_text(color = 'red', bold = TRUE)
```
````

```
# Test

The **officedown** package is
`r ftext('awesome', ft)`!
```

Besides functions in **officer**, **officedown** also allows you to use some special

HTML comments to perform **officer** tasks. For example, the function officer::block_pour_docx() can be used to import an external Word document into the current document, and alternatively, you can use the HTML
comment in R Markdown:

```
<!---BLOCK_POUR_DOCX{file: 'my-file.docx'}--->
```

That is equivalent to the inline R expression:

```
`r block_pour_docx(file = 'my-file.docx')`
```

Other things you may do with **officedown** and **officer** include the following:

- Insert page breaks.

- Put content in a multi-column layout.

- Change paragraph settings.

- Insert a table of contents.

- Change the orientation of a section (landscape or portrait).

To learn more about **officedown**, please check out its documentation at
https://davidgohel.github.io/officedown/.

9

Multiple Output Formats

One main advantage of R Markdown is that it can create multiple output formats from a single source, which could be one or multiple Rmd documents. For example, this book was written in R Markdown, and compiled to two formats: PDF for printing, and HTML for the online version.

Sometimes it can be challenging to make an output element of a code chunk work for all output formats. For example, it is extremely simple to create a rounded and circular image in HTML output with a single CSS rule (`img { border-radius: 50%; }`), but not so straightforward in LaTeX output (typically it will involve TikZ graphics).

Sometimes it is just impossible for an output element to work for all output formats. For example, you can easily create a GIF animation with the **gifski** package (Ooms, 2018) (see Section 4.14), and it will work perfectly for HTML output, but embedding such an animation in LaTeX output is not possible without extra steps of processing the GIF file and using extra LaTeX packages.

This chapter provides a few examples that can work for multiple formats. If a certain feature is only available to a specific output format, we will show you how to conditionally enable or disable it based on the output format.

9.1 LaTeX or HTML output

LaTeX and HTML are two commonly used output formats. The function `knitr::is_latex_output()` tells you if the output format is LaTeX (including Pandoc output formats `latex` and `beamer`). Similarly, the function `knitr::is_html_output` tells you if the output format is HTML. By default, these Pandoc output formats are considered HTML formats: `markdown`, `epub`, `html`, `html4`, `html5`, `revealjs`, `s5`, `slideous`, and `slidy`. If you do not think a certain Pandoc format is HTML, you may use the `excludes` argument to exclude it, e.g.,

```
# do not treat markdown as an HTML format
knitr::is_html_output(excludes = "markdown")
## [1] FALSE
```

If a certain output element can only be generated in LaTeX or HTML, you can use these functions to conditionally generate it. For example, when a table is too big on a PDF page, you may include the table in an environment of a smaller font size, but such a LaTeX environment certainly will not work for HTML output, so it should not be included in HTML output (if you want to tweak the font size for HTML output, you may use CSS). Below is a full example:

```
---
title: Render a table in a tiny environment
output:
  pdf_document: default
  html_document: default
---

```{r, setup, include=FALSE}
knitr::opts_chunk$set(echo = FALSE)
options(knitr.table.format = function() {
  if (knitr::is_latex_output()) 'latex' else 'pandoc'
})
```

The LaTeX environment `tiny` is only generated for LaTeX output.

```{r, include=knitr::is_latex_output()}
knitr::asis_output('\n\n\\begin{tiny}')
```

```{r}
knitr::kable(mtcars)
```

```{r, include=knitr::is_latex_output()}
```
```

```
knitr::asis_output('\\end{tiny}\n\n')
```

By comparison, below is the table with the normal font size.

````
```{r}
knitr::kable(mtcars)
```
````

The key in the above example is the chunk option `include` = `knitr::is_latex_output()`. That is, the environment \begin{tiny} \end{tiny} is only included when the output format is LaTeX. The two tables in the example will look identical when the output format is not LaTeX.

In Section 5.1, we used these functions to change the text color for HTML and LaTeX output. In Section 4.14, we showed an animation example, which also used this trick. The code chunk that generated the animation for HTML output and static images for LaTeX output is like this:

````
```{r animation.hook=if (knitr::is_html_output()) 'gifski'}
for (i in 1:2) {
  pie(c(i %% 2, 6), col = c('red', 'yellow'), labels = NA)
}
```
````

These conditional functions can be used anywhere. You can use them in other chunk options (e.g., `eval` for conditional evaluation of the chunk), or in your R code, e.g.,

````
```{r, eval=knitr::is_html_output(), echo=FALSE}
cat('You will only see me in HTML output.')
```
````

````
```{r}
if (knitr::is_latex_output()) {
  knitr::asis_output('\n\n\\begin{tiny}')
}
```
````

9.2   Display HTML widgets

HTML widgets (https://htmlwidgets.org) are typically interactive JavaScript applications, which only work in HTML output. If you knit an Rmd document containing HTML widgets to a non-HTML format such as PDF or Word, you may get an error message like this:

```
Error: Functions that produce HTML output found in document
targeting X output. Please change the output type of this
document to HTML. Alternatively, you can allow HTML output in
non-HTML formats by adding this option to the YAML front-matter
of your rmarkdown file:

  always_allow_html: yes

Note however that the HTML output will not be visible in
non-HTML formats.
```

There is actually a better solution than the one mentioned in the above error message, but it involves extra packages. You can install the **webshot** package (Chang, 2019) in R and also install PhantomJS:

```
install.packages("webshot")
webshot::install_phantomjs()
```

Then if you knit an Rmd document with HTML widgets to a non-HTML format, the HTML widgets will be displayed as static screenshots. The screenshots are automatically taken in **knitr**. Section 2.10[1] of the **bookdown** book contains more information on finer control over the screenshots.

9.3   Embed a web page

If you have the **webshot** package (Chang, 2019) and PhantomJS installed (see Section 9.2), you can embed any web page in the output document through

---

[1]https://bookdown.org/yihui/bookdown/html-widgets.html

`knitr::include_url()`. When you pass a URL of a web page to this function in a code chunk, it will generate an `<iframe>` (inline frame) if the output format is HTML, and a screenshot of the web page for other output formats. You can view the actual page in the inline frame. For example, Figure 9.1 should show you my homepage if you are reading the online version of this book, otherwise you will see a static screenshot instead.

```
knitr::include_url("https://yihui.org")
```

About •
Blog •
关于 •
日志 •

I'm a software engineer working at RStudio, PBC. I earned my PhD from the Department of Statistics, Iowa State University. My thesis was *Dynamic Graphics and Reporting for Statistics*, advised by Di Cook and Heike Hofmann. I have developed a few R packages either seriously or for fun (or both), such as knitr, animation, bookdown, blogdown, pagedown, xaringan, and tinytex. I founded a Chinese website called "Capital of Statistics" in 2006, which has grown into a large online community on statistics. I initiated the Chinese R conference in 2008. I'm a big fan of GitHub, LyX and Pandoc. I hate IE. I fall asleep when I see beamer slides, and I yell at people who use \textbf{} to write \title{}. I know I cannot eat code, so I cook almost every day to stay away from my computer for two hours.

这是谢益辉的个人主页。2013 年底我从 Ames 村办大学统计系毕业，终于解决了人生前 30 年被问最多的问题："你怎么还没毕业？"目前就职于 RStudio。我支持开源，喜欢折腾网站和代码，是一个高度自我驱动的人。打羽毛球爱勾对角，打乒乓球像太极，网球满场子捡球，篮球容易被撞飞，攀岩一次，腿软。宅，口重，嗜辣，屡教不改。智商中等偏下，对麻将和三国杀有不可逾越的认知障碍，实变函数课上曾被老师叫醒。略好读书，偶尔也在网上乱翻帖子，对诗词楹联比较感兴趣，目前比较中意的一联是：千秋邈矣独留我；百战归来再读书。最喜欢的一首词是：

深情似海，问相逢初度，是何年纪？依约而今还记取，不是前生尘世。放学花前，题诗石上，春水园亭里。逢君一笑，人间无此欢喜。

元夜苍狗着云，红羊散劫，惘惘休提起。寒气渐多真气少，泪浸心灵何已。千古声名，百年担负，事事违初意。心头阁住，儿时那种情味。

© Yihui Xie 2005 - 2020

FIGURE 9.1: Embed Yihui's homepage as an iframe or screenshot.

Most chunk options related to figures also work for `knitr::include_url()`, such as `out.width` and `fig.cap`.

If you have published a Shiny app publicly on a server, you can use `knitr::include_app()` to include it, which works in the same way as `include_url()`. Section 2.11[2] of the **bookdown** book (Xie, 2016) contains more details about `include_app()` and `include_url()`.

---

[2]`https://bookdown.org/yihui/bookdown/web-pages-and-shiny-apps.html`

9.4   Multiple figures side by side

You can place multiple figures side by side using the `fig.show="hold"`
along with the `out.width` option. In the example below, we have set
`out.width="50%"` (see Figure 9.2 for the output):

```
```{r, figures-side, fig.show="hold", out.width="50%"}
par(mar = c(4, 4, .1, .1))
plot(cars)
plot(mpg ~ hp, data = mtcars, pch = 19)
```
```

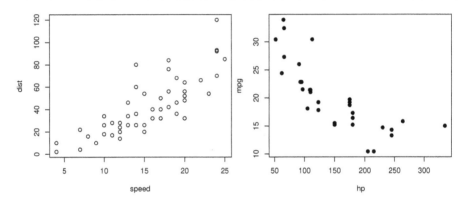

FIGURE 9.2: Side-by-side figures.

This simple approach works for both PDF and HTML output.

If you want to use sub-figures when there are multiple plots in a figure, you
may see Section 6.6, but please note that sub-figures are only supported in
LaTeX output.

9.5   Write raw content (*)

The technique introduced in Section 6.11 is actually a general technique. You
can protect any complex raw content in Markdown by specifying the content
as "raw." For example, if you want to write raw HTML content, you can use
the attribute `=html`:

````
```{=html}
<p>Any <strong>raw</strong> HTML content works here.
For example, here is a Youtube video:</p>

<iframe width="100%" height="400"
  src="https://www.youtube.com/embed/s3JldKoA0zw?rel=0"
  frameborder="0" allow="autoplay; encrypted-media"
  allowfullscreen></iframe>
```
````

The attribute name is the Pandoc output format name. If you want to know the output format name, you may check the output of the code chunk below inside an Rmd document:

````
```{r}
knitr:::pandoc_to()
```
````

Please note that raw content is only visible to a specific output format. For example, raw LaTeX content will be ignored when the output format is HTML.

***

9.6   Custom blocks (*)

Section 2.7[3] of the **bookdown** book mentioned how we can use custom blocks in R Markdown to customize the appearance of blocks of content. This can be a useful way to make some content stand out from your report or book, to make sure that your readers take away the key points from your work. Examples of how these blocks could be used include:

- display a warning message to make sure users are using up-to-date packages before running your analysis;

- add a link at the beginning of your document to your GitHub repository containing the source;

- highlight key results and findings from your analysis.

---

[3]https://bookdown.org/yihui/bookdown/custom-blocks.html

In this section, we will explain how to create your own custom blocks for both PDF and HTML output. They can both use the same formatting syntax in the R Markdown document, but require different configurations.

9.6.1 Syntax

The syntax for custom blocks is based on Pandoc's fenced Div blocks.[4] Div blocks are very powerful, but there is a problem at the moment: they mainly work for HTML output and do not work for LaTeX output.

Since version 1.16 of the **rmarkdown** package, it has been possible to convert Div blocks to both HTML and LaTeX. For HTML output, all attributes of the block will become attributes of the <div> tag. For example, a Div can have an ID (after #), one or multiple classes (class names are written after .), and other attributes. The following Div block

```
::: {#hello .greeting .message width="40%"}
Hello **world**!
:::
```

will be converted to the HTML code below:

```
<div id="hello" class="greeting message" width="40%">
  Hello <strong>world</strong>!
</div>
```

For LaTeX output, the first class name will be used as the LaTeX environment name. You should also provide an attribute named data-latex in the Div block, which will be the arguments of the environment. This attribute can be an empty string if the environment does not need arguments. We show two simple examples below. The first example uses the verbatim environment in LaTeX, which does not have any arguments:

```
::: {.verbatim data-latex=""}
We show some _verbatim_ text here.
:::
```

Its LaTeX output will be:

---

[4]https://pandoc.org/MANUAL.html#divs-and-spans

```
\begin{verbatim}
We show some \emph{verbatim} text here.
\end{verbatim}
```

When the block is converted to HTML, the HTML code will be:

```
<div class="verbatim">
We show some <em>verbatim</em> text here.
</div>
```

The second example uses the `center` and `minipage` environments to display some text in a centered box of half of the page width.

```
:::: {.center data-latex=""}

::: {.minipage data-latex="{.5\linewidth}"}
This paragraph will be centered on the page, and
its width is 50% of the width of its parent element.
:::

::::
```

Note that we nested the `minipage` block in the `center` block. You need more colons for a parent block to include a child block. In the above example, we used four colons (you can use five or more) for the `center` block. The two blocks will be converted to the LaTeX code below:

```
\begin{center}
\begin{minipage}{.5\linewidth}
This paragraph will be centered on the page, and
its width is 50\% of the width of its parent element.
\end{minipage}
\end{center}
```

It is up to the user to define the appearance of their `<div>` blocks via CSS for the HTML output. Similarly, for LaTeX output, you may use the command `\newenvironment` to define the environment if it has not been defined, or `\renewenvironment` to redefine an existing environment in LaTeX. In the LaTeX definitions, you can decide on the appearance of these blocks in PDF.

These customizations will normally be contained in their own files such as style.css or preamble.tex, and then included within the YAML options:

```
---
output:
  html_document:
    css: style.css
  pdf_document:
    includes:
      in_header: preamble.tex
---
```

Next we will demonstrate a few more advanced custom blocks that use custom CSS rules and LaTeX environments. You may find an additional example in Section 5.8, in which we arranged multiple blocks in a multi-column layout.

9.6.2   Adding a shaded box

First, we show how to include content in a shaded box. The box has a black background with an orange frame with rounded corners. The text in the box is in white.

For HTML output, we define these rules in a CSS file. If you are unfamiliar with CSS, there are plenty of free online tutorials, e.g., https://www.w3schools.com/css/.

```
.blackbox {
  padding: 1em;
  background: black;
  color: white;
  border: 2px solid orange;
  border-radius: 10px;
}
.center {
  text-align: center;
}
```

For LaTeX output, we create a new environment named blackbox and based on the LaTeX package **framed**, with a black background and white text:

```
\usepackage{color}
\usepackage{framed}
\setlength{\fboxsep}{.8em}

\newenvironment{blackbox}{
  \definecolor{shadecolor}{rgb}{0, 0, 0}  % black
  \color{white}
  \begin{shaded}}
 {\end{shaded}}
```

We used the **framed** package in this book because it is fairly lightweight, but it is not possible to draw a colored frame with rounded corners with this package. To achieve the latter, you will need more sophisticated LaTeX packages such as **tcolorbox** (https://ctan.org/pkg/tcolorbox), which offers a set of very flexible options for creating shaded boxes. You can find many examples in its documentation. The LaTeX environment below will create a shaded box of similar appearance to the above CSS example:

```
\usepackage{tcolorbox}

\newtcolorbox{blackbox}{
  colback=black,
  colframe=orange,
  coltext=white,
  boxsep=5pt,
  arc=4pt}
```

Now we can use our custom box in both PDF and HTML output formats. The source code of the box is:

```
:::: {.blackbox data-latex=""}
::: {.center data-latex=""}
**NOTICE!**
:::


Thank you for noticing this **new notice**! Your noticing it has
been noted, and _will be reported to the authorities_!
::::
```

The output is:

> **NOTICE!**
>
> Thank you for noticing this **new notice**! Your noticing it has been noted, and *will be reported to the authorities*!

9.6.3 Including icons

We can make custom blocks even more visually appealing by including images in them. Images can also be an effective way to convey the content of the block. For the following example, we assume that we are working within a directory structure below, which is a simplified version of what is used to build this book:

```
directory/
├── your-report.Rmd
├── style.css
├── preamble.tex
└── images/
        └── ├── important.png
            ├── note.png
            └── caution.png
```

We show the source code and output of the example before we explain how everything works:

```
::: {.infobox .caution data-latex="{caution}"}
**NOTICE!**

Thank you for noticing this **new notice**! Your noticing it has
been noted, and _will be reported to the authorities_!
:::
```

The output is:

> **NOTICE!**
>
> Thank you for noticing this **new notice**! Your noticing it has been noted, and *will be reported to the authorities*!

For the HTML output, we can add an image to the box through the background-image property in CSS. We insert the image into the background, and add enough padding on the left-hand side to avoid the text overlapping with this image. If you are using local images, the file path to the images is provided relative to the CSS file. For example:

```
.infobox {
  padding: 1em 1em 1em 4em;
  margin-bottom: 10px;
  border: 2px solid orange;
  border-radius: 10px;
  background: #f5f5f5 5px center/3em no-repeat;
}


.caution {
  background-image: url("images/caution.png");
}
```

Note that we used two class names, .infobox and .caution, on the outer block. The infobox class will be used to define the shaded box with a colored border, and the caution class will be used to include the image. The advantage of using two classes is that we can define more blocks with different icons without repeating the setup of the shaded box. For example, if we need a warning box, we only need to define the following CSS rule without repeating rules in .infobox:

```
.warning {
  background-image: url("images/warning.png");
}
```

Then you can create a warning box with the Markdown source code below:

```
:::: {.infobox .warning data-latex="warning"}

Include the actual content here.

::::
```

For the PDF output, we can create an infobox environment based on the blackbox environment defined in the previous example, and add the icon to the left side of the box. There are multiple ways of including images in a La-TeX environment. Here is only one of them (it does not precisely reproduce the box style defined in the CSS above):

```
\newenvironment{infobox}[1]
  {
  \begin{itemize}
  \renewcommand{\labelitemi}{
    \raisebox{-.7\height}[0pt][0pt]{
      {\setkeys{Gin}{width=3em,keepaspectratio}
        \includegraphics{images/#1}}
    }
  }
  \setlength{\fboxsep}{1em}
  \begin{blackbox}
  \item
  }
  {
  \end{blackbox}
  \end{itemize}
  }
```

Below we show more example blocks with different icons:

NOTICE!

Thank you for noticing this **new notice**! Your noticing it has been noted, and *will be reported to the authorities!*

NOTICE!

Thank you for noticing this **new notice**! Your noticing it has been noted, and *will be reported to the authorities!*

NOTICE!

Thank you for noticing this **new notice**! Your noticing it has been noted, and *will be reported to the authorities!*

NOTICE!

Thank you for noticing this **new notice**! Your noticing it has been noted, and *will be reported to the authorities*!

Alternatively, you may use the LaTeX package **awesomebox**[5] to generate boxes with icons in the PDF output. This package gives you a much larger number of icons to choose from. We give a brief example below: please refer to the package documentation for the possible LaTeX environments and their arguments.

```
---
title: Awesome Boxes
output:
  pdf_document:
    extra_dependencies: awesomebox
---
```

A note box:

```
::: {.noteblock data-latex=""}
Thank you for noticing this **new notice**! Your noticing it has
been noted, and _will be reported to the authorities_!
:::
```

We define an R function `box_args()` to generate the arguments for the box:

```{r}
box_args <- function(
  vrulecolor = 'white',
  hrule = c('\\abLongLine', '\\abShortLine', ''),
  title = '', vrulewidth = '0pt',
  icon = 'Bomb', iconcolor = 'black'
) {
  hrule <- match.arg(hrule)
  sprintf(
```

---

[5]https://ctan.org/pkg/awesomebox

```
    '[%s][%s][\\textbf{%s}]{%s}{\\fa%s}{%s}',
    vrulecolor, hrule, title, vrulewidth, icon, iconcolor
  )
}
```

Pass some arguments to the `awesomeblock` environment through an inline R expression:

```
::: {.awesomeblock data-latex="`r box_args(title = 'NOTICE!')`"}
Thank you for noticing this **new notice**!

Your noticing it has been noted, and _will be reported to
the authorities_!
:::
```

10

Tables

Tables are one of the primary ways in which we can communicate results in a report. You may often desire to tweak their appearance to suit your particular needs. In this chapter, we will introduce techniques that can be used to customize tables. This chapter aims to do the following:

- Show all features of the table-generating function `knitr::kable()`.

- Highlight more advanced customization of tables using the **kableExtra** package (Zhu, 2019).

- Provide a list of other packages that produce tables.

10.1 The function `knitr::kable()`

The `kable()` function in **knitr** is a very simple table generator, and is simple by design. It only generates tables for strictly rectangular data such as matrices and data frames. You cannot heavily format the table cells or merge cells. However, this function does have a large number of arguments for you to customize the appearance of tables:

```
kable(x, format, digits = getOption("digits"), row.names = NA,
  col.names = NA, align, caption = NULL, label = NULL,
  format.args = list(), escape = TRUE, ...)
```

10.1.1 Supported table formats

In most cases, `knitr::kable(x)` may be enough if you only need a simple table for the data object x. The `format` argument is automatically set according to the **knitr** source document format. Its possible values are `pipe` (tables with columns separated by pipes), `simple` (Pandoc's simple tables), `latex`

(LaTeX tables), html (HTML tables), and rst (reStructuredText tables). For
R Markdown documents, kable() uses the pipe format for tables by default,
which looks like this:

```
knitr::kable(head(mtcars[, 1:4]), "pipe")
```

```
|                    |   mpg| cyl| disp|  hp|
|:-------------------|-----:|---:|----:|---:|
|Mazda RX4           |  21.0|   6|  160| 110|
|Mazda RX4 Wag       |  21.0|   6|  160| 110|
|Datsun 710          |  22.8|   4|  108|  93|
|Hornet 4 Drive      |  21.4|   6|  258| 110|
|Hornet Sportabout   |  18.7|   8|  360| 175|
|Valiant             |  18.1|   6|  225| 105|
```

You can also generate simple tables, or tables in HTML, LaTeX, and reStructuredText:

```
knitr::kable(head(mtcars[, 1:4]), "simple")
```

```
                     mpg   cyl   disp    hp
-------------------  ----  ----  -----  ----
Mazda RX4            21.0     6    160   110
Mazda RX4 Wag        21.0     6    160   110
Datsun 710           22.8     4    108    93
Hornet 4 Drive       21.4     6    258   110
Hornet Sportabout    18.7     8    360   175
Valiant              18.1     6    225   105
```

```
knitr::kable(mtcars[1:2, 1:2], "html")
```

```
<table>
 <thead>
  <tr>
   <th style="text-align:left;">   </th>
   <th style="text-align:right;"> mpg </th>
   <th style="text-align:right;"> cyl </th>
  </tr>
```

```
  </thead>
<tbody>
  <tr>
   <td style="text-align:left;"> Mazda RX4 </td>
   <td style="text-align:right;"> 21 </td>
   <td style="text-align:right;"> 6 </td>
  </tr>
  <tr>
   <td style="text-align:left;"> Mazda RX4 Wag </td>
   <td style="text-align:right;"> 21 </td>
   <td style="text-align:right;"> 6 </td>
  </tr>
</tbody>
</table>
```

```r
knitr::kable(head(mtcars[, 1:4]), "latex")
```

```
\begin{tabular}{l|r|r|r|r}
\hline
  & mpg & cyl & disp & hp\\
\hline
Mazda RX4 & 21.0 & 6 & 160 & 110\\
\hline
Mazda RX4 Wag & 21.0 & 6 & 160 & 110\\
\hline
Datsun 710 & 22.8 & 4 & 108 & 93\\
\hline
Hornet 4 Drive & 21.4 & 6 & 258 & 110\\
\hline
Hornet Sportabout & 18.7 & 8 & 360 & 175\\
\hline
Valiant & 18.1 & 6 & 225 & 105\\
\hline
\end{tabular}
```

```r
knitr::kable(head(mtcars[, 1:4]), "rst")
```

```
=================  ====  ===  ====  ===
\                   mpg  cyl  disp   hp
=================  ====  ===  ====  ===
Mazda RX4          21.0    6   160  110
Mazda RX4 Wag      21.0    6   160  110
Datsun 710         22.8    4   108   93
Hornet 4 Drive     21.4    6   258  110
Hornet Sportabout  18.7    8   360  175
Valiant            18.1    6   225  105
=================  ====  ===  ====  ===
```

Please note that only the formats pipe and simple are portable, i.e., they work for any output document format. Other table formats only work for specific output formats, e.g., format = 'latex' only works for LaTeX output documents. Using a specific table format will give you more control, at the price of sacrificing portability.

If you only need one table format that is not the default format for a document, you can set the global R option knitr.table.format, e.g.,

```
options(knitr.table.format = "latex")
```

This option can also be a function that returns the format string or NULL. In the case of NULL, **knitr** will try to automatically decide the appropriate format. For example, we can use the latex format only when the output format is LaTeX:

```
options(knitr.table.format = function() {
  if (knitr::is_latex_output())
    "latex" else "pipe"
})
```

10.1.2   Change column names

The names of columns in a data frame may not be the same as what we want to display to readers. In R, the column names of data often do not use spaces to separate words but dots or underscores instead. This may not feel natural when we read them in a table. We can use the col.names argument to replace the column names with a vector of new names. For example, we substitute the dots with spaces in the column names of the `iris` data:

```r
iris2 <- head(iris)
knitr::kable(iris2, col.names = gsub("[.]", " ", names(iris)))
```

Sepal Length	Sepal Width	Petal Length	Petal Width	Species
5.1	3.5	1.4	0.2	setosa
4.9	3.0	1.4	0.2	setosa
4.7	3.2	1.3	0.2	setosa
4.6	3.1	1.5	0.2	setosa
5.0	3.6	1.4	0.2	setosa
5.4	3.9	1.7	0.4	setosa

The `col.names` argument can take an arbitrary character vector (not necessarily the modified column names via functions like `gsub()`), as long as the length of the vector is equal to the number of columns of the data object, e.g.,

```r
knitr::kable(
  iris,
  col.names = c('We', 'Need', 'Five', 'Names', 'Here')
)
```

10.1.3 Specify column alignment

To change the alignment of the table columns, you can use either a vector of values consisting of characters `l` (left), `c` (center), and `r` (right) or a single multi-character string for alignment, so `kable(..., align = c('c', 'l'))` can be shortened to `kable(..., align = 'cl')`. By default, numeric columns are right-aligned, and other columns are left-aligned. Here is an example:

```r
# left, center, center, right, right
knitr::kable(iris2, align = "lccrr")
```

TABLE 10.1: An example table caption.

Sepal.Length	Sepal.Width	Petal.Length	Petal.Width	Species
5.1	3.5	1.4	0.2	setosa
4.9	3.0	1.4	0.2	setosa
4.7	3.2	1.3	0.2	setosa
4.6	3.1	1.5	0.2	setosa
5.0	3.6	1.4	0.2	setosa
5.4	3.9	1.7	0.4	setosa

Sepal.Length	Sepal.Width	Petal.Length	Petal.Width	Species
5.1	3.5	1.4	0.2	setosa
4.9	3.0	1.4	0.2	setosa
4.7	3.2	1.3	0.2	setosa
4.6	3.1	1.5	0.2	setosa
5.0	3.6	1.4	0.2	setosa
5.4	3.9	1.7	0.4	setosa

10.1.4   Add a table caption

You can add a caption to the table via the `caption` argument, e.g. (see Table 10.1 for the output),

```
knitr::kable(iris2, caption = "An example table caption.")
```

As we mentioned in Section 4.7, a table can be cross-referenced when it has a caption and the output format is from **bookdown**.

10.1.5   Format numeric columns

You can set the maximum number of decimal places via the `digits` argument (which will be passed to the `round()` function), and other formatting arguments via `format.args` (to be passed to the `format()` function in base R). First we show a few simple examples of `round()` and `format()` so you will understand how the arguments work later in `kable()`:

```
round(1.234567, 0)
## [1] 1
round(1.234567, digits = 1)
```

```
## [1] 1.2
round(1.234567, digits = 3)
## [1] 1.235
format(1000, scientific = TRUE)
## [1] "1e+03"
format(10000.123, big.mark = ",")
## [1] "10,000"
```

Then we round and format numbers in a table:

```
d <- cbind(X1 = runif(3), X2 = 10^c(3, 5, 7), X3 = rnorm(3,
    0, 1000))
# at most 4 decimal places
knitr::kable(d, digits = 4)
```

X1	X2	X3
0.6517	1e+03	-869.5843
0.0513	1e+05	-1182.8496
0.9654	1e+07	69.3775

```
# round columns separately
knitr::kable(d, digits = c(5, 0, 2))
```

X1	X2	X3
0.65170	1e+03	-869.58
0.05128	1e+05	-1182.85
0.96539	1e+07	69.38

```
# do not use the scientific notation
knitr::kable(d, digits = 3, format.args = list(scientific = FALSE))
```

X1	X2	X3
0.652	1000	-869.584
0.051	100000	-1182.850
0.965	10000000	69.377

```
# add commas to big numbers
knitr::kable(d, digits = 3, format.args = list(big.mark = ",",
    scientific = FALSE))
```

X1	X2	X3
0.652	1,000	-869.584
0.051	100,000	-1,182.850
0.965	10,000,000	69.377

10.1.6   Display missing values

By default, missing values (i.e., NA) are displayed as the character string NA in the table. You can replace them with other values or choose not to display anything (i.e., leave the NA cells empty) with the global R option knitr.kable.NA, e.g., we make NA cells empty in the second table and display ** in the third table below:

```
d[rbind(c(1, 1), c(2, 3), c(3, 2))] <- NA
knitr::kable(d)  # NA is displayed by default
```

X1	X2	X3
NA	1e+03	-869.58
0.0513	1e+05	NA
0.9654	NA	69.38

```
# replace NA with empty strings
opts <- options(knitr.kable.NA = "")
knitr::kable(d)
```

X1	X2	X3
	1e+03	-869.58
0.0513	1e+05	
0.9654		69.38

```
options(knitr.kable.NA = "**")
knitr::kable(d)
```

X1	X2	X3
**	1e+03	-869.58
0.0513	1e+05	**
0.9654	**	69.38

```
options(opts)  # restore global R options
```

10.1.7 Escape special characters

If you are familiar with HTML or LaTeX, you know that there are a few special characters in these languages. To generate safe output, `kable()` will escape these special characters by default via the argument `escape` = `TRUE`, which means all characters will be generated verbatim, and special characters lose their special meanings. For example, > will be substituted with > for HTML tables, and _ will be escaped as _ for LaTeX tables. If you are an expert and know how to use special characters properly, you may disable this argument via `escape` = `FALSE`. In the second table below, we include a few LaTeX math expressions that contain special characters $, \, and _:

```
m <- lm(dist ~ speed, data = cars)
d <- coef(summary(m))
knitr::kable(d)
```

	Estimate	Std. Error	t value	Pr(>|t|)
(Intercept)	-17.579	6.7584	-2.601	0.0123
speed	3.932	0.4155	9.464	0.0000

```
# add a few math expressions to row and column names
rownames(d) <- c("$\\beta_0$", "$\\beta_1$")
colnames(d)[4] <- "$P(T > |t|)$"
knitr::kable(d, escape = FALSE)
```

	Estimate	Std. Error	t value	$P(T > \|t\|)$
β_0	-17.579	6.7584	-2.601	0.0123
β_1	3.932	0.4155	9.464	0.0000

Without `escape` = `FALSE`, special characters will either be escaped or substituted. For example, $ is escaped as \$, _ is escaped as _, and \ is substituted with \textbackslash{}:

```
knitr::kable(d, format = "latex", escape = TRUE)
```

```
\begin{tabular}{l|r|r|r|r}
\hline
```

```
 & Estimate & Std. Error & t value & \$P(T > |t|)\$\\
\hline
\$\textbackslash{}beta\_0\$ & -17.579 & 6.7584 & -2.601 & 0.0123\\
\hline
\$\textbackslash{}beta\_1\$ & 3.932 & 0.4155 & 9.464 & 0.0000\\
\hline
\end{tabular}
```

Other common special LaTeX characters include #, %, &, {, and }. Common special HTML characters include &, <, >, and ". You need to be cautious when generating tables with escape = FALSE, and make sure you are using the special characters in the right way. It is a very common mistake to use escape = FALSE and include % or _ in column names or the caption of a LaTeX table without realizing that they are special.

If you are not sure how to properly escape special characters, there are two internal helper functions in **knitr**. Below are some examples:

```
knitr:::escape_latex(c("100%", "# a comment", "column_name"))
```

```
## [1] "100\\%"           "\\# a comment" "column\\_name"
```

```
knitr:::escape_html(c("<address>", "x = \"character\"",
  "a & b"))
```

```
## [1] "&lt;address&gt;"
## [2] "x = &quot;character&quot;"
## [3] "a &amp; b"
```

10.1.8   Multiple tables side by side

You can pass a list of data frames or matrices to kable() to generate multiple tables side by side. For example, Table 10.2 contains two tables generated from the code below:

```
d1 <- head(cars, 3)
d2 <- head(mtcars[, 1:3], 5)
knitr::kable(
  list(d1, d2),
```

TABLE 10.2: Two tables placed side by side.

speed	dist		mpg	cyl	disp
4	2	Mazda RX4	21.0	6	160
4	10	Mazda RX4 Wag	21.0	6	160
7	4	Datsun 710	22.8	4	108
		Hornet 4 Drive	21.4	6	258
		Hornet Sportabout	18.7	8	360

```
  caption = 'Two tables placed side by side.',
  booktabs = TRUE, valign = 't'
)
```

Please note that this feature only works for HTML and PDF output.

If you want to be able to customize each table individually when placing them side by side, you may use the `kables()` function (the plural form of `kable()`), and pass a list of `kable()` objects to it. For example, we change the column names in the left table and set the number of decimal places to zero in the right table in Table 10.3:

```
# data objects d1 and d2 are from the previous code chunk
knitr::kables(
  list(
    # the first kable() to change column names
    knitr::kable(
      d1, col.names = c('SPEED', 'DISTANCE'), valign = 't'
    ),
    # the second kable() to set the digits option
    knitr::kable(d2, digits = 0, valign = 't')
  ),
  caption = 'Two tables created by knitr::kables().'
)
```

10.1.9 Generate multiple tables from a for-loop (*)

One common confusion about `kable()` is that it does not work inside for-loops. This problem is not specific to `kable()` but exists in many other pack-

TABLE 10.3: Two tables created by knitr::kables().

SPEED	DISTANCE		mpg	cyl	disp
4	2	Mazda RX4	21	6	160
4	10	Mazda RX4 Wag	21	6	160
7	4	Datsun 710	23	4	108
		Hornet 4 Drive	21	6	258
		Hornet Sportabout	19	8	360

ages, too. The reason is a little complicated. In case you are interested in the technicality, it is explained in the blog post "The Ghost Printer behind Top-level R Expressions."[1]

You may expect the following code chunk to generate three tables, but it will not:

```{r}
for (i in 1:3) {
  knitr::kable(head(iris))
}
```

You have to explicitly print the `kable()` results, and apply the chunk option `results = 'asis'`, e.g.,

```{r, results='asis'}
for (i in 1:3) {
  print(knitr::kable(head(iris)))
}
```

In general, when you generate output from a `for`-loop, we recommend that you add a few line breaks (\n) or an HTML comment (<!-- -->) after each output element to clearly separate all output elements, e.g.,

```{r, results='asis'}
for (i in 1:3) {
  print(knitr::kable(head(iris), caption = 'A caption.'))
```

---

[1]https://yihui.org/en/2017/06/top-level-r-expressions/

```
  cat('\n\n<!-- -->\n\n')
}
```

Without the separators, Pandoc may be fail to detect the individual elements. For example, when a plot is followed immediately by a table, the table will not be recognized:

```
![](logo.png)
                    mpg   cyl   disp    hp
-------------------  -----  ----  -----  ----
Mazda RX4           21.0     6    160   110
Mazda RX4 Wag       21.0     6    160   110
```

But it will be if there is a clear separation like this (note that we added an empty line below the image):

```
![](logo.png)

                    mpg   cyl   disp    hp
-------------------  -----  ----  -----  ----
Mazda RX4           21.0     6    160   110
Mazda RX4 Wag       21.0     6    160   110
```

or

```
![](logo.png)

<!-- -->

                    mpg   cyl   disp    hp
-------------------  -----  ----  -----  ----
Mazda RX4           21.0     6    160   110
Mazda RX4 Wag       21.0     6    160   110
```

10.1.10 Customize LaTeX tables (*)

If the only output format you need is LaTeX, there are a few extra options you can use in `kable()`. Note that these options will be ignored in other types of output such as HTML. Unless you have set the table format option globally (see Section 10.1.1), you will have to use the format argument of kable() explicitly in the examples of this section, e.g.,

```
knitr::kable(iris2, format = "latex", booktabs = TRUE)
```

When you assign a caption to a table (see Section 10.1.4), kable() will use the table environment to include the table, i.e.,

```
\begin{table}
% the table body (usually the tabular environment)
\end{table}
```

You can change this environment via the table.envir argument, e.g.,

```
knitr::kable(cars[1:2, ], format = "latex", table.envir = "figure")
```

```
\begin{figure}
\begin{tabular}{r|r}
\hline
speed & dist\\
\hline
4 & 2\\
\hline
4 & 10\\
\hline
\end{tabular}
\end{figure}
```

The floating position of the table is controlled by the argument position. For example, we can try to force a table to float to the bottom of a page via position = "!b":

```
knitr::kable(cars[1:2, ], format = "latex", table.envir = "table",
  position = "!b")
```

```
\begin{table}[!b]
\begin{tabular}{r|r}
```

```
\hline
speed & dist\\
\hline
4 & 2\\
\hline
4 & 10\\
\hline
\end{tabular}
\end{table}
```

When a table has a caption, you can also assign a short caption to it via the `caption.short` argument, e.g.,

```
knitr::kable(iris2, caption = "A long long long caption!",
  caption.short = "A short one.")
```

The short caption goes into the square brackets of the `\caption[]{}` command in LaTeX, and is often used in the List of Tables of the PDF output document (if the short caption is not provided, the full caption is displayed there).

If you are familiar with the LaTeX package **booktabs**[2] for publication-quality tables, you can set `booktabs = TRUE`, e.g.,

```
iris3 <- head(iris, 10)
knitr::kable(iris3, format = "latex", booktabs = TRUE)
```

---

[2]https://ctan.org/pkg/booktabs

Sepal.Length	Sepal.Width	Petal.Length	Petal.Width	Species
5.1	3.5	1.4	0.2	setosa
4.9	3.0	1.4	0.2	setosa
4.7	3.2	1.3	0.2	setosa
4.6	3.1	1.5	0.2	setosa
5.0	3.6	1.4	0.2	setosa
5.4	3.9	1.7	0.4	setosa
4.6	3.4	1.4	0.3	setosa
5.0	3.4	1.5	0.2	setosa
4.4	2.9	1.4	0.2	setosa
4.9	3.1	1.5	0.1	setosa

Please note that when you need additional LaTeX packages such as **booktabs** for an R Markdown document, you have to declare these packages in YAML (see Section 6.4 for how).

Depending on whether the argument `booktabs` is TRUE or FALSE (default), the table appearance is different. For `booktabs = FALSE`:

- Table columns are separated by vertical lines. You can explicitly remove the vertical lines via the `vline` argument, e.g., `knitr::kable(iris, vline = "")` (the default is `vline = "|"`). You can set this option as a global R option so you do not need to set it for every single table, e.g., `options(knitr.table.vline = "")`.

- The horizontal lines can be defined via arguments `toprule`, `midrule`, `linesep`, and `bottomrule`. Their default values are all `\hline`.

For `booktabs = TRUE`:

- There are no vertical lines in the table, but you can add these lines via the `vline` argument.

- The table only has horizontal lines for the table header and the bottom row. The default argument values are `toprule = "\\toprule"`, `midrule = "\\midrule"`, and `bottomrule = "\\bottomrule"`. A line space is added to every five rows by default. This is controlled by the argument `linesep`, which defaults to `c("", "", "", "", "\\addlinespace")`. If you want to add a space to every three rows, you can do this:

```
knitr::kable(iris3, format = "latex", linesep = c("", "",
  "\\addlinespace"), booktabs = TRUE)
```

Sepal.Length	Sepal.Width	Petal.Length	Petal.Width	Species
5.1	3.5	1.4	0.2	setosa
4.9	3.0	1.4	0.2	setosa
4.7	3.2	1.3	0.2	setosa
4.6	3.1	1.5	0.2	setosa
5.0	3.6	1.4	0.2	setosa
5.4	3.9	1.7	0.4	setosa
4.6	3.4	1.4	0.3	setosa
5.0	3.4	1.5	0.2	setosa
4.4	2.9	1.4	0.2	setosa
4.9	3.1	1.5	0.1	setosa

If you want to remove the line spaces altogether, you may use `linesep` = ''.

Sometimes your table may be longer than a page. In this case, you can use the argument `longtable` = `TRUE`, which uses the LaTeX package **longtable**[3] to span your table to multiple pages.

Tables are center-aligned by default when they are included in a table environment (i.e., when the table has a caption). If you do not want to center a table, use the argument `centering` = `FALSE`.

10.1.11 Customize HTML tables (*)

If you want to customize tables generated via `knitr::kable(format = "html")`, there is only one extra argument besides the common arguments mentioned in previous sections: `table.attr`. This argument allows you to add arbitrary attributes to the `<table>` tag. For example:

```
knitr::kable(mtcars[1:2, 1:2], table.attr = "class=\"striped\"",
  format = "html")
```

---

[3]https://ctan.org/pkg/longtable

```html
<table class="striped">
 <thead>
  <tr>
   <th style="text-align:left;">    </th>
   <th style="text-align:right;"> mpg </th>
   <th style="text-align:right;"> cyl </th>
  </tr>
 </thead>
<tbody>
  <tr>
   <td style="text-align:left;"> Mazda RX4 </td>
   <td style="text-align:right;"> 21 </td>
   <td style="text-align:right;"> 6 </td>
  </tr>
  <tr>
   <td style="text-align:left;"> Mazda RX4 Wag </td>
   <td style="text-align:right;"> 21 </td>
   <td style="text-align:right;"> 6 </td>
  </tr>
</tbody>
</table>
```

We added a class striped to the table. However, a class name is not enough to change the appearance of a table. You have to define CSS rules for the class. For example, to make a striped table that has different colors for odd and even rows, you can add a light gray background to even or odd rows:

```css
.striped tr:nth-child(even) { background: #eee; }
```

The above CSS rule means all rows (i.e., the <tr> tags) with even row numbers (:nth-child(even)) that are children of an element with the striped class will have a background color #eee.

A little bit of CSS can make a plain HTML table look decent. Figure 10.1 is a screenshot of an HTML table to which the following CSS rules are applied:

```css
table {
  margin: auto;
  border-top: 1px solid #666;
```

```
  border-bottom: 1px solid #666;
}
table thead th { border-bottom: 1px solid #ddd; }
th, td { padding: 5px; }
thead, tfoot, tr:nth-child(even) { background: #eee; }
```

Sepal.Length	Sepal.Width	Petal.Length	Petal.Width	Species
5.1	3.5	1.4	0.2	setosa
4.9	3.0	1.4	0.2	setosa
4.7	3.2	1.3	0.2	setosa
4.6	3.1	1.5	0.2	setosa
5.0	3.6	1.4	0.2	setosa
5.4	3.9	1.7	0.4	setosa

FIGURE 10.1: A striped table created with HTML and CSS.

10.2 The kableExtra package

The **kableExtra** package (Zhu, 2019) is designed to extend the basic functionality of tables produced using `knitr::kable()` (see Section 10.1). Since `knitr::kable()` is simple by design (please feel free to read this as "Yihui is lazy"), it definitely has a lot of missing features that are commonly seen in other packages, and **kableExtra** has filled the gap perfectly. The most amazing thing about **kableExtra** is that most of its table features work for both HTML and PDF formats (e.g., making striped tables like the one in Figure 10.1).

This package can be installed from CRAN as usual, or you may try the development version on GitHub (`https://github.com/haozhu233/kableExtra`):

```
# install from CRAN
install.packages("kableExtra")
```

```
# install the development version
remotes::install_github("haozhu233/kableExtra")
```

It has extensive documentation at https://haozhu233.github.io/
kableExtra/, which provides a lot of examples on how the kable() output
can be customized for either HTML or LaTeX output. We recommend that
you read its documentation by yourself, and will only present a handful of
examples in this section.

The **kableExtra** package features the pipe operator, %>%. You can pipe the
kable() output to the styling functions of **kableExtra**, e.g.,

```
library(knitr)
library(kableExtra)
kable(iris) %>%
  kable_styling(latex_options = "striped")
```

10.2.1   Set the font size

The function kable_styling() in **kableExtra** allows you to style the whole
table. For example, you can specify the alignment of the table on the page, the
width, and the font size of the table. Below is an example of using a smaller
font size:

```
kable(head(iris, 5), booktabs = TRUE) %>%
  kable_styling(font_size = 8)
```

Sepal.Length	Sepal.Width	Petal.Length	Petal.Width	Species
5.1	3.5	1.4	0.2	setosa
4.9	3.0	1.4	0.2	setosa
4.7	3.2	1.3	0.2	setosa
4.6	3.1	1.5	0.2	setosa
5.0	3.6	1.4	0.2	setosa

10.2.2   Style specific rows/columns

The functions row_spec() and column_spec() can be used to style individual rows and columns, respectively. In the example below, we make the first
row bold and italic, add a black background to the second and third rows

while changing the font color to white, underline the fourth row and change its typeface, rotate the fifth row, and strike out the fifth column:

```r
kable(head(iris, 5), align = 'c', booktabs = TRUE) %>%
  row_spec(1, bold = TRUE, italic = TRUE) %>%
  row_spec(2:3, color = 'white', background = 'black') %>%
  row_spec(4, underline = TRUE, monospace = TRUE) %>%
  row_spec(5, angle = 45) %>%
  column_spec(5, strikeout = TRUE)
```

Sepal.Length	Sepal.Width	Petal.Length	Petal.Width	Species
5.1	*3.5*	*1.4*	*0.2*	*setosa*
4.9	3.0	1.4	0.2	setosa
4.7	3.2	1.3	0.2	setosa
4.6	3.1	1.5	0.2	setosa
5.0	3.6	1.4	0.2	setosa

Similarly, you can style individual cells with the `cell_spec()` function.

10.2.3 Group rows/columns

Rows and columns can be grouped via the functions `pack_rows()` and `add_header_above()`, respectively. You can also collapse rows via `collapse_rows()`, so one cell can span multiple rows. Below is an example that shows a custom table header with grouped columns:

```r
iris2 <- iris[1:5, c(1, 3, 2, 4, 5)]
names(iris2) <- gsub('[.].+', '', names(iris2))
kable(iris2, booktabs = TRUE) %>%
  add_header_above(c("Length" = 2, "Width" = 2, " " = 1)) %>%
  add_header_above(c("Measurements" = 4, "More attributes" = 1))
```

Measurements				More attributes
Length		Width		
Sepal	Petal	Sepal	Petal	Species
5.1	1.4	3.5	0.2	setosa
4.9	1.4	3.0	0.2	setosa
4.7	1.3	3.2	0.2	setosa
4.6	1.5	3.1	0.2	setosa
5.0	1.4	3.6	0.2	setosa

For the named vector in add_header_above(), the names are the text to be shown in the table header, and the integer values of the vector indicate how many columns a name should span, e.g., "Length" = 2 means Length should span two columns.

Below is an example of pack_rows(). The meaning of its index argument is similar to the argument of add_header_above() as we just explained before.

```
iris3 <- iris[c(1:2, 51:54, 101:103), ]
kable(iris3[, 1:4], booktabs = TRUE) %>% pack_rows(
  index = c("setosa" = 2, "versicolor" = 4, "virginica" = 3)
)
```

	Sepal.Length	Sepal.Width	Petal.Length	Petal.Width
setosa				
1	5.1	3.5	1.4	0.2
2	4.9	3.0	1.4	0.2
versicolor				
51	7.0	3.2	4.7	1.4
52	6.4	3.2	4.5	1.5
53	6.9	3.1	4.9	1.5
54	5.5	2.3	4.0	1.3
virginica				
101	6.3	3.3	6.0	2.5
102	5.8	2.7	5.1	1.9
103	7.1	3.0	5.9	2.1

10.2.4 Scaling down wide tables in LaTeX

There are a few features that are specific to the HTML or LaTeX output format. For example, landscape pages only make sense in LaTeX, so the `land-scape()` function in **kableExtra** only works for LaTeX output. Below we show an example to scale down a table to fit the page (otherwise it would be too wide):

```
tab <- kable(tail(mtcars, 5), booktabs = TRUE)
tab  # original table (too wide)
```

	mpg	cyl	disp	hp	drat	wt	qsec	vs	am	gear	carb
Lotus Europa	30.4	4	95.1	113	3.77	1.513	16.9	1	1	5	2
Ford Pantera L	15.8	8	351.0	264	4.22	3.170	14.5	0	1	5	4
Ferrari Dino	19.7	6	145.0	175	3.62	2.770	15.5	0	1	5	6
Maserati Bora	15.0	8	301.0	335	3.54	3.570	14.6	0	1	5	8
Volvo 142E	21.4	4	121.0	109	4.11	2.780	18.6	1	1	4	2

```
tab %>%
  kable_styling(latex_options = "scale_down")
```

	mpg	cyl	disp	hp	drat	wt	qsec	vs	am	gear	carb
Lotus Europa	30.4	4	95.1	113	3.77	1.513	16.9	1	1	5	2
Ford Pantera L	15.8	8	351.0	264	4.22	3.170	14.5	0	1	5	4
Ferrari Dino	19.7	6	145.0	175	3.62	2.770	15.5	0	1	5	6
Maserati Bora	15.0	8	301.0	335	3.54	3.570	14.6	0	1	5	8
Volvo 142E	21.4	4	121.0	109	4.11	2.780	18.6	1	1	4	2

You will not see any differences in the above two tables if you are viewing the HTML version.

10.3 Other packages for creating tables

There are many other R packages that can be used to generate tables. The main reason that I introduced `kable()` (Section 10.1) and **kableExtra** (Section 10.2) is not that they are better than other packages, but because I'm familiar with only them.[4] Next I will list the packages that I'm aware of but not very familiar with. You can check them out by yourself, and decide which one fits your purpose best.

- **flextable** (Gohel, 2020a) and **huxtable** (Hugh-Jones, 2020): If you are looking for a table package that supports the widest range of output formats, **flextable** and **huxtable** are probably the two best choices. They all support HTML, LaTeX, and Office formats, and contain most common table features (e.g., conditional formatting). More information about **flextable** can be found at `https://davidgohel.github.io/flextable/`, and the documentation of **huxtable** is at `https://hughjonesd.github.io/huxtable/`.

- **gt** (Iannone et al., 2020b): Allows you to compose a table by putting together different parts of the table, such as the table header (title and subtitle), the column labels, the table body, row group labels, and the table footer. Some parts are optional. You can also format numbers and add background shading to cells. Currently **gt** mainly supports HTML output.[5] You can find more information about it at `https://gt.rstudio.com`.

- **formattable** (Ren and Russell, 2016): Provides some utility functions to format numbers (e.g., `percent()` and `accounting()`), and also functions to style table columns (e.g., format the text, annotate numbers with background shading or color bars, or add icons in cells). Like **gt**, this package also primarily supports the HTML format. You can find more information about it from its GitHub project at `https://github.com/renkun-ken/formattable`.

- **DT** (Xie et al., 2020a): As its author, I think I'm familiar with this package, but I did not introduce it in a separate section because it only supports the HTML format. **DT** is built on top of the JavaScript library **DataTables**, which can turn a static table into an interactive table on an HTML page. You may sort, search, and paginate the table. **DT** also supports formatting the cells, works with Shiny to build interactive applications, and has included a large number of **DataTables** extensions (e.g., you may export the table to Excel, or interactively reorder columns). See the package repository for more information: `https://github.com/rstudio/DT`.

---

[4]Frankly speaking, I rarely use tables by myself, so I'm not highly motivated to learn how to create sophisticated tables.

[5]If you need the support for other output formats such as LaTeX and Word, the **gtsummary** package (Sjoberg et al., 2020) has made some extensions based on **gt** that look very promising: `https://github.com/ddsjoberg/gtsummary`.

- **reactable** (Lin, 2020): Similar to **DT**, this package also creates interactive tables based on a JavaScript library. Frankly speaking, it looks better than **DT** in several aspects in my eyes (such as row grouping and aggregation, and embedding HTML widgets). Had **reactable** existed in 2015, I would not have developed **DT**. That said, **reactable** does not contain all the features of **DT**, so you may read its documentation and see which one fits your purpose better: `https://glin.github.io/reactable/`.

- **rhandsontable** (Owen, 2018): Also similar to **DT**, and has an Excel feel (e.g., you can edit data directly in the table). Visit `https://jrowen.github.io/rhandsontable/` to learn more about it.

- **pixiedust** (Nutter, 2020): Features creating tables for models (such as linear models) converted through the **broom** package (Robinson et al., 2020). It supports Markdown, HTML, and LaTeX output formats. Its repository is at `https://github.com/nutterb/pixiedust`.

- **stargazer** (Hlavac, 2018): Features formatting regression models and summary statistics tables. The package is available on CRAN at `https://cran.r-project.org/package=stargazer`.

- **xtable** (Dahl et al., 2019): Perhaps the oldest package for creating tables—the first release was made in 2000. It supports both LaTeX and HTML formats. The package is available on CRAN at `https://cran.r-project.org/package=xtable`.

I'm not going to introduce the rest of packages, but will just list them here: **tables** (Murdoch, 2020), **pander** (Daróczi and Tsegelskyi, 2018), **tangram** (Garbett, 2020), **ztable** (Moon, 2018), and **condformat** (Oller Moreno, 2020).

11

Chunk Options

As illustrated in Figure 2.1, the R package **knitr** plays a critical role in R Markdown. In this chapter and the next three chapters, we show some recipes related to **knitr**.

There are more than 50 chunk options that can be used to fine-tune the behavior of **knitr** when processing R chunks. Please refer to the online documentation at `https://yihui.org/knitr/options/` for the full list of options. For your convenience, we have also provided a copy of the documentation in Appendix A of this book.

In the following sections, we only show examples of applying chunk options to individual code chunks. However, please be aware of the fact that any chunk options can also be applied globally to a whole document, so you do not have to repeat the options in every single code chunk. To set chunk options globally, call `knitr::opts_chunk$set()` in a code chunk (usually the first one in the document), e.g.,

```
```{r, include=FALSE}
knitr::opts_chunk$set(
  comment = "#>", echo = FALSE, fig.width = 6
)
```
```

11.1   Use variables in chunk options

Usually chunk options take constant values (e.g., `fig.width = 6`), but they can actually take values from arbitrary R expressions, no matter how simple or complicated the expressions are. A special case is a variable passed to a chunk option (note that a variable is also an R expression). For example, you can define a figure width in a variable in the beginning of a document, and use it later in other code chunks, so you will be able to easily change the width in the future:

````
```{r}
my_width <- 7
```
````

````
```{r, fig.width=my_width}
plot(cars)
```
````

Below is an example of using an if-else statement in a chunk option:

````
```{r}
fig_small <- FALSE   # change to TRUE for larger figures
width_small <- 4
width_large <- 8
```
````

````
```{r, fig.width=if (fig_small) width_small else width_large}
plot(cars)
```
````

And we have one more example below in which we evaluate (i.e., execute) a code chunk only if a required package is available:

````
```{r, eval=require('leaflet')}
library(leaflet)
leaflet() %>% addTiles()
```
````

In case you do not know it, require('package') returns TRUE if the package is available (and FALSE if not).

11.2 Do not stop on error

Sometimes you may want to show errors on purpose (e.g., in an R tutorial). By default, errors in the code chunks of an Rmd document will halt R. If you

want to show the errors without stopping R, you may use the chunk option
`error = TRUE,` e.g.,

```
```{r, error=TRUE}
1 + "a"
```
```

You will see the error message in the output document after you compile the
Rmd document:

```
Error in 1 + "a": non-numeric argument to binary operator
```

In R Markdown, `error = FALSE` is the default, which means R should stop
on error when running the code chunks.

11.3 Multiple graphical output formats for the same plot

In most cases, you may want one image format for one plot, such as `png` or
`pdf`. The image format is controlled by the chunk option `dev` (i.e., the graphical device to render the plots). This option can take a vector of device names,
e.g.,

```
```{r, dev=c('png', 'pdf', 'svg', 'tiff')}
plot(cars)
```
```

Only the first format is used in the output document, but the images corresponding to the rest of formats are also generated. This can be useful when
you are required to submit figures of different formats additionally (e.g., you
have shown a `png` figure in the report but the `tiff` format of the same figure
is also required).

Note that by default, plot files are typically deleted after the output document
is rendered. To preserve these files, please see Section 16.5.

11.4   Cache time-consuming code chunks

When a code chunk is time-consuming to run, you may consider caching it via the chunk option cache = TRUE. When the cache is turned on, **knitr** will skip the execution of this code chunk if it has been executed before and nothing in the code chunk has changed since then. When you modify the code chunk (e.g., revise the code or the chunk options), the previous cache will be automatically invalidated, and **knitr** will cache the chunk again.

For a cached code chunk, its output and objects will be automatically loaded from the previous run, as if the chunk were executed again. Caching is often helpful when loading results is much faster than computing the results. However, there is no free lunch. Depending on your use case, you may need to learn more about how caching (especially cache invalidation[1]) works, so you can take full advantage of it without confusing yourself as to why sometimes **knitr** invalidates your cache too often and sometimes there is not enough invalidation.

The most appropriate use case of caching is to save and reload R objects that take too long to compute in a code chunk, and the code does not have any side effects, such as changing global R options via options() (such changes will not be cached). If a code chunk has side effects, we recommend that you do not cache it.

As we briefly mentioned earlier, the cache depends on chunk options. If you change any chunk options (except the option include), the cache will be invalidated. This feature can be used to solve a common problem. That is, when you read an external data file, you may want to invalidate the cache when the data file is updated. Simply using cache = TRUE is not enough:

```
```{r import-data, cache=TRUE}
d <- read.csv('my-precious.csv')
```
```

You have to let **knitr** know if the data file has been changed. One way to do it is to add another chunk option cache.extra = file.mtime('my-precious.csv') or more rigorously, cache.extra = tools::md5sum('my-precious.csv'). The former means if the modification time of the file

---

[1]https://yihui.org/en/2018/06/cache-invalidation/

has been changed, we need to invalidate the cache. The latter means if the content of the file has been modified, we update the cache. Note that cache.extra is not a built-in **knitr** chunk option. You can use any other name for this option, as long as it does not conflict with built-in option names.

Similarly, you can associate the cache with other information such as the R version (cache.extra = getRversion()), the date (cache.extra = Sys.Date()), or your operating system (cache.extra = Sys.info()[['sysname']]), so the cache can be properly invalidated when these conditions change.

We do not recommend that you set the chunk option cache = TRUE globally in a document. Caching can be fairly tricky. Instead, we recommend that you enable caching only on individual code chunks that are surely time-consuming and do not have side effects.

If you are not happy with **knitr**'s design for caching, you can certainly cache objects by yourself. Below is a quick example:

```
if (file.exists("results.rds")) {
  res <- readRDS("results.rds")
} else {
  res <- compute_it()  # a time-consuming function
  saveRDS(res, "results.rds")
}
```

In this case, the only (and also simple) way to invalidate the cache is to delete the file results.rds. If you like this simple caching mechanism, you may use the function xfun::cache_rds() introduced in Section 14.9.

11.5 Cache a code chunk for multiple output formats

When caching is turned on via the chunk option cache = TRUE, **knitr** will write R objects generated in a code chunk to a cache database, so they can be reloaded the next time. The path to the cache database is determined by the chunk option cache.path. By default, R Markdown uses different cache paths for different output formats, which means a time-consuming code chunk will be fully executed for each output format. This may be inconvenient, but there is a reason for this default behavior: the output of a code chunk can be dependent on the specific output format. For example, when you generate a plot, the output for the plot could be Markdown code like `![text](path/to/image.png)` when the output format is `word_document`, or HTML code like `<img src="path/to/image.png" />` when the output format is `html_document`.

When a code chunk does not have any side effects (such as plots), it is safe to use the same cache database for all output formats, which can save you time. For example, when you read a large data object or run a time-consuming model, the result does not depend on the output format, so you can use the same cache database. You can specify the path to the database via the chunk option `cache.path` on a code chunk, e.g.,

````
```{r important-computing, cache=TRUE, cache.path="cache/"}
```
````

By default, `cache.path` = `"INPUT_cache/FORMAT/"` in R Markdown, where `INPUT` is the input filename, and `FORMAT` is the output format name (e.g., `html`, `latex`, or `docx`).

11.6 Cache large objects

When the chunk option `cache` = `TRUE`, cached objects will be lazy-loaded into the R session, which means an object will not be read from the cache database until it is actually used in the code. This can save you some memory when not all objects are used later in the document. For example, if you read a large data object but only use a subset in the subsequent analysis, the original data object will not be loaded from the cache database:

````
```{r, read-data, cache=TRUE}
full <- read.csv("HUGE.csv")
rows <- subset(full, price > 100)
# next we only use `rows`
```

```{r}
````
````

```
plot(rows)
```

However, when an object is too large, you may run into an error like this:

```
Error in lazyLoadDBinsertVariable(vars[i], ...
  long vectors not supported yet: ...
Execution halted
```

If this problem occurs, you can try to turn off the lazy-loading via the chunk option `cache.lazy` = `FALSE`. All objects in this chunk will be immediately loaded into memory.

11.7 Hide code, text output, messages, or plots

By default, **knitr** displays all possible output from a code chunk, including the source code, text output, messages, warnings, and plots. You can hide them individually using the corresponding chunk options.

Hide source code:

````
```{r, echo=FALSE}
1 + 1
```
````

Hide text output (you can also use `results = FALSE`):

````
```{r, results='hide'}
print("You will not see the text output.")
```
````

Hide messages:

````
```{r, message=FALSE}
message("You will not see the message.")
```
````

Hide warning messages:

````
```{r, warning=FALSE}
# this will generate a warning but it will be suppressed
1:2 + 1:3
```
````

Hide plots:

````
```{r, fig.show='hide'}
plot(cars)
```
````

Note that the plot will be generated in the above chunk. It is just not displayed in the output.

One frequently asked question about **knitr** is how to hide package loading messages. For example, when you library(tidyverse) or library(ggplot2), you may see some loading messages. Such messages can also be suppressed by the chunk option message = FALSE.

You can also selectively show or hide these elements by indexing them. In the following example, we only show the fourth and fifth expressions of the R source code (note that a comment counts as one expression), the first two messages, and the second and third warnings:

````
```{r, echo=c(4, 5), message=c(1, 2), warning=2:3}
# one way to generate random N(0, 1) numbers
x <- qnorm(runif(10))
# but we can just use rnorm() in practice
x <- rnorm(10)
x

for (i in 1:5) message('Here is the message ', i)

for (i in 1:5) warning('Here is the warning ', i)
```
````

You can use negative indices, too. For example, echo = -2 means to exclude the second expression of the source code in the output.

Similarly, you can choose which plots to show or hide by using indices for the fig.keep option. For example, fig.keep = 1:2 means to keep the first two plots. There are a few shortcuts for this option: fig.keep = "first" will only keep the first plot, fig.keep = "last" only keeps the last plot, and fig.keep = "none" discards all plots. Note that the two options fig.keep = "none" and fig.show = "hide" are different: the latter will generate plots but only hide them, and the former will not generate plot files at all.

For source code blocks in the html_document output, if you do not want to completely omit them (echo = FALSE), you may see Section 7.5 for how to fold them on the page, and allow users to unfold them by clicking the unfolding buttons.

11.8   Hide everything from a chunk

Sometimes we may want to execute a code chunk without showing any output at all. Instead of using separate options mentioned in Section 11.7, we can suppress the entire output of the code chunk using a single option include = FALSE, e.g.,

```
```{r, include=FALSE}
# any R code here
```
```

With include=FALSE, the code chunk will be evaluated (unless eval=FALSE), but the output will be completely suppressed—you will not see any code, text output, messages, or plots.

11.9   Collapse text output blocks into source blocks

If you feel there is too much spacing between text output blocks and source code blocks in the output, you may consider collapsing the text output into the source blocks with the chunk option `collapse` = TRUE. This is what the output looks like when `collapse` = TRUE:

```
1 + 1
## [1] 2
1:10
##  [1]  1  2  3  4  5  6  7  8  9 10
```

Below is the same chunk but it does not have the option `collapse` = TRUE (the default is FALSE):

```
1 + 1
```

```
## [1] 2
```

```
1:10
```

```
##  [1]  1  2  3  4  5  6  7  8  9 10
```

11.10   Reformat R source code

When you set the chunk option `tidy` = TRUE, the R source code will be reformatted by the `tidy_source()` function in the **formatR** package (Xie, 2019a). The `tidy_source()` can reformat the code in several aspects, such as adding spaces around most operators, indenting the code properly, and replacing the assignment operator = with <-. The chunk option `tidy.opts` can be a list of arguments to be passed to formatR::`tidy_source()`, e.g.,

````
```{r, tidy=TRUE, tidy.opts=list(arrow=TRUE, indent=2)}
# messy R code...
1+              1
x=1:10#some users prefer '<-' as the assignment operator
if(TRUE){
print('Hello world!') # indent by 2 spaces
}
```
````

The output:

```
# messy R code...
1 + 1
x <- 1:10   #some users prefer '<-' as the assignment operator
if (TRUE) {
  print("Hello world!")   # indent by 2 spaces
}
```

In Section 5.3, we mentioned how to control the width of text output. If you want to control the width of the source code, you may try the width.cutoff argument when tidy = TRUE, e.g.,

```
```{r, tidy=TRUE, tidy.opts=list(width.cutoff=50)}
# a long expression
1+1+1+1+1+1+1+1+1+1+1+1+1+1+1+1+1+1+1+1+1+1+
1+1+1+1+1+1+1+1+1+1+1+1+1+1+1+1+1+1+1+1+1+1+1
```
```

The output:

```
# a long expression
1 + 1 + 1 + 1 + 1 + 1 + 1 + 1 + 1 + 1 + 1 + 1 +
    1 + 1 + 1 + 1 + 1 + 1 + 1 + 1 + 1 + 1 + 1 +
    1 + 1 + 1 + 1 + 1 + 1 + 1 + 1 + 1 + 1 + 1 +
    1 + 1 + 1 + 1 + 1 + 1 + 1 + 1 + 1 + 1
```

Please read the help page ?formatR::tidy_source to know the possible arguments, and also see https://yihui.org/formatR/ for examples and limitations of this function.

Alternatively, you may use the **styler** package (Müller and Walthert, 2020) to reformat your R code if you set the chunk option tidy = 'styler'. The R code will be formatted with the function styler::style_text(). The **styler** package has richer features than **formatR**. For example, it can align function arguments and works with the pipe operator %>%. The chunk option tidy.opts can also be used to pass additional arguments to styler::style_text(), e.g.,

```
```{r, tidy='styler', tidy.opts=list(strict=FALSE)}
# align the assignment operators
```
```

```
a   <- 1#one variable
abc <- 2#another variable
```

By default, `tidy` = `FALSE` and your R code will not be reformatted.

11.11   Output text as raw Markdown content (*)

By default, text output from code chunks will be written out verbatim with two leading hashes (see Section 11.12). The text is verbatim because **knitr** puts it in fenced code blocks. For example, the raw output of the code `1:5` from **knitr** is:

```
## [1] 1 2 3 4 5
```

Sometimes you may not want verbatim text output, but treat text output as Markdown content instead. For example, you may want to write out a section header with `cat('# This is a header')`, but the raw output is:

```
## # This is a header
```

You do not want the text to be in a fenced code block (or the leading hashes). That is, you want the raw output to be exactly the character string passed to `cat()`:

```
# This is a header
```

The solution to this problem is the chunk option `results` = `'asis'`. This option tells **knitr** not to wrap your text output in verbatim code blocks, but treat it "as is." This can be particularly useful when you want to generate content dynamically from R code. For example, you may generate the list of column names of the `iris` data from the following code chunk with the option `results` = `'asis'`:

```r
cat(paste0("- `", names(iris), "`"), sep = "\n")
```

- Sepal.Length
- Sepal.Width
- Petal.Length
- Petal.Width
- Species

The hyphen (-) is the syntax for unordered lists in Markdown. The backticks are optional. You can see the verbatim output of the above chunk without the results = 'asis' option:

```r
cat(paste0("- `", names(iris), "`"), sep = "\n")
```

```
- `Sepal.Length`
- `Sepal.Width`
- `Petal.Length`
- `Petal.Width`
- `Species`
```

Below is a full example that shows how you can generate section headers, paragraphs, and plots in a for-loop for all columns of the mtcars data:

```
---
title: Generate content programmatically
---


With the chunk option `results = 'asis'`, you can
write out text as raw Markdown content, which can
also be mixed with plots.

```{r, mtcars-plots, results='asis'}
for (i in names(mtcars)) {
  cat('\n\n# Summary of the variable `', i, '`\n\n')
  x <- mtcars[, i]
  if (length(unique(x)) <= 6) {
    cat('`', i, '` is a categorical variable.\n\n')
    plot(table(x), xlab = i, ylab = 'Frequency', lwd = 10)
  } else {
    cat('Histogram for the continuous variable `', i, '`.\n\n')
```
```

```
    hist(x, xlab = i, main = '')
  }
}
```

Please note that we added line breaks (\n) excessively in the code. That is because we want different elements to be separated clearly in the Markdown content. It is harmless to use an excessive number of line breaks between different elements, whereas it can be problematic if there are not enough line breaks. For example, there is much ambiguity in the Markdown text below:

```
# Is this a header?
Is this a paragraph or a part of the header?
![How about this image?](foo.png)
# How about this line?
```

With more empty lines (which could be generated by cat('\n')), the ambiguity will be gone:

```
# Yes, a header!

And definitely a paragraph.

![An image here.](foo.png)

# Absolutely another header
```

The cat() function is not the only function that can generate text output. Another commonly used function is print(). Please note that print() is often *implicitly* called to print objects, which is why you see output after typing out an object or value in the R console. For example, when you type 1:5 in the R console and hit the Enter key, you see the output because R actually called print(1:5) implicitly. This can be highly confusing when you fail to generate output inside an expression (such as a for-loop) with objects or values that would otherwise be correctly printed if they were typed in the R console. This topic is quite technical, and I have written the blog post "The Ghost Printer behind Top-level R Expressions"[2] to explain it. If you are not interested in the technical details, just remember this rule: if you do not see

---

[2]https://yihui.org/en/2017/06/top-level-r-expressions/

output from a `for`-loop, you should probably print objects explicitly with the `print()` function.

11.12 Remove leading hashes in text output

By default, R code output will have two hashes `##` inserted in front of the text output. We can alter this behavior through the `comment` chunk option, which defaults to a character string `"##"`. We can use an empty string if we want to remove the hashes. For example:

````
```{r, comment=""}
1:100
```
````

Of course, you can use any other character values, e.g., `comment = "#>"`. Why does the `comment` option default to hashes? That is because `#` indicates comments in R. When the text output is commented out, it will be easier for you to copy all the code from a code chunk in a report and run it by yourself, without worrying about the fact that text output is not R code. For example, in the code chunk below, you can copy all four lines of text and run them safely as R code:

```
1 + 1
## [1] 2
2 + 2
## [1] 4
```

If you remove the hashes via `comment = ""`, it will not be easy for you to run all the code, because if you copy the four lines, you will have to manually remove the second and fourth lines:

```
1 + 1
[1] 2
2 + 2
[1] 4
```

One argument in favor of `comment = ""` is that it makes the text output look familiar to R console users. In the R console, you do not see hashes in the

beginning of lines of text output. If you want to truly mimic the behavior of
the R console, you can actually use comment = "" in conjunction with prompt
= TRUE, e.g.,

```
```{r, comment="", prompt=TRUE}
1 + 1
if (TRUE) {
  2 + 2
}
```
```

The output should look fairly familiar to you if you have ever typed and run
code in the R console, since the source code contains the prompt character
> and the continuation character +:

```
> 1 + 1
[1] 2
> if (TRUE) {
+   2 + 2
+ }
[1] 4
```

11.13   Add attributes to text output blocks (*)

In Section 7.3, we showed some examples of styling source and text output
blocks based on the chunk options class.source and class.output. Actually, there is a wider range of similar options in **knitr**, such as class.message,
class.warning, and class.error. These options can be used to add class
names to the corresponding text output blocks, e.g., class.error adds
classes to error messages when the chunk option error = TRUE (see Section
11.2). The most common application of these options may be styling the output blocks with CSS rules defined according to the class names, as demonstrated by the examples in Section 7.3.

Typically, a text output block is essentially a fenced code block, and its Markdown source looks like this:

```
```{.className}
lines of output
```
```

When the output format is HTML, it is usually[3] converted to:

```
<pre class="className">
<code>lines of output</code>
</pre>
```

The class.* options control the class attribute of the <pre> element, which is the container of the text output blocks that we mentioned above.

In fact, the class is only one of the possible attributes of the <pre> element in HTML. An HTML element may have many other attributes, such as the width, height, and style, etc. The chunk options attr.*, including attr.source, attr.output, attr.message, attr.warning, and attr.error, allow you to add arbitrary attributes to the text output blocks. For example, with attr.source = 'style="background: pink;"', you may change the background color of source blocks to pink. The corresponding fenced code block will be:

```
```{style="background: pink;"}
...
```
```

And the HTML output will be:

```
<pre style="background: pink;">
...
</pre>
```

You can find more examples in Section 5.7 and Section 12.3.

As a technical note, the chunk options class.* are just special cases of attr.*, e.g., class.source = 'numberLines' is equivalent to attr.source = '.numberLines' (note the leading dot here), but attr.source can take ar-

---

[3]It could also be converted to <div class="className"></div>. You may view the source of the HTML output document to make sure.

bitrary attribute values, e.g., `attr.source = c('.numberLines', 'start-From="11"')`.

These options are mostly useful to HTML output. There are cases in which the attributes may be useful to other output formats, but these cases are relatively rare. The attributes need to be supported by either Pandoc (such as the `.numberLines` attribute, which works for both HTML and LaTeX output), or a third-party package (usually via a Lua filter, as introduced in Section 4.20).

11.14 Post-process plots (*)

After a plot is generated from a code chunk, you can post-process the plot file via the chunk option `fig.process`, which should be a function that takes the file path as the input argument and returns a path to the processed plot file. This function can have an optional second argument `options`, which is a list of the current chunk options.

Below we show an example of adding an R logo to a plot using the extremely powerful **magick** package (Ooms, 2020). If you are not familiar with this package, we recommend that you read its online documentation or package vignette, which contains lots of examples. First, we define a function `add_logo()`:

```r
add_logo <- function(path, options) {
  # the plot created from the code chunk
  img <- magick::image_read(path)
  # the R logo
  logo <- file.path(R.home("doc"), "html", "logo.jpg")
  logo <- magick::image_read(logo)
  # the default gravity is northwest, and users can change
  # it via the chunk option magick.gravity
  if (is.null(g <- options$magick.gravity))
    g <- "northwest"
  # add the logo to the plot
  img <- magick::image_composite(img, logo, gravity = g)
  # write out the new image
  magick::image_write(img, path)
```

```
    path
}
```

Basically the function takes the path of an R plot, adds an R logo to it, and saves the new plot to the original path. By default, the logo is added to the upper-left corner (northwest) of the plot, but users can customize the location via the custom chunk option magick.gravity (this option name can be arbitrary).

Now we apply the above processing function to the code chunk below with chunk options fig.process = add_logo and magick.gravity = "northeast", so the logo is added to the upper-right corner. See Figure 11.1 for the actual output.

```
par(mar = c(4, 4, 0.1, 0.1))
hist(faithful$eruptions, breaks = 30, main = "", col = "gray",
  border = "white")
```

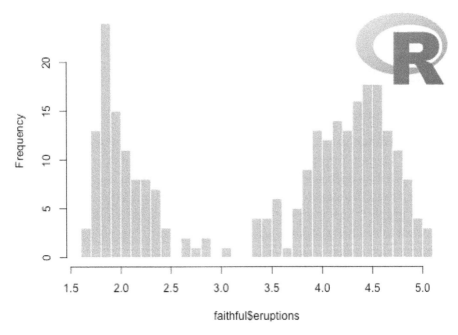

FIGURE 11.1: Add the R logo to a plot via the chunk option fig.process.

After you get more familiar with the **magick** package, you may come up with more creative and useful ideas to post-process your R plots.

Finally, we show one more application of the `fig.process` option. The `pdf2png()` function below converts a PDF image to PNG. In Section 11.15, we have an example of using the `tikz` graphical device to generate plots. The problem is that this device generates PDF plots, which will not work for non-LaTeX output documents. With the chunk options `dev = "tikz"` and `fig.process = pdf2png`, we can show the PNG version of the plot in Figure 11.2.

```
pdf2png <- function(path) {
  # only do the conversion for non-LaTeX output
  if (knitr::is_latex_output())
    return(path)
  path2 <- xfun::with_ext(path, "png")
  img <- magick::image_read_pdf(path)
  magick::image_write(img, path2, format = "png")
  path2
}
```

11.15   High-quality graphics (*)

The **rmarkdown** package has set reasonable default graphical devices for different output formats. For example, HTML output formats use the `png()` device, so **knitr** will generate PNG plot files, and PDF output formats use the `pdf()` device, etc. If you are not satisfied with the quality of the default graphical devices, you can change them via the chunk option `dev`. All possible devices supported by **knitr** are: `"bmp"`, `"postscript"`, `"pdf"`, `"png"`, `"svg"`, `"jpeg"`, `"pictex"`, `"tiff"`, `"win.metafile"`, `"cairo_pdf"`, `"cairo_ps"`, `"quartz_pdf"`, `"quartz_png"`, `"quartz_jpeg"`, `"quartz_tiff"`, `"quartz_gif"`, `"quartz_psd"`, `"quartz_bmp"`, `"CairoJPEG"`, `"CairoPNG"`, `"CairoPS"`, `"CairoPDF"`, `"CairoSVG"`, `"CairoTIFF"`, `"Cairo_pdf"`, `"Cairo_png"`, `"Cairo_ps"`, `"Cairo_svg"`, `"svglite"`, `"ragg_png"`, and `"tikz"`.

Usually, a graphical device name is also a function name. If you want to know more about a device, you can read the R help page. For example, you can type ?svg in the R console to know the details about the svg device, which is included in base R. Note that the quartz_xxx devices are based on the quartz() function, and they are only available on macOS. The CairoXXX devices are from the add-on R package **Cairo** (Urbanek and Horner, 2020), the Cairo_xxx devices are from the **cairoDevice** package (Lawrence, 2019), the svglite device is from the **svglite** package (Wickham et al., 2020c), and tikz is a device in the **tikzDevice** package (Sharpsteen and Bracken, 2020). If you want to use devices from an add-on package, you have to install the package first.

Usually, vector graphics have higher quality than raster graphics, and you can scale vector graphics without loss of quality. For HTML output, you may consider using dev = "svg" or dev = "svglite" for SVG plots. Note that SVG is a vector graphics format, and the default png device produces a raster graphics format.

For PDF output, if you are really picky about the typeface in your plots, you may use dev = "tikz", because it offers native support for LaTeX, which means all elements in a plot, including text and symbols, are rendered in high quality through LaTeX. Figure 11.2 shows an example of writing LaTeX math expressions in an R plot rendered with the chunk option dev = "tikz".

```
par(mar = c(4, 4, 2, .1))
curve(dnorm, -3, 3, xlab = '$x$', ylab = '$\\phi(x)$',
      main = 'The density function of $N(0, 1)$')
text(-1, .2, cex = 3, col = 'blue',
  '$\\phi(x)=\\frac{1}{\\sqrt{2\\pi}}e^{\\frac{-x^2}{2}}$')
```

Note that base R actually supports math expressions, but they are not rendered via LaTeX (see ?plotmath for details). There are several advanced options to tune the typesetting details of the tikz device. You may see ?tikzDevice::tikz for the possibilities. For example, if your plot contains multibyte characters, you may want to set the option:

```
options(tikzDefaultEngine = "xetex")
```

That is because xetex is usually better than the default engine pdftex in processing multibyte characters in LaTeX documents.

There are two major disadvantages of the tikz device. First, it requires a La-

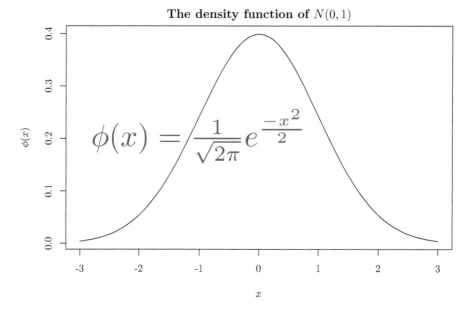

FIGURE 11.2: A plot rendered via the tikz device.

TeX installation, but this may not be too bad (see Section 1.2). You also need a few LaTeX packages, which can be easily installed if you are using TinyTeX:

```
tinytex::tlmgr_install(c("pgf", "preview", "xcolor"))
```

Second, it is often significantly slower to render the plots, because this device generates a LaTeX file and has to compile it to PDF. If you feel the code chunk is time-consuming, you may enable caching by the chunk option `cache = TRUE` (see Section 11.4).

For Figure 11.2, we also used the chunk option `fig.process = pdf2png`, where the function `pdf2png` is defined in Section 11.14 to convert the PDF plot to PNG when the output format is not LaTeX. Without the conversion, you may not be able to view the PDF plot in the online version of this book in the web browser.

11.16 Step-by-step plots with low-level plotting functions (*)

For R graphics, there are two types of plotting functions: high-level plotting functions create new plots, and low-level functions add elements to existing plots. You may see Chapter 12 ("Graphical procedures") of the R manual *An Introduction to R*[4] for more information.

By default, **knitr** does not show the intermediate plots when a series of low-level plotting functions are used to modify a previous plot. Only the last plot on which all low-level plotting changes have been made is shown.

It can be useful to show the intermediate plots, especially for teaching purposes. You can set the chunk option `fig.keep = 'low'` to keep low-level plotting changes. For example, Figure 11.3 and Figure 11.4 are from a single code chunk with the chunk option `fig.keep = 'low'`, although they appear to be from two code chunks. We also assigned different figure captions to them with the chunk option `fig.cap = c('A scatterplot ...', 'Adding a regression line...')`.

```
par(mar = c(4, 4, 0.1, 0.1))
plot(cars)
```

```
fit <- lm(dist ~ speed, data = cars)
abline(fit)
```

If you want to keep modifying a plot in a *different* code chunk, please see Section 14.5.

11.17 Customize the printing of objects in chunks (*)

By default, objects in code chunks are printed through the `knitr::knit_print()` function, which is by and large just `print()` in base R. The `knit_print()` function is an S3 generic function, which means you can extend it by yourself by registering S3 methods on it. The following

---

[4]https://cran.r-project.org/doc/manuals/r-release/R-intro.html

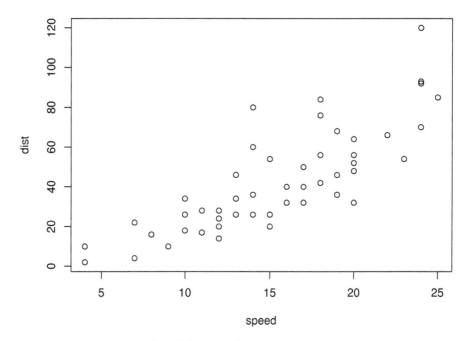

FIGURE 11.3: A scatterplot of the cars data.

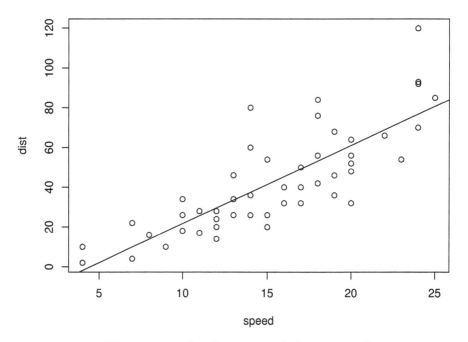

FIGURE 11.4: Adding a regression line to an existing scatterplot.

is an example that shows how to automatically print data frames as tables
via knitr::kable():

```
---
title: Use a custom `knit_print` method to print data frames
---


First, we define a `knit_print` method, and register it:

```{r}
knit_print.data.frame = function(x, ...) {
  res = paste(c("", "", knitr::kable(x)), collapse = "\n")
  knitr::asis_output(res)
}

registerS3method(
  "knit_print", "data.frame", knit_print.data.frame,
  envir = asNamespace("knitr")
)
```


Now we can test this custom printing method on data frames.
Note that you no longer need to call `knitr::kable()`
explicitly.

```{r}
head(iris)
```

```{r}
head(mtcars)
```

```

You can learn more about the knit_print() function in the **knitr** package
vignette:

```
vignette("knit_print", package = "knitr")
```

The **printr** package (Xie, 2017) has provided a few S3 methods to automatically print R objects as tables if possible. All you need is `library(printr)` in an R code chunk, and all methods will be automatically registered.

If you find this technique too advanced for you, some R Markdown output formats such as `html_document` and `pdf_document` also provide an option `df_print`, which allows you to customize the printing behavior of data frames. For example, if you want to print data frames as tables via `knitr::kable()`, you may set the option:

```
---
output:
  html_document:
    df_print: kable
---
```

Please see the help pages of the output format functions (e.g., `?rmark-down::html_document`) to determine whether an output format supports the `df_print` option and, if so, what the possible values are.

In fact, you can completely replace the printing function `knit_print()` through the chunk option `render`, which can take any function to print objects. For example, if you want to print objects using the **pander** package, you may set the chunk option `render` to the function `pander::pander()`:

````
```{r, render=pander::pander}
iris
```
````

The `render` option gives you complete freedom on how to print your R objects.

11.18   Option hooks (*)

Sometimes you may want to change certain chunk options dynamically according to the values of other chunk options. You may use the object `opts_hooks` to set up an *option hook* to do it. An option hook is a function associated with the option and to be executed when a corresponding chunk option is not NULL. This function takes the list of options for the current chunk as the input argument, and should return the (potentially modified) list. For example, we can tweak the `fig.width` option so that it is always no smaller than `fig.height`:

```
knitr::opts_hooks$set(fig.width = function(options) {
  if (options$fig.width < options$fig.height) {
    options$fig.width <- options$fig.height
  }
  options
})
```

Because `fig.width` will never be NULL, this hook function is always executed before a code chunk to update its chunk options. For the code chunk below, the actual value of `fig.width` will be 6 instead of the initial 5 if the above option hook has been set up:

```
```{r fig.width = 5, fig.height = 6}
plot(1:10)
```
```

As another example, we rewrite the last example in Section 11.12 so we can use a single chunk option console = TRUE to imply comment = " " and prompt = TRUE. Note that console is not a built-in **knitr** chunk option but a custom and arbitrary option name instead. Its default value will be NULL. Below is a full example:

```
```{r, include=FALSE}
knitr::opts_hooks$set(console = function(options) {
  if (isTRUE(options$console)) {
    options$comment <- ''; options$prompt <- TRUE
  }
  options
})
```
```

Default output:

```
```{r}
1 + 1
if (TRUE) {
```
```

```
  2 + 2
}
```
```

Output with `console = TRUE`:

```
```{r, console=TRUE}
1 + 1
if (TRUE) {
  2 + 2
}
```
```

The third example is about how to automatically add line numbers to any output blocks, including source code blocks, text output, messages, warnings, and errors. We have mentioned in Section 5.7 how to use chunk options such as attr.source and attr.output to add line numbers. Here we want to use a single chunk option (numberLines in this example) to control the blocks to which we want to add line numbers.

```
knitr::opts_hooks$set(
  numberLines = function(options) {
    attrs <- paste0("attr.", options$numberLines)
    options[attrs] <- lapply(options[attrs], c, ".numberLines")
    options
  }
)

knitr::opts_chunk$set(
  numberLines = c(
    "source", "output", "message", "warning", "error"
  )
)
```

Basically, the option hook numberLines appends the attribute .numberLines to output blocks, and the chunk option numberLines set via opts_chunk$set() makes sure that the option hook will be executed.

With the above setup, you can use the chunk option numberLines on a code
```

chunk to decide which of its output blocks will have line numbers, e.g., numberLines = c('source', 'output'). Specifying numberLines = NULL re-
moves line numbers completely.

You may wonder how this approach differs from setting the chunk options directly, e.g., just knitr::opts_chunk$set(attr.source = '.num-
berLines') like we did in Section 5.7. The advantage of using the option
hooks here is that they only *append* the attribute .numberLines to chunk options, which means they will not *override* existing chunk option values, e.g.,
the source code block of the chunk below will be numbered (with the above
setup), and the numbers start from the second line:

```
```{r, attr.source='startFrom="2"'}
# this comment line will not be numbered
1 + 1
```
```

It is equivalent to:

```
```{r, attr.source=c('startFrom="2"', '.numberLines'}
# this comment line will not be numbered
1 + 1
```
```

12

Output Hooks (*)

With the **knitr** package, you have control over every piece of output from your code chunks, such as source code, text output, messages, and plots. The control is achieved through "output hooks." Output hooks are a series of functions that take a piece of output as the input (typically a character vector), and return a character vector to be written to the output document. This may not be easy to understand for now, but hopefully you can see the idea more clearly with a small example below explaining how the output of a simple code chunk is rendered through **knitr**'s output hooks.

Consider this code chunk with one line of code:

````
```{r}
1 + 1
```
````

After **knitr** evaluates the code chunk, it gets two output elements, and both are stored as character strings: the source code "1 + 1", and the text output "[1] 2". These character strings will be further processed by chunk hooks for the desired output format. For example, for Markdown documents, **knitr** will wrap the source code in a fenced code block with a language name. This is done through the source hook, which more or less looks like this function:

```
# for the above case, `x` is a character string '1 + 1'
function(x, options) {
  # the little 'r' here indicates the language name
  paste(c("```r", x, "```"), collapse = "\n")
}
```

Similarly, the text output is processed by the output hook that looks like this function:

```
function(x, options) {
  paste(c("```", x, "```"), collapse = "\n")
}
```

So the final output of the above code chunk is:

```
```r
1 + 1
```

```

```
[1] 2
```

The actual hooks are more complicated than the two functions above, but
the idea is the same. You may obtain the actual hooks from the object
knit_hooks via the get() method, e.g.,

```
# for meaningful output, the code below should be
# executed *inside* a code chunk of a knitr document
knitr::knit_hooks$get("source")
knitr::knit_hooks$get("output")
# or knitr::knit_hooks$get(c('source', 'output'))
```

Unless you are truly interested in making contributions to the **knitr** package, we do not recommend that you read the source code of these built-in
hooks. If you are interested, this code can be found in the scripts named in
the form hooks-*.R at https://github.com/yihui/knitr/tree/master/R
(e.g., hooks-md.R contains hooks for R Markdown documents). As a **knitr**
user, it usually suffices if you know how to create custom output hooks by
taking advantage of the built-in hooks. You will learn that in several examples in this chapter, and we show the basic idea below.

A custom output hook is registered through the set() method of
knit_hooks. Because this method will override the existing default
hook, we recommend that you save a copy of an existing hook, process the
output elements in your own way, and pass the results to the default hook.
The usual syntax is:

```
# using local() is optional here (we just want to avoid
# creating unnecessary global variables like `hook_old`)
local({
  hook_old <- knitr::knit_hooks$get("NAME")  # save the old hook
  knitr::knit_hooks$set(NAME = function(x, options) {
    # now do whatever you want to do with x, and pass the
    # new x to the old hook
    hook_old(x, options)
  })
})
```

Here, NAME is the name of the hook, which can be one of the following values:

- source: processing the source code.

- output: processing text output.

- warning: processing warnings (usually from warning()).

- message: processing messages (usually from message()).

- error: processing error messages (usually from stop()).

- plot: processing plot file paths.

- inline: processing output from inline R expressions.

- chunk: processing output from the whole chunk.

- document: processing the whole document.

The meaning of the argument x in the hook functions is explained in the above list. For the options argument of a hook, it denotes the chunk options (as a list) for the current code chunk. For example, if you set foo = TRUE on a chunk, you can obtain its value via options$foo in the hook. The options argument is not available to the inline and document hooks.

Output hooks give you the ultimate control over every single piece of your chunk and document output. Compared with chunk options, which often have predefined purposes, output hooks can be much more powerful since they are user-defined functions, and you can do anything you want in functions.

12.1   Redact source code

Sometimes we may not want to fully display our source code in the report. For example, you may have a password in a certain line of code. We mentioned in Section 11.7 that you can use the chunk option echo to select which expressions in the R code to display (e.g., show the second expression via echo = 2). In this section, we provide a more flexible method that does not require you to specify the indices of expressions.

The basic idea is that you add a special comment to the code (e.g., # SE-CRET!!). When this comment is detected in a line of code, you omit that line. Below is a full example using the source hook:

```
---
title: Using the `source` hook to hide certain lines of code
---


First, we set up a `source` hook to exclude the lines of code
that contain the string `# SECRET!!` at the end.

```{r, include=FALSE}
local({
  hook_source <- knitr::knit_hooks$get('source')
  knitr::knit_hooks$set(source = function(x, options) {
    x <- x[!grepl('# SECRET!!$', x)]
    hook_source(x, options)
  })
})
```


Now we can test the new hook. When you knit this document, you
will not see the lines with the special comment `# SECRET!!`.

```{r}
1 + 1  # normal code to be displayed

# please use your real username and password
auth <- httr::authenticate("user", "passwd")
```
```

```
auth <- httr::authenticate("yihui", "horsebattery")  # SECRET!!
httr::GET("http://httpbin.org/basic-auth/user/passwd", auth)
```

The key part in the above source hook is this line, which matches the trailing comment # SECRET!! in the source code vector x via grepl() and exclude the matches:

```
x <- x[!grepl("# SECRET!!$", x)]
```

Precisely speaking, the above hook will exclude whole *expressions* containing the trailing comment # SECRET!!, instead of individual lines, because x is actually a vector of R expressions. For example, for the code chunk below:

```
1 + 1
if (TRUE) {
  # SECRET!!
  1:10
}
```

The value of x in the source hook is:

```
c("1 + 1", "if (TRUE) { # SECRET!!\n  1:10\n}")
```

If you want to hide lines instead of expressions of R code, you will have to split x into individual lines. You may consider using the function xfun::split_lines(). The body of the hook function will be:

```
x <- xfun::split_lines(x)   # split into individual lines
x <- x[!grepl("# SECRET!!$", x)]
x <- paste(x, collapse = "\n")   # combine into a single string
hook_source(x, options)
```

This example shows you how to manipulate the source code string, and grepl() is certainly not the only choice of string manipulation. In Section 12.2, we will show another example.

12.2   Add line numbers to source code

In this section, we show an example of defining a `source` hook to add line numbers as comments to the source code. For example, for this code chunk:

```
```{r}
if (TRUE) {
  x <- 1:10
  x + 1
}
```
```

We want the output to be:

```
if (TRUE) {       # 1
  x <- 1:10       # 2
  x + 1           # 3
}                 # 4
```

The full example is below:

```
---
title: Add line numbers to source code
---

We set up a `source` hook to add line numbers to the source
code. The numbers appear in comments at the end of each line.

```{r, include=FALSE}
local({
  hook_source <- knitr::knit_hooks$get('source')
  knitr::knit_hooks$set(source = function(x, options) {
    x <- xfun::split_lines(x)
    n <- nchar(x, 'width')
    i <- seq_along(x)   # line numbers
    n <- n + nchar(i)
    s <- knitr:::v_spaces(max(n) - n)
    x <- paste(x, s, ' # ', i, sep = '', collapse = '\n')
```
```

```
    hook_source(x, options)
  })
})
```

Now we can test the new hook. When you knit this document, you
will see line numbers in trailing comments.

```{r}
if (TRUE) {
  x <- 1:10
  x + 1
}
```

The main trick in the above example is to determine the number of spaces
needed before the comment on each line, so the comments can align to the
right. The number depends on the widths of each line of code. We leave it to
readers to digest the code in the hook function. Note that an internal function `knitr:::v_spaces()` is used to generate spaces of specified lengths,
e.g.,

```
knitr:::v_spaces(c(1, 3, 6, 0))
```

```
## [1] " "     "   "    "      " ""
```

The method introduced in Section 5.7 may be the actual way in which you
want to add line numbers to source code. The syntax is cleaner, and it works
for both source code and text output blocks. The above `source` hook trick
mainly aims to show you one possibility of manipulating the source code
with a custom function.

12.3 Scrollable text output

In Section 7.4, we showed how to restrict the heights of code blocks and text
output blocks via CSS. In fact, there is a simpler method with the chunk options `attr.source` and `attr.output` to add the `style` attribute to the fenced

code blocks in the Markdown output (see Section 11.13 for more information on these options). For example, for this code chunk with the `attr.output` option:

```
```{r, attr.output='style="max-height: 100px;"'}
1:300
```
```

Its Markdown output will be:

```
```r
1:300
```
```

```
```{style="max-height: 100px;"}
##  [1]   1   2   3   4   5   6   7   8   9  10
## [11]  11  12  13  14  15  16  17  18  19  20
##  ... ...
```
```

Then the text output block will be converted to HTML by Pandoc:

```
<pre style="max-height: 100px;">
<code>##  [1]   1   2   3   4   5   6   7   8   9  10
## [11]  11  12  13  14  15  16  17  18  19  20
##  ... ...</code>
</pre>
```

To learn more about Pandoc's fenced code blocks, please read its manual at `https://pandoc.org/MANUAL.html#fenced-code-blocks`.

The `attr.source` and `attr.output` options have made it possible for us to specify maximum heights for individual code chunks. However, the syntax is a little clunky, and requires a better understanding of CSS and Pandoc's Markdown syntax. Below we show an example of a custom `output` hook that works with a custom chunk option `max.height`, so you will only need to set the chunk option like `max.height = "100px"` instead of `attr.output = 'style="max-height: 100px;"'`. In this example, we only manipulate the `options` argument, but not the `x` argument.

```
---
title: Scrollable code blocks
output:
  html_document:
    highlight: tango
---
```

We set up an `output` hook to add a `style` attribute to the text output when the chunk option `max.height` is set.

````
```{r, include=FALSE}
options(width = 60)
local({
  hook_output <- knitr::knit_hooks$get('output')
  knitr::knit_hooks$set(output = function(x, options) {
    if (!is.null(options$max.height)) options$attr.output <- c(
      options$attr.output,
      sprintf('style="max-height: %s;"', options$max.height)
    )
    hook_output(x, options)
  })
})
```
````

Without the `max.height` option, you will see the full output, e.g.,

````
```{r}
1:100
```
````

Now we set `max.height` to `100px`. You will see a scrollbar in the text output because its height is larger than 100px.

````
```{r, max.height='100px'}
1:100
```
````

Essentially the `max.height` option is converted to the

`attr.output` option. It works even if the `attr.output`
option is present, i.e., it will not override the
`attr.output` option, e.g., we show line numbers on the left
side of the text output via the `.numberLines` attribute:

````
```{r, max.height='100px', attr.output='.numberLines'}
1:100
```
````

Figure 12.1 shows the output. Note that in the last code chunk with the chunk
option `attr.output`, the option will not be overridden by `max.height` because we respect existing attributes by combining them with the `style` attribute generated by `max.height`:

```
options$attr.output <- c(
  options$attr.output,
  sprintf('style="max-height: %s;"', options$max.height)
)
```

You can use a similar trick in the `source` hook to limit the height of source
code blocks.

12.4   Truncate text output

When the text output from a code chunk is lengthy, you may want to only
show the first few lines. For example, when printing a data frame of a few
thousand rows, it may not be helpful to show the full data, and the first few
lines may be enough. Below we redefine the `output` hook so that we can control the maximum number of lines via a custom chunk option `out.lines`:

```
# save the built-in output hook
hook_output <- knitr::knit_hooks$get("output")

# set a new output hook to truncate text output
knitr::knit_hooks$set(output = function(x, options) {
  if (!is.null(n <- options$out.lines)) {
```

Without the `max.height` option, you will see the full output, e.g.,

```
1:100
```

```
##   [1]   1   2   3   4   5   6   7   8   9  10  11  12  13
##  [14]  14  15  16  17  18  19  20  21  22  23  24  25  26
##  [27]  27  28  29  30  31  32  33  34  35  36  37  38  39
##  [40]  40  41  42  43  44  45  46  47  48  49  50  51  52
##  [53]  53  54  55  56  57  58  59  60  61  62  63  64  65
##  [66]  66  67  68  69  70  71  72  73  74  75  76  77  78
##  [79]  79  80  81  82  83  84  85  86  87  88  89  90  91
##  [92]  92  93  94  95  96  97  98  99 100
```

Now we set `max.height` to `100px`. You will see a scrollbar in the text output because its height is larger than 100px.

```
1:100
```

```
##   [1]   1   2   3   4   5   6   7   8   9  10  11  12  13
##  [14]  14  15  16  17  18  19  20  21  22  23  24  25  26
##  [27]  27  28  29  30  31  32  33  34  35  36  37  38  39
##  [40]  40  41  42  43  44  45  46  47  48  49  50  51  52
##  [53]  53  54  55  56  57  58  59  60  61  62  63  64  65
```

Essentially the `max.height` option is converted to the `attr.output` option. It works even if the `attr.output` option is present, i.e., it will not override the `attr.output` option, e.g., we show line numbers on the left side of the text output via the `.numberLines` attribute:

```
1:100
```

```
1  ##   [1]   1   2   3   4   5   6   7   8   9  10  11  12  13
2  ##  [14]  14  15  16  17  18  19  20  21  22  23  24  25  26
3  ##  [27]  27  28  29  30  31  32  33  34  35  36  37  38  39
4  ##  [40]  40  41  42  43  44  45  46  47  48  49  50  51  52
5  ##  [53]  53  54  55  56  57  58  59  60  61  62  63  64  65
```

FIGURE 12.1: An example of scrollable text output, with its height specified in the chunk option max.height.

```
    x <- xfun::split_lines(x)
    if (length(x) > n) {
      # truncate the output
      x <- c(head(x, n), "....\n")
    }
    x <- paste(x, collapse = "\n")
  }
  hook_output(x, options)
})
```

The basic idea of the above hook function is that if the number of lines of the text output is greater than the threshold set in the chunk option out.lines (stored in the variable n in the function body), we only keep the first n lines and add an ellipsis (....) to indicate the output is truncated.

Now we can test the new output hook by setting the chunk option out.lines = 4 on the chunk below:

```
print(cars)
```

```
##      speed dist
## 1       4     2
## 2       4    10
## 3       7     4
....
```

And you see four lines of output as expected. Since we have stored the original output hook in hook_output, we can restore it by calling the set() method again:

```
knitr::knit_hooks$set(output = hook_output)
```

As an exercise for readers, you may try to truncate the output in a different way: given the chunk option out.lines to determine the maximum number of lines, can you truncate the output in the middle instead of the end? For example, if out.lines = 10, you extract the first and last five lines, and add .... in the middle like this:

```
##      speed dist
## 1       4     2
```

```
## 2       4    10
## 3       7     4
## 4       7    22
....
## 46     24    70
## 47     24    92
## 48     24    93
## 49     24   120
## 50     25    85
```

Please note that the last line in the output (i.e., the argument x of the hook function) might be an empty line, so you may need something like c(head(x, n/2), '....', tail(x, n/2 + 1)) (+ 1 to take the last empty line into account).

12.5   Output figures in the HTML5 format

By default, plots in R Markdown are included in the tag <img src="..." /> in a <p> or <div> tag in the HTML output. This example below shows how to use the HTML5 <figure> tag to display plots.

```
---
title: Output figures in `<figure>` tags
output: html_document
---


Given a plot file path `x` and a figure caption in the chunk
option `options$fig.cap`, we want to write the plot in the
HTML5 tag in this form:

```html
<figure>
  <img src="PATH" alt="CAPTION" />
  <figcaption>CAPTION</figcaption>
</figure>
```
```

Now we redefine the `plot` hook (only when the output format is HTML):

```{r}
if (knitr::is_html_output()) knitr::knit_hooks$set(
  plot = function(x, options) {
    cap  <- options$fig.cap  # figure caption
    tags <- htmltools::tags
    as.character(tags$figure(
      tags$img(src = x, alt = cap),
      tags$figcaption(cap)
    ))
  }
)
```

The plot from the code chunk below will be placed in the
`<figure>` tag:

```{r, fig.cap='A scatterplot for the cars data.'}
par(mar = c(4.5, 4.5, .2, .2))
plot(cars, pch = 19, col = 'red')
```

We add some CSS styles to "see" the `<figure>` and
`<figcaption>` tags better (the `figure` has a dashed
border, and the caption has a light pink background):

```{css, echo=FALSE}
figure {
  border: 2px dashed red;
  margin: 1em 0;
}
figcaption {
  padding: .5em;
  background: lightpink;
  font-size: 1.3em;
  font-variant: small-caps;
```

```
}
```

The figure output is shown in Figure 12.2. Note that we actually overrode the default plot hook in this example, while most other examples in this chapter build custom hooks on top of the default hooks. You should completely override default hooks only when you are sure you want to ignore some built-in features of the default hooks. For example, the plot hook function in this case did not consider possible chunk options like out.width = '100%' or fig.show = 'animate'.

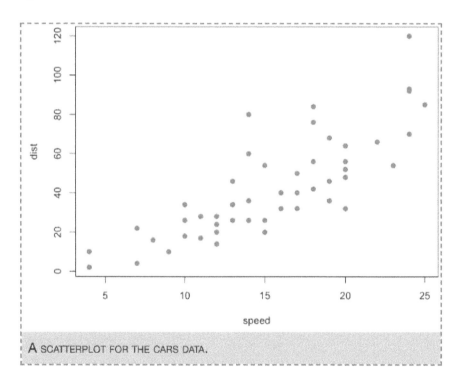

A SCATTERPLOT FOR THE CARS DATA.

FIGURE 12.2: A figure in the HTML5 figure tag.

This example shows you what you can possibly do with the plot file path x in the plot hook. If all you need is to customize the style of figures, you do not have to use the HTML5 tags. Usually the default plot hook will output images in the HTML code like this:

```
<div class="figure">
  <img src="PATH" />
  <p class="caption">CAPTION</p>
</div>
```

So you can just define css rules for `div.figure` and `p.caption`.

13

Chunk Hooks (*)

A chunk hook is a function that is triggered by a chunk option when the value of this chunk option is not NULL. Chunk hooks provide a way for you to execute additional tasks beyond running the code in a chunk. For example, you may want to post-process plots (e.g., Section 13.1 and Section 13.2), or record the time taken by a code chunk (Section 13.3). Such tasks may not be essential to the computing or analysis in the report, but they can be useful for other purposes (e.g., enhance plots or help you identify the most time-consuming chunks).

You can use chunk hooks purely for their side effects (e.g., only printing out certain information to the console), or for their returned values, which will be written to the output document if the value is a character value.

Like output hooks (see Chapter 12), chunk hooks are also registered via the object knitr::knit_hooks. Please note that the names of output hooks are reserved by **knitr**, so you must not use these names for your custom chunk hooks:

```
names(knitr:::.default.hooks)
```

```
##  [1] "source"            "output"
##  [3] "warning"           "message"
##  [5] "error"             "plot"
##  [7] "inline"            "chunk"
##  [9] "text"              "evaluate.inline"
## [11] "evaluate"          "document"
```

A chunk hook is associated with a chunk option of the same name. For example, you can register a chunk hook with the name greet:

```
knitr::knit_hooks$set(greet = function(before) {
  if (before)
```

```
    "Hello!" else "Bye!"
})
```

We will explain the arguments of the hook function in a moment. Now we set the chunk option greet = TRUE for the chunk below:

```
```{r, greet=TRUE}
1 + 1
```
```

And you will see that "Hello!" appears before the chunk, and "Bye!" appears after the chunk in the output below (which is because they are character values):

```
    Hello!
1 + 1

## [1] 2
    Bye!
```

A chunk hook function can possibly take four arguments: before, options, envir, and name. In other words, it can be of this form:

```
function(before, options, envir, name) {

}
```

All four arguments are optional. You can have four, three, two, one, or even no arguments. In the above example, we used one argument (i.e., before). The meanings of these arguments are:

- before: Whether the chunk hook is currently being executed before or after the code chunk itself is executed. Note that a chunk hook is executed twice for every code chunk (once before with hook(before = TRUE) and once after with hook(before = FALSE).

- options: The list of chunk options for the current code chunk, e.g., list(fig.width = 5, echo = FALSE, ...).

- envir: The environment in which the chunk hook is evaluated.

- name: The name of the chunk option that triggered the chunk hook.

As we mentioned in the beginning of this chapter, non-character values returned by chunk hooks are silently ignored, and character values are written to the output document.

13.1 Crop plots

The chunk hook knitr::hook_pdfcrop() can be used to crop PDF and other types of plot files, i.e., remove the extra margins in plots. To enable it, set this hook via knit_hooks$set() in a code chunk, and turn on the corresponding chunk option, e.g.,

```
knitr::knit_hooks$set(crop = knitr::hook_pdfcrop)
```

Then you can use the chunk option crop = TRUE to crop plots in a code chunk.

The hook hook_pdfcrop() calls the external program pdfcrop to crop PDF files. This program often comes with a LaTeX distribution (e.g., TeX Live or MiKTeX). You can check if it is available in your system via:

```
# if the returned value is not empty, it is available
Sys.which("pdfcrop")
```

```
##                     pdfcrop
## "/usr/local/bin/pdfcrop"
```

If you are using the LaTeX distribution TinyTeX (see Section 1.2), and pdfcrop is not available in your system, you may install it via tiny-tex::tlmgr_install('pdfcrop').

For non-PDF plot files such as PNG or JPEG files, this hook function calls the R package **magick** (Ooms, 2020) for cropping. You need to make sure this R package has been installed. Figure 13.1 shows a plot that is not cropped, and Figure 13.2 shows the same plot but has been cropped.

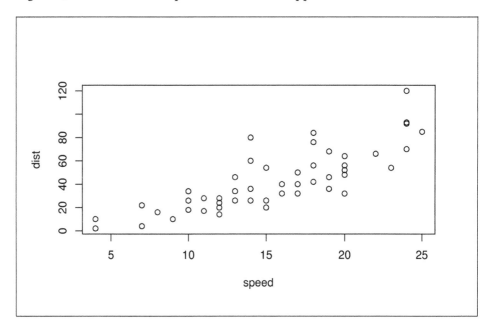

FIGURE 13.1: A plot that is not cropped.

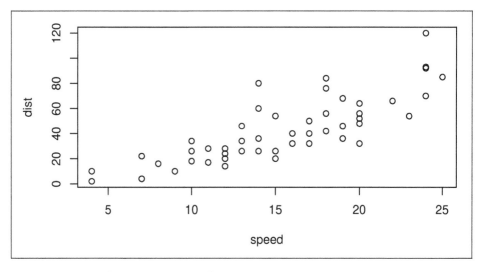

FIGURE 13.2: A plot that is cropped.

13.2 Optimize PNG plots

If you have installed the program OptiPNG (http://optipng.sourceforge.
net), you may use the hook knitr::hook_optipng() to optimize PNG plot
files to a smaller size without losing the image quality.

```
knitr::knit_hooks$set(optipng = knitr::hook_optipng)
```

After you set up this hook, you can use the chunk option optipng to pass
command-line arguments to OptiPNG, e.g., optipng = '-o7'. These
command-line arguments are optional, which means you can just use optipng = '' to enable the hook for a code chunk. Please see the user manual
on the website of OptiPNG to know the possible arguments.

Note that macOS users can easily install OptiPNG with Homebrew (https:
//brew.sh): brew install optipng.

13.3 Report how much time each chunk takes to run

By default, **knitr** provides a text-based progress bar to show you the knitting
progress. If you want more precise timing information about the chunks,
you may register a custom chunk hook to record the time for each chunk.
Here is an example hook:

```
knitr::knit_hooks$set(time_it = local({
  now <- NULL
  function(before, options) {
    if (before) {
      # record the current time before each chunk
      now <<- Sys.time()
    } else {
      # calculate the time difference after a chunk
      res <- difftime(Sys.time(), now)
      # return a character string to show the time
      paste("Time for this code chunk to run:", res)
    }
```

```
  }
}))
```

Then you can time a chunk with the chunk option time_it, e.g.,

```
```{r, time_it = TRUE}
Sys.sleep(2)
```
```

If you want to time all code chunks, you can certainly set the option globally: knitr::opts_chunk$set(time_it = TRUE).

In the above hook function, you can also output more information from the chunk options (i.e., the options argument of the function). For example, you may print out the chunk label in the returned value:

```
paste("Time for the chunk", options$label, "to run:", res)
```

Or you may record the time without printing it out in the hook:

```
all_times <- list()  # store the time for each chunk
knitr::knit_hooks$set(time_it = local({
  now <- NULL
  function(before, options) {
    if (before) {
      now <<- Sys.time()
    } else {
      res <- difftime(Sys.time(), now)
      all_times[[options$label]] <<- res
    }
  }
}))
```

Then you can access all the time information in the object all_times. This object is a named list with the names being chunk labels, and element values being the execution time for each chunk.

Lastly, as a technical note, we want to explain the use of the local() function in the previous hooks because some readers may not be familiar with it. This function allows you to run code in a "local" environment. The main benefit is that variables created in the code are local to that environment, so they will not pollute the outer environment (usually the global environment). For example, we created a variable now in local(), and used it in the time_it hook function. In the hook function, we update the value of now via the double arrow <<- instead of the normal assignment operator <-. This is because <<- assigns a value to a variable in the parent environment (which is the environment in local() in this case), and <- can only assign values to variables in the current environment. Before each code chunk is evaluated, the local variable now records the current time. After each code chunk is evaluated, we calculate the time difference between the current time and now. Note that local() returns the last value in the expression passed to it, which is a (hook) function in this case. In short, local() can make your workspace cleaner by not exposing variables that are only used locally but unused in the global environment. If you do not mind creating a variable now in the global environment, you can choose not to use local().

13.4 Show the chunk header in the output

Sometimes you may want to show the original code chunk header to your readers. For example, when you write an R Markdown tutorial, you may want to show both the chunk output and the chunk options that you used to generate the output, so your readers can learn how to do it by themselves.

The original chunk options are actually stored as a character string in the chunk option params.src. After you know this, you may write a chunk hook to add params.src to the output. Below is a full example:

```
---
title: Show chunk headers in the output
---

Set up a chunk hook named `wrapper` to wrap the chunk
output inside the original chunk header and footer.

```{r, setup, include=FALSE}
knitr::knit_hooks$set(wrapper = function(before, options) {
  # the original chunk might be indented
  if (is.null(indent <- options$indent)) indent <- ''
```
```

```
  # hide the wrapper=TRUE option
  opts <- gsub(', wrapper=TRUE', '', options$params.src)

  if (before) {
    # add the header
    sprintf('\n\n%s````\n```{r,%s}\n````\n', indent, opts)
  } else {
    # add the footer
    sprintf('\n\n%s````\n```\n````\n', indent)
  }
})
```

Now we apply the hook via the chunk option `wrapper=TRUE`.
Remember to put `wrapper=TRUE` at the end of the header, and
it has to be `wrapper=TRUE` precisely (e.g., not `wrapper=T`),
following a comma and a space, unless you adjust the `gsub()`
call in the above hook.

```
```{r, test-label, collapse=TRUE, wrapper=TRUE}
1 + 1
plot(cars)
```
```

You should see the original chunk header appear in
the output. The hook should also work when the chunk
is indented, e.g.,

- One bullet.

  ```
  ```{r, eval=TRUE, wrapper=TRUE}
  2 + 2
  ```
  ```

- Another bullet.

Basically, we restored the chunk header from `options$params.src` by
putting this string inside ```` ```{r, } ````. Then we wrapped this line in a pair of
four backticks, so it can be displayed verbatim in the output. Note that the

original code chunk might be indented (e.g., when it is nested in a list item), so we also need to add the proper indentation, which is stored in the chunk option `options$indent`.

The output of the bullet list at the end of the above example will be like this:

- One bullet.

  ```` ```{r, eval=TRUE} ````

  ```
  2 + 2
  ```

  ```
  ## [1] 4
  ```

  ```` ``` ````

- Another bullet.

You can see that the code chunk was evaluated, and the chunk header was also added.

13.5 Embed an interactive 3D plot with rgl

The **rgl** package (Adler and Murdoch, 2020) can be used to generate interactive 3D plots. These plots can still be interactive if they are saved to the WebGL format, which can be done through a hook function `rgl::hook_webgl()`. Below is an example that shows you how to set up **rgl** and **knitr** so 3D plots can be saved while preserving the interactivity:

```
---
title: Embed 3D plots with rgl
output: html_document
---
```

```
Set up a hook to save **rgl** plots:
```

````
```{r, setup}
library(rgl)
knitr::knit_hooks$set(webgl = hook_webgl)
```
````

See if it works for this 3D plot after we enable the hook
via the chunk option `webgl = TRUE`:

````
```{r, test-rgl, webgl=TRUE}
x <- sort(rnorm(1000))
y <- rnorm(1000)
z <- rnorm(1000) + atan2(x,y)
plot3d(x, y, z, col = rainbow(1000))
```
````

You should get an interactive 3D scatterplot like Figure 13.3 after you compile this example. Note that the interactive plots only work when the output format is HTML.

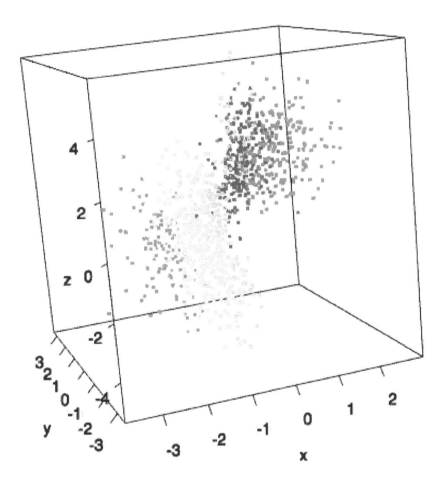

FIGURE 13.3: A 3D scatterplot generated from the rgl package.

14

Miscellaneous knitr Tricks

Besides chunk options (Chapter 11), output hooks (Chapter 12), and chunk hooks (Chapter 13), there are other useful functions and tricks in **knitr**. We introduce these tricks in this chapter, such as how to reuse code chunks, exit knitting early, display a plot in a custom place, and so on.

14.1 Reuse code chunks

You can freely reuse code chunks anywhere in your source document without cut-and-paste. The key is to label your code chunks, so you can refer to them with labels in other places. There are three ways to reuse code chunks.

14.1.1 Embed one chunk in another chunk (*)

You can embed one code chunk in another code chunk by enclosing its label in <<>>. Then **knitr** will automatically expand the string <<label>> to the actual code. For example, you can create an R function in this way:

We define a function to convert Fahrenheit to Celsius.

````
```{r, f2c}
F2C <- function(x) {
  <<check-arg>>
  <<convert>>
}
```
````

First, we check if the input value is numeric:

````
```{r, check-arg, eval=FALSE}
````
````

```
  if (!is.numeric(x)) stop("The input must be numeric!")
```

Then we do the actual conversion:

```{r, convert, eval=FALSE}
  (x - 32) * 5/ 9
```

This is based on one of the main ideas of Literate Programming,[1] which was proposed by Donald Knuth. The advantage of this technique is that you can split (complex) code into smaller parts, write each part in a separate code chunk, and explain them with narratives. All parts can be composed into the main code chunk to be executed.

For the above example, the first code chunk (with the label f2c) will become:

```{r, f2c}
F2C <- function(x) {
  if (!is.numeric(x)) stop("The input must be numeric!")
  (x - 32) * 5/ 9
}
```

You can embed an arbitrary number of other code chunks in one code chunk. The embedding can also be recursive. For example, you may embed chunk A in chunk B, and chunk B in chunk C. Then chunk C will include code from chunk A via chunk B.

The marker <<label>> does not have to be on a separate line. It can be embedded anywhere in a code chunk.

14.1.2   Use the same chunk label in another chunk

If you want to use exactly the same code chunk two or more times, you may define the chunk with a label, and create more code chunks with the same label but leave the chunk content empty, e.g.,

---

[1]https://en.wikipedia.org/wiki/Literate_programming

Here is a code chunk that is not evaluated:

````
```{r, chunk-one, eval=FALSE}
1 + 1
2 + 2
```
````

Now we actually evaluate it:

````
```{r, chunk-one, eval=TRUE}
```
````

We used the chunk label "chunk-one" twice in the above example, and the second chunk just reuses code from the first chunk.

We recommend that you do not use this method to run a code chunk more than once to generate plots (or other files), because plot files created from a later chunk may overwrite files from a previous chunk. It is okay if only one of such chunks uses the chunk option eval = TRUE, and all other chunks use eval = FALSE.

14.1.3 Use reference labels (*)

The chunk option ref.label takes a vector of chunk labels to retrieve the content of these chunks. For example, the code chunk with the label chunk-a is the combination of chunk-c and chunk-b below:

````
```{r chunk-a, ref.label=c('chunk-c', 'chunk-b')}
```
````

````
```{r chunk-b}
# this is the chunk b
1 + 1
```
````

````
```{r chunk-c}
# this is the chunk c
2 + 2
```
````

In other words, `chunk-a` is essentially this:

```{r chunk-a}
# this is the chunk c
2 + 2
# this is the chunk b
1 + 1
```

The chunk option `ref.label` has provided a very flexible way of reorganizing code chunks in a document without resorting to cut-and-paste. It does not matter if the code chunks referenced are before or after the code chunk that uses `ref.label`. An early code chunk can reference a later chunk.

There is an application of this chunk option in Section 4.19.

14.2 Use an object before it is created (*)

All code in a **knitr** document, including the code in code chunks and inline R expressions, is executed in linear order from beginning to end. In theory, you cannot use a variable before it is assigned a value. However, in certain cases, we may want to mention the value of a variable earlier in the document. For example, it is common to present a result in the abstract of an article, but the result is actually computed later in the document. Below is an example that illustrates the idea but will not compile:

```
---
title: An important report
abstract: >
  In this analysis, the average value of
  `x` is `r mx`.
---
```

```
We create the object `mx` in the following chunk:
```

```{r}
x <- 1:100
```

```
mx <- mean(x)
```

To solve this problem, the value of the object has to be saved somewhere and loaded the next time when the document is compiled. Please note that this means the document has to be compiled at least twice. Below is one possible solution using the saveRDS() function:

```{r, include=FALSE}
mx <- if (file.exists('mean.rds')) {
  readRDS('mean.rds')
} else {
  "The value of `mx` is not available yet"
}
```

```
---
title: An important report
abstract: >
  In this analysis, the average value of
  `x` is `r mx`.
---

We create the object `mx` in the following chunk:

```{r}
x <- 1:100
mx <- mean(x)
saveRDS(mx, 'mean.rds')
```

The first time you compile this document, you will see the phrase "The value of mx is not available yet" in the abstract. Later, when you compile it again, you will see the actual value of mx.

The function knitr::load_cache() is an alternative solution, which allows you to load the value of an object from a specific code chunk after the chunk has been cached. The idea is similar to the above example, but it will save you the effort of manually saving and loading an object, because the object
```

is automatically saved to the cache database, and you only need to load it via
`load_cache()`. Below is the simplified example:

```
---
title: An important report
abstract: >
  In this analysis, the average value of
  `x` is `r knitr::load_cache('mean-x', 'mx')`.
---

We create the object `mx` in the following chunk:

```{r mean-x, cache=TRUE}
x <- 1:100
mx <- mean(x)
```
```

In this example, we added a chunk label `mean-x` to the R code chunk (which
is passed to the `load_cache()` function), and cached it using the chunk option `cache = TRUE`. All objects in this code chunk will be saved to the cache
database. Again, you will have to compile this document at least twice, so
the object `mx` can be correctly loaded from the cache database. If the value of
`mx` is not going to be changed in the future, you do not need to compile the
document one more time.

If you do not specify the object name in the second argument to
`load_cache()`, the whole cache database will be loaded into the current environment. You can then use any objects that were in the cache
database before these objects are created later in the document, e.g.,

```
knitr::load_cache("mean-x")
x   # the object `x`
mx  # the object `mx`
```

14.3 Exit knitting early

Sometimes we may want to exit knitting early and not at the end of the document. For example, we may be working on some analysis and only wish to

share the first half of the results, or we may still be working on code at the bottom that is not yet complete. In these situations, we could consider using the `knit_exit()` function in a code chunk, which will end the knitting process after that chunk.

Below is a simple example, where we have a very simple chunk followed by a more time-consuming one:

````
```{r}
1 + 1
knitr::knit_exit()
```
````

```
You will only see the above content in the output.
```

````
```{r}
Sys.sleep(100)
```
````

Normally you have to wait for 100 seconds, but since we have called `knit_exit()`, the rest of the document will be ignored.

14.4 Generate a plot and display it elsewhere

Normally plots generated in a code chunk are displayed beneath the code chunk, but you can choose to show them elsewhere and (optionally) hide them in the code chunk. Below is an example:

```
We generate a plot in this code chunk but do not show it:
```

````
```{r cars-plot, dev='png', fig.show='hide'}
plot(cars)
```
````

```
After another paragraph, we introduce the plot:
```

```
![A nice plot.](`r knitr::fig_chunk('cars-plot', 'png')`)
```

In the code chunk, we used the chunk option `fig.show='hide'` to hide the plot temporarily. Then in another paragraph, we called the function `knitr::fig_chunk()` to retrieve the path of the plot file, which is usually like `test_files/figure-html/cars-plot-1.png`. You need to pass the chunk label and the graphical device name to `fig_chunk()` for it to calculate the plot file path.

You may see `https://stackoverflow.com/a/46305297/559676` for an application of `fig_chunk()` to **blogdown** websites. This function works for any R Markdown output formats. It can be particularly helpful for presenting plots on slides, because the screen space is often limited on slide pages. You may present code on a slide, and reveal the plot on a different slide.

14.5 Modify a plot in a previous code chunk

By default, **knitr** opens a new graphical device to record plots for each new code chunk. This brings a problem: you cannot easily modify a plot from a previous code chunk, because the previous graphical device has been closed. This is usually problematic for base R graphics (not so for grid graphics such as those created from **ggplot2** (Wickham et al., 2020a) because plots can be saved to R objects). For example, if we draw a plot in one code chunk, and add a line to the plot in a later chunk, R will signal an error saying that a high-level plot has not been created, so it could not add the line.

If you want the graphical device to remain open for all code chunks, you may set a **knitr** package option in the beginning of your document device:

```
knitr::opts_knit$set(global.device = TRUE)
```

Please note that it is `opts_knit` instead of the more frequently used `opts_chunk`. You may see the Stack Overflow post `https://stackoverflow.com/q/17502050` for an example.

When you no longer need this global graphical device, you can set the option to `FALSE`. Here is a full example:

```
---
title: "Using a global graphical device to record plots"
---
```

First, turn on a global graphical device:

```{r, include=FALSE}
knitr::opts_knit$set(global.device = TRUE)
```

Draw a plot:

```{r}
par(mar = c(4, 4, 0.1, 0.1))
plot(cars)
```

Add a line to the plot in the previous code chunk:

```{r}
fit <- lm(dist ~ speed, data = cars)
abline(fit)
```

No longer use the global device:

```{r, include=FALSE}
knitr::opts_knit$set(global.device = FALSE)
```

Draw another plot:

```{r}
plot(pressure, type = 'b')
```

14.6   Save a group of chunk options and reuse them (*)

If you frequently use some chunk options, you may save them as a group and reuse them later only using the group name. This can be done with `knitr::opts_template$set(name = list(options))`. Then you can use the chunk option `opts.label` to refer to the group name. For example:

```{r, setup, include=FALSE}
knitr::opts_template$set(fullwidth = list(
  fig.width = 10, fig.height = 6,
  fig.retina = 2, out.width = '100%'
))
```

```{r, opts.label='fullwidth'}
plot(cars)
```

With `opts.label = 'fullwidth'`, **knitr** will read chunk options from `knitr::opts_template`, and apply them to the current chunk. This can save you some typing effort. If a chunk option is to be used globally in a document, you should consider setting it globally (see Chapter 11).

You can override options read from `opts.label`, e.g., if you set `fig.height = 7` in the chunk below, the actual `fig.height` will be 7 instead of 6.

```{r, opts.label='fullwidth', fig.height=7}
plot(cars)
```

You can save an arbitrary number of grouped options, e.g., `knitr::opts_template$set(group1 = list(...), group2 = list(...))`.

14.7 Use `knitr::knit_expand()` to generate Rmd source

The function `knitr::knit_expand()` "expands" an expression in `{{ }}` (by default) to its value, e.g.,

```
knitr::knit_expand(text = "The value of `pi` is {{pi}}.")
## [1] "The value of `pi` is 3.14159265358979."
knitr::knit_expand(
  text = "The value of `a` is {{a}}, so `a + 1` is {{a+1}}.",
  a = round(rnorm(1), 4)
)
## [1] "The value of `a` is -0.1636, so `a + 1` is 0.8364."
```

This means that if you have an Rmd document that contains some dynamic parts in `{{ }}`, you may apply `knit_expand()` on the document, and then call `knit()` to compile it. For example, here is a template document named `template.Rmd`:

```
# Regression on {{i}}

```{r lm-{{i}}}
lm(mpg ~ {{i}}, data = mtcars)
```
```

We can build linear regression models using `mpg` against all other variables one by one in the `mtcars` dataset:

```
```{r, echo=FALSE, results='asis'}
src = lapply(setdiff(names(mtcars), 'mpg'), function(i) {
  knitr::knit_expand('template.Rmd')
})
res = knitr::knit_child(text = unlist(src), quiet = TRUE)
cat(res, sep = '\n')
```
```

If you find it difficult to understand this example, please see Section 11.11 for the meaning of the chunk option `results = 'asis'`, and Section 16.4 for the usage of `knitr::knit_child()`.

14.8   Allow duplicate labels in code chunks (*)

By default, **knitr** does not allow duplicate code chunk labels in the document. Duplicate labels will result in an error when the document is knitted. This occurs most frequently when a code chunk is copied and pasted within a document. You may have seen an error message like this:

```
processing file: myfile.Rmd
Error in parse_block(g[-1], g[1], params.src, markdown_mode) :
  Duplicate chunk label 'cars'
Calls: <Anonymous> ... process_file -> split_file -> lapply ->
  FUN -> parse_block
Execution halted
```

However, there are scenarios where we may wish to allow duplicate labels. For example, if we have one parent document parent.Rmd in which we knit the child document multiple times, it will fail:

```
# settings
settings <- list(...)

# run once
knit_child("useful_analysis.Rmd")

# new settings
settings <- list(...)

# run again
knit_child("useful_analysis.Rmd")
```

In this scenario, we can allow duplicate labels by setting this global option in R *before* the child document is knitted:

```
options(knitr.duplicate.label = "allow")
```

If you want to allow duplicate labels in the main document instead of the child document, you have to set this option *before* knitr::knit() is called. One possible way to achieve that is to set the option in your ~/.Rprofile file (see the help page ?Rprofile for more information).

You should set this option with caution. As with most error messages, they are there for a reason. Allowing duplicate chunks can create silent problems with figures and cross references. For example, in theory, if two code chunks have the same label and both chunks generate plots, their plot files will overwrite each other (without error or warning messages), because the filenames of plots are determined by the chunk labels. With the option `knitr.duplicate.label = "allow"`, **knitr** will silently change the duplicate labels by adding numeric suffixes. For example, for the two code chunks:

```
```{r, test}
plot(1:10)
```
```

```
```{r, test}
plot(10:1)
```
```

The second label will be silently changed to `test-1`. This may avoid overwriting the plot from the chunk with the label `test`, but it also makes the chunk label unpredictable, so you may have difficulties in cross-referencing figures (see Section 4.7), because the cross references are also based on chunk labels.

14.9 A more transparent caching mechanism

If you feel the caching mechanism of **knitr** introduced in Section 11.4 is too complicated (it is!), you may consider a simpler caching mechanism based on the function `xfun::cache_rds()`, e.g.,

```
xfun::cache_rds({
  # write your time-consuming code in this expression
})
```

The tricky thing about **knitr**'s caching is how it decides when to invalidate the cache. For `xfun::cache_rds()`, it is much clearer: the first time you pass an R expression to this function, it evaluates the expression and saves the result to a `.rds` file; the next time you run `cache_rds()` again, it reads the `.rds` file and returns the result immediately without evaluating the expression again. The most obvious way to invalidate the cache is to delete the .rds file. If you do not want to manually delete it, you may call xfun::cache_rds() with the argument rerun = TRUE.

When xfun::cache_rds() is called inside a code chunk in a **knitr** source document, the path of the .rds file is determined by the chunk option cache.path and the chunk label. For example, for a code chunk with the chunk label foo in the Rmd document input.Rmd:

````
```{r, foo}
res <- xfun::cache_rds({
  Sys.sleep(3)
  1:10
})
```
````

The path of the .rds file will be of the form input_cache/FORMAT/foo_HASH.rds, where FORMAT is the Pandoc output format name (e.g., html or latex), and HASH is an MD5 hash that contains 32 hexadecimal digits (consisting a-z and 0-9), e.g., input_cache/html/foo_7a3f22c4309d400eff95de0e8bddac71.rds.

As documented on the help page ?xfun::cache_rds, there are two common cases in which you may want to invalidate the cache: 1) the code in the expression to be evaluated has changed; 2) the code uses an external variable, and the value of that variable has changed. Next we will explain how these two ways of cache invalidation work, as well as how to keep multiple copies of the cache corresponding to different versions of the code.

14.9.1 Invalidate the cache by changing code in the expression

When you change the code in cache_rds() (e.g., from cache_rds({x + 1}) to cache_rds({x + 2})), the cache will be automatically invalidated and the expression will be re-evaluated. However, please note that changes in white spaces or comments do not matter. Or generally speaking, as long as the change does not affect the parsed expression, the cache will not be invalidated. For example, the two expressions passed to cache_rds() below are essentially identical:

```
res <- xfun::cache_rds({
  Sys.sleep(3  );
```

```
  x<-1:10;   # semi-colons won't matter
  x+1;
})
```

```
res <- xfun::cache_rds({
  Sys.sleep(3)
  x <- 1:10   # a comment
  x +
    1   # feel free to make any changes in white spaces
})
```

Hence if you have executed cache_rds() on the first expression, the second expression will be able to take advantage of the cache. This feature is helpful because it allows you make cosmetic changes in your code without invalidating the cache.

If you are not sure if two versions of code are equivalent, you may try the parse_code() below:

```
parse_code <- function(expr) {
  deparse(substitute(expr))
}
# white spaces and semi-colons do not matter
parse_code({x+1})
```

```
## [1] "{"          "    x + 1" "}"
```

```
parse_code({ x   +    1; })
```

```
## [1] "{"          "    x + 1" "}"
```

```
# left arrow and right arrow are equivalent
identical(parse_code({x <- 1}), parse_code({1 -> x}))
```

```
## [1] TRUE
```

14.9.2   Invalidate the cache by changes in global variables

There are two types of variables in an expression: global variables and local variables. Global variables are those created outside the expression, and local variables are those created inside the expression. If the value of a global variable in the expression has changed, your cached result will no longer reflect the result that you would obtain by running the expression again. For example, in the expression below, if y has changed, you are most likely to want to invalidate the cache and rerun the expression, otherwise you still get the result from the old value of y:

```
y <- 2

res <- xfun::cache_rds({
  x <- 1:10
  x + y
})
```

To invalidate the cache when y has changed, you may let cache_rds() know through the hash argument that y needs to be considered when deciding if the cache should be invalidated:

```
res <- xfun::cache_rds({
  x <- 1:10
  x + y
}, hash = list(y))
```

When the value of the hash argument is changed, the 32-digit hash in the cache filename (as mentioned earlier) will change accordingly, therefore the cache will be invalidated. This provides a way to specify the cache's dependency on other R objects. For example, if you want the cache to be dependent on the version of R, you may specify the dependency like this:

```
res <- xfun::cache_rds({
  x <- 1:10
  x + y
}, hash = list(y, getRversion()))
```

Or if you want the cache to depend on when a data file was last modified:

```
res <- xfun::cache_rds({
  x <- read.csv("data.csv")
```

```
    x[[1]] + y
}, hash = list(y, file.mtime("data.csv")))
```

If you do not want to provide this list of global variables to the `hash` argument, you may try `hash = "auto"` instead, which tells `cache_rds()` to try to figure out all global variables automatically and use a list of their values as the value for the `hash` argument, e.g.,

```
res <- xfun::cache_rds({
    x <- 1:10
    x + y + z  # y and z are global variables
}, hash = "auto")
```

This is equivalent to:

```
res <- xfun::cache_rds({
    x <- 1:10
    x + y + z  # y and z are global variables
}, hash = list(y = y, z = z))
```

The global variables are identified by `codetools::findGlobals()` when `hash = "auto"`, which may not be completely reliable. You know your own code the best, so we recommend that you specify the list of values explicitly in the `hash` argument if you want to be completely sure which variables can invalidate the cache.

14.9.3 Keep multiple copies of the cache

Since the cache is typically used for time-consuming code, perhaps you should invalidate it conservatively. You might regret invalidating the cache too soon or aggressively, because if you should need an older version of the cache again, you would have to wait for a long time for the computing to be redone.

The `clean` argument of `cache_rds()` allows you to keep older copies of the cache if you set it to `FALSE`. You can also set the global R option `options(xfun.cache_rds.clean = FALSE)` if you want this to be the default behavior throughout the entire R session. By default, `clean = TRUE` and `cache_rds()` will try to delete the older cache every time. Setting `clean =`

FALSE can be useful if you are still experimenting with the code. For example, you can cache two versions of a linear model:

```
model <- xfun::cache_rds({
  lm(dist ~ speed, data = cars)
}, clean = FALSE)

model <- xfun::cache_rds({
  lm(dist ~ speed + I(speed^2), data = cars)
}, clean = FALSE)
```

After you decide which model to use, you can set clean = TRUE again, or delete this argument (so the default TRUE is used).

14.9.4 Comparison with knitr's caching

You may wonder when to use **knitr**'s caching (i.e., set the chunk option cache = TRUE), and when to use xfun::cache_rds() in a **knitr** source document. The biggest disadvantage of xfun::cache_rds() is that it does not cache side effects (but only the value of the expression), whereas **knitr** does. Some side effects may be useful, such as printed output or plots. For example, in the code below, the text output and the plot will be lost when cache_rds() loads the cache the next time, and only the value 1:10 will be returned:

```
xfun::cache_rds({
  print("Hello world!")
  plot(cars)
  1:10
})
```

By comparison, for a code chunk with the option cache = TRUE, everything will be cached:

````
```{r, cache=TRUE}
print("Hello world!")
plot(cars)
1:10
```
````

The biggest disadvantage of **knitr**'s caching (and also what users complain most frequently about) is that your cache might be inadvertently invalidated, because the cache is determined by too many factors. For example, any changes in chunk options can invalidate the cache,[2] but some chunk options may not be relevant to the computing. In the code chunk below, changing the chunk option `fig.width = 6` to `fig.width = 10` should not invalidate the cache, but it will:

```
```{r, cache=TRUE, fig.width=6}
# there are no plots in this chunk
x <- rnorm(1000)
mean(x)
```
```

Actually, **knitr** caching is quite powerful and flexible, and its behavior can be tweaked in many ways. As its author, I often doubt if it is worth introducing these lesser-known features, because you may end up spending much more time on learning and understanding how the cache works than the time the actual computing takes.

In case it is not clear, `xfun::cache_rds()` is a general way for caching the computing, and it works anywhere, whereas **knitr**'s caching only works in **knitr** documents.

---

[2]This is the default behavior, and you can change it. See `https://yihui.org/knitr/demo/cache/` for how you can make the cache more granular, so not all chunk options affect the cache.

15

Other Languages

Besides the R language, many other languages are supported in R Markdown through the **knitr** package. The language name is indicated by the first word in the curly braces after the three opening backticks. For example, the little r in ```` ```{r} ```` indicates that the code chunk contains R code, and ```` ```{python} ```` is a Python code chunk. In this chapter, we show a few languages that you may not be familiar with.

In **knitr**, each language is supported through a language engine. Language engines are essentially functions that take the source code and options of a chunk as the input, and return a character string as the output. They are managed through the object `knitr::knit_engines`. You may check the existing engines via:

```
names(knitr::knit_engines$get())
```

```
##  [1] "awk"       "bash"      "coffee"    "gawk"
##  [5] "groovy"    "haskell"   "lein"      "mysql"
##  [9] "node"      "octave"    "perl"      "psql"
## [13] "Rscript"   "ruby"      "sas"       "scala"
## [17] "sed"       "sh"        "stata"     "zsh"
## [21] "highlight" "Rcpp"      "tikz"      "dot"
## [25] "c"         "cc"        "fortran"   "fortran95"
## [29] "asy"       "cat"       "asis"      "stan"
## [33] "block"     "block2"    "js"        "css"
## [37] "sql"       "go"        "python"    "julia"
## [41] "sass"      "scss"
```

At the moment, most code chunks of non-R languages are executed independently. For example, all bash code chunks in the same document are executed separately in their own sessions, so a later bash code chunk cannot use variables created in a previous bash chunk, and the changed working directory (via cd) will not be persistent across different bash chunks. Only R,

Python, and Julia code chunks are executed in the same session. Please note that all R code chunks are executed in the same R session, and all Python code chunks are executed in the same Python session, etc. The R session and the Python session are two different sessions, but it is possible to access or manipulate objects of one session from another session (see Section 15.2).

Section 2.7[1] of the *R Markdown Definitive Guide* (Xie et al., 2018) shows examples of using Python, Shell, SQL, Rcpp, Stan, JavaScript, CSS, Julia, C, and Fortran code in R Markdown. In this chapter, we will show more language engines, and you may find more examples in the repository at `https://github.com/yihui/knitr-examples` (look for filenames that contain the word "engine").

First, let's reveal how a language engine works by registering a custom language engine.

15.1   Register a custom language engine (*)

You can register a custom language engine via the method `knitr::knit_engines$set()`. It accepts a function as its input, e.g.,

```r
knitr::knit_engines$set(foo = function(options) {
  # the source code is in options$code; just do whatever
  # you want with it
})
```

This registers the `foo` engine, and you will be able to use a code chunk that starts with ```` ```{foo} ````.

The engine function has one argument, `options`, which is a list of chunk options of the code chunk. You can access the source code of the chunk as a character vector in `options$code`. For example, for the code chunk:

```r
```{foo}
1 + 1
2 + 2
```
```

---

[1]`https://bookdown.org/yihui/rmarkdown/language-engines.html`

The code element of options would be a character vector c('1 + 1', '2 + 2').

Language engines do not really have to deal with computer languages, but can process any text in a code chunk. First, we show a simple example of an engine that converts the content of a code chunk to uppercase:

```r
knitr::knit_engines$set(upper = function(options) {
  code <- paste(options$code, collapse = "\n")
  if (options$eval)
    toupper(code) else code
})
```

The key is that we apply the function toupper to the "code," and return the result as a single character string (by concatenating all lines of code by \n). Note that toupper() is applied only when the chunk option eval = TRUE, otherwise the original string is returned. This shows you how to make use of chunk options like eval inside the engine function. Similarly, you may consider adding if (options$results == 'hide') return() to the function body to hide the output when the chunk option results = 'hide'. Below is an example chunk that uses the upper engine, with its output:

```
```{upper}
Hello, **knitr** engines!
```
```

HELLO, **KNITR** ENGINES!

Next we show an example of an alternative Python engine[2] named py. This engine is implemented by simply calling the python command via the R function system2():

---

[2] In practice, you should use the built-in python engine instead, which is based on the **reticulate** package and supports Python code chunks much better (see Section 15.2).

```
knitr::knit_engines$set(py = function(options) {
  code <- paste(options$code, collapse = '\n')
  out  <- system2(
    'python', c('-c', shQuote(code)), stdout = TRUE
  )
  knitr::engine_output(options, code, out)
})
```

To fully understand the above engine function, you need to know the following:

1. Given Python code as a character string (code in the above function), we can execute the code via a command-line call `python -c 'code'`. That is what `system2()` does. We collect the (text) output by specifying `stdout = TRUE` in `system2()`.

2. You can pass the chunk options, source code, and text output to the function `knitr::engine_output()` to generate the final output. This function deals with common chunk options like `echo = FALSE` and `results = 'hide'`, so you do not need to take care of these cases.

A lot of language engines in **knitr** are defined in this way (i.e., using `system2()` to execute commands corresponding to languages). If you are curious about the technical details, you may check out the source code of most language engines in the R source code here: `https://github.com/yihui/knitr/blob/master/R/engine.R`.

Now we can use the new engine py, e.g.,

````
```{py}
print(1 + 1)
```
````

```
## 2
```

You can even override existing language engines in **knitr** via `knitr::knit_engines$set()`, if you are sure that your versions are necessary or better than the existing ones. Usually we do not recommend that you do this because it may surprise users who are familiar with existing engines, but we want to make you aware of this possibility anyway.

15.2 Run Python code and interact with Python

We know you love Python, so let's make it super clear: R Markdown and **knitr** do support Python.

To add a Python code chunk to an R Markdown document, you can use the chunk header ```` ```{python} ````, e.g.,

````
```{python}
print("Hello Python!")
```
````

You can add chunk options to the chunk header as usual, such as `echo = FALSE` or `eval = FALSE`. Plots drawn with the **matplotlib** package in Python are also supported.

The Python support in R Markdown and **knitr** is based on the **reticulate** package (Ushey et al., 2020), and one important feature of this package is that it allows two-way communication between Python and R. For example, you may access or create Python variables from the R session via the object `py` in **reticulate**:

````
```{r, setup}
library(reticulate)
```
````

Create a variable `x` in the Python session:

````
```{python}
x = [1, 2, 3]
```
````

Access the Python variable `x` in an R code chunk:

````
```{r}
py$x
```
````

Create a new variable `y` in the Python session using R,
and pass a data frame to `y`:

````
```{r}
py$y <- head(cars)
```
````

Print the variable `y` in Python:

````
```{python}
print(y)
```
````

For more information about the **reticulate** package, you may see its documentation at https://rstudio.github.io/reticulate/.

15.3   Execute content conditionally via the asis engine

As its name indicates, the asis engine writes out the chunk content as is. The advantage of using this engine is that you can include some content conditionally—the display of the chunk content is decided by the chunk option echo. When echo = FALSE, the chunk will be hidden. Below is a simple example:

````
```{r}
getRandomNumber <- function() {
  sample(1:6, 1)
}
```
````

```
```{asis, echo = getRandomNumber() == 4}
According to https://xkcd.com/221/, we just generated
a **true** random number!
```
```

The text in the `asis` chunk will be displayed only if the condition `getRandom-Number() == 4` is (randomly) true.

15.4 Execute Shell scripts

You can run Shell scripts via the `bash` or `sh` or `zsh` engine, depending on which shell you prefer. Below is a `bash` example, with the chunk header ```` ```{bash} ````:

```
ls *.Rmd | head -n 5
```

```
## 00-authors.Rmd
## 01-installation.Rmd
## 02-overview.Rmd
## 03-basics.Rmd
## 04-content.Rmd
```

Please note that `bash` is invoked with the R function `system2()`. It will ignore profile files like `~/.bash_profile` and `~/.bash_login`, in which you may have defined command aliases or modified environment variables like the `PATH` variable. If you want these profile files to be executed just like when you use the terminal, you may pass the argument `-l` to `bash` via `engine.opts`, e.g.,

```
```{bash, engine.opts='-l'}
echo $PATH
```
```

If you want to enable the `-l` argument globally for all `bash` chunks, you may set it in the global chunk option in the beginning of your document:

```
knitr::opts_chunk$set(engine.opts = list(bash = "-l"))
```

You can also pass other arguments to bash by providing them as a character vector to the chunk option engine.opts.

15.5   Visualization with D3

The R package **r2d3** (Luraschi and Allaire, 2018) is an interface to D3 visualizations. This package can be used in R Markdown documents as well as other applications (e.g., Shiny). To use it in R Markdown, you can either call its function r2d3() in a code chunk, or use its d3 engine. The latter requires you to understand the D3 library and JavaScript, which are beyond the scope of this book, and we will leave it to readers to learn them. Below is an example of using the d3 engine to draw a bar chart:

```
---
title: Generate a chart with D3
output: html_document
---


First, load the package **r2d3** to set up the `d3` engine
for **knitr** automatically:

```{r setup}
library(r2d3)
```


Now we can generate data in R, pass it to D3, and draw
the chart:

```{d3, data=runif(30), options=list(color='steelblue')}
svg.selectAll('rect')
  .data(data)
  .enter()
    .append('rect')
      .attr('width', function(d) { return d * 672; })
```
```

```
    .attr('height', '10px')
    .attr('y', function(d, i) { return i * 16; })
    .attr('fill', options.color);
```
```

## 15.6 Write the chunk content to a file via the cat engine

Sometimes it could be useful to write the content of a code chunk to an external file, and use this file later in other code chunks. Of course, you may do this via the R functions like writeLines(), but the problem is that when the content is relatively long, or contains special characters, the character string that you would pass to writeLines() may look awkward. Below is an example of writing a long character string to a file my-file.txt:

```
writeLines("This is a long character string.
It has multiple lines. Remember to escape
double quotes \"\", but 'single quotes' are OK.
I hope you not to lose your sanity when thinking
about how many backslashes you need, e.g., is it
'\t' or '\\t' or '\\\\t'?",
  con = "my-file.txt")
```

This problem has been greatly alleviated since R 4.0.0, because R started to support raw strings in r"( )" (see the help page ?Quotes), and you do not need to remember all the rules about special characters. Even with raw strings, it can still be a little distracting for readers to see a long string written to a file explicitly in a code chunk.

The cat engine in **knitr** has provided a way for you to present text content in a code chunk and/or write it to an external file, without thinking about all the rules about R's character strings (e.g., you need double backslashes when you need a literal backslash).

To write the chunk content to a file, specify the file path in the chunk option engine.opts, e.g., engine.opts = list(file = 'path/to/file'). Under the hood, the list of values specified in engine.opts will be passed to the function base::cat(), and file is one of the arguments of base::cat().
```

Next we will present three examples to illustrate the use of the cat engine.

15.6.1 Write to a CSS file

As shown in Section 7.3, you can embed a css code chunk in an Rmd document to style elements with CSS. An alternative way is to provide a custom CSS file to Pandoc via the css option of some R Markdown output formats such as html_document. The cat engine can be used to write this CSS file from Rmd.

This example below shows how to generate a file custom.css from a chunk in the document, and pass the file path to the css option of the html_document format:

```
---
title: "Create a CSS file from a code chunk"
output:
  html_document:
    css: custom.css
---

The chunk below will be written to `custom.css`, which
will be used during the Pandoc conversion.

```{cat, engine.opts = list(file = "my_custom.css")}
h2 {
  color: blue;
}
```

And this title will blue
```

The only difference between the css code chunk approach and this approach is that the former approach writes the CSS code in place (i.e., in the place of the code chunk), which is inside the <body> tag of the output document, and the latter approach writes CSS to the <head> area of the output document. There will not be any practical visual differences in the output document.

15.6.2   Include LaTeX code in the preamble

In Section 6.1, we introduced how to add LaTeX code to the preamble, which requires an external .tex file. This file can also be generated from Rmd, and here is an example:

```
---
title: "Create a .tex file from a chunk"
author: "Jane Doe"
classoption: twoside
output:
  pdf_document:
    includes:
      in_header: preamble.tex
---


# How it works

Write a code chunk to a file `preamble.tex` to define
the header and footer of the PDF output document:

```{cat, engine.opts=list(file = 'preamble.tex')}
\usepackage{fancyhdr}
\usepackage{lipsum}
\pagestyle{fancy}
\fancyhead[CO,CE]{This is fancy header}
\fancyfoot[CO,CE]{And this is a fancy footer}
\fancyfoot[LE,RO]{\thepage}
\fancypagestyle{plain}{\pagestyle{fancy}}
```


\lipsum[1-15]

More random content

\lipsum[16-30]
```

In the LaTeX code in the cat code chunk above, we have defined the header and footer of the PDF document. If we also want to show the author name in the footer, we can append the author information to preamble.tex in another `cat` code chunk with options `engine.opts` `=` `list(file` `=` `'preamble.tex',` `append` `=` `TRUE)` and `code` `=` `sprintf('\\fancyfoot[LO,RE]{%s}',` `rmarkdown::metadata$author)`. To understand how this works, recall that we mentioned earlier in this section that `engine.opts` is passed to `base::cat()` (so `append` `=` `TRUE` is passed to `cat()`), and you may understand the chunk option `code` by reading Section 16.2.

15.6.3   Write YAML data to a file and also display it

By default, the content of the `cat` code chunk will not be displayed in the output document. If you also want to display it after writing it out, set the chunk option `class.source` to a language name. The language name is used for syntax highlighting. In the example below, we specify the language to be `yaml`:

```
```{cat, engine.opts=list(file='demo.yml'), class.source='yaml'}
a:
  aa: "something"
  bb: 1
b:
  aa: "something else"
  bb: 2
```
```

Its output is displayed below, and it also generated a file `demo.yml`.

```
a:
  aa: "something"
  bb: 1
b:
  aa: "something else"
  bb: 2
```

To show the file `demo.yml` is really generated, we can try to read it into R with the **yaml** package (Stephens et al., 2020):

```
xfun::tree(yaml::read_yaml("demo.yml"))
```

```
## List of 2
```

```
##   |-a:List of 2
##   |   |-aa: chr "something"
##   |   |-bb: int 1
##   |-b:List of 2
##       |-aa: chr "something else"
##       |-bb: int 2
```

15.7 Run SAS code

You may run SAS (https://www.sas.com) code using the sas engine. You
need to either make sure the SAS executable is in your environment variable PATH, or (if you do not know what PATH means) provide the full path
to the SAS executable via the chunk option engine.path, e.g., engine.path
= "C:\\Program Files\\SASHome\\x86\\SASFoundation\\9.3\\sas.exe".
Below is an example to print out "Hello World":

````
```{sas}
data _null_;
put 'Hello, world!';
run;
```
````

15.8 Run Stata code

You can run Stata (https://www.stata.com) code with the stata engine if
you have installed Stata. Unless the stata executable can be found via the
environment variable PATH, you need to specify the full path to the executable
via the chunk option engine.path, e.g., engine.path = "C:/Program Files
(x86)/Stata15/StataSE-64.exe". The following is a quick example:

````
```{stata}
sysuse auto
summarize
```
````

The stata engine in **knitr** is quite limited. Doug Hemken has substantially extended it in the **Statamarkdown** package, which is available on GitHub at `https://github.com/Hemken/Statamarkdown`. You may find tutorials about this package by searching online for "Stata R Markdown."

15.9 Create graphics with Asymptote

Asymptote (`https://asymptote.sourceforge.io`) is a powerful language for vector graphics. You may write and run Asymptote code in R Markdown with the asy engine if you have installed Asymptote (see its website for instructions on the installation). Below is an example copied from the repository `https://github.com/vectorgraphics/asymptote`, and its output is shown in Figure 15.1:

```
import graph3;
import grid3;
import palette;
settings.prc = false;

currentprojection=orthographic(0.8,1,2);
size(500,400,IgnoreAspect);

real f(pair z) {return cos(2*pi*z.x)*sin(2*pi*z.y);}

surface s=surface(f,(-1/2,-1/2),(1/2,1/2),50,Spline);

surface S=planeproject(unitsquare3)*s;
S.colors(palette(s.map(zpart),Rainbow()));
draw(S,nolight);
draw(s,lightgray+opacity(0.7));

grid3(XYZgrid);
```

Note that for PDF output, you may need some additional LaTeX packages, otherwise you may get an error that looks like this:

```
! LaTeX Error: File `ocgbase.sty' not found.
```

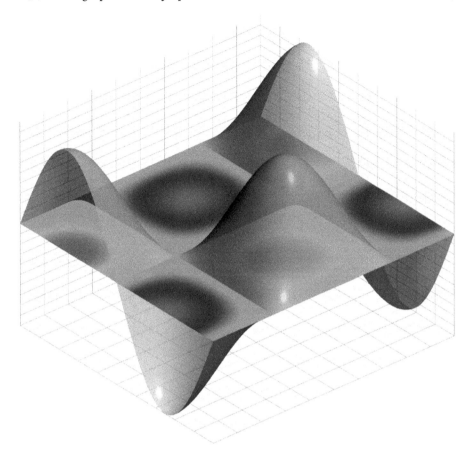

FIGURE 15.1: A 3D graph made with Asymptote.

If such an error occurs, please see Section 1.3 for how to install the missing LaTeX packages.

In the asy chunk above, we used the setting `settings.prc = false`. Without this setting, Asymptote generates an interactive 3D graph when the output format is PDF. However, the interactive graph can only be viewed in Acrobat Reader. If you use Acrobat Reader, you can interact with the graph. For example, you can rotate the 3D surface in Figure 15.1 with your mouse.

15.9.1 Generate data in R and read it in Asymptote

Now we show an example in which we first save data generated in R to a CSV file (below is an R code chunk):

```
x <- seq(0, 5, l = 100)
y <- sin(x)
writeLines(paste(x, y, sep = ","), "sine.csv")
```

Then read it in Asymptote, and draw a graph based on the data as shown in Figure 15.2 (below is an asy code chunk):

```
import graph;
size(400,300,IgnoreAspect);
settings.prc = false;

// import data from csv file
file in=input("sine.csv").line().csv();
real[][] a=in.dimension(0,0);
a=transpose(a);

// generate a path
path rpath = graph(a[0],a[1]);
path lpath = (1,0)--(5,1);

// find intersection
pair pA=intersectionpoint(rpath,lpath);

// draw all
draw(rpath,red);
draw(lpath,dashed + blue);
dot("$\delta$",pA,NE);
xaxis("$x$",BottomTop,LeftTicks);
yaxis("$y$",LeftRight,RightTicks);
```

15.10   Style HTML pages with Sass/SCSS

Sass (https://sass-lang.com) is a CSS extension language that allows you to create CSS rules in much more flexible ways than you'd do with plain CSS. Please see its official documentation if you are interested in learning it.

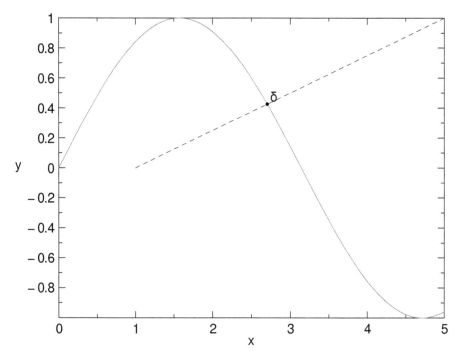

FIGURE 15.2: Pass data from R to Asymptote to draw a graph.

The R package **sass** (Cheng et al., 2020) can be used to compile Sass to CSS. Based on the **sass** package, **knitr** includes two language engines: sass and scss (corresponding to the Sass and SCSS syntax, respectively) to compile code chunks to CSS. Below is a scss code chunk, with the chunk header ```` ```{scss} ````:

```scss
$font-stack: "Comic Sans MS", cursive, sans-serif;
$primary-color: #00FF00;

.book.font-family-1 {
  font: 100% $font-stack;
  color: $primary-color;
}
```

You can also use the sass engine, and the Sass syntax is slightly different with the SCSS syntax, e.g.,

```{sass}
$font-stack: "Comic Sans MS", cursive, sans-serif
$primary-color: #00FF00

.book.font-family-1
  font: 100% $font-stack
  color: $primary-color
```

If you are reading the HTML version of this section,[3] you will notice that the font for this page has been changed to Comic Sans, which might be surprising, but please do not panic—you are not having a stroke.[4]

The sass/scss code chunks are compiled through the `sass::sass()` function. Currently you can customize the output style for the CSS code via the chunk option `engine.opts`, e.g., `engine.opts = list(style = "expanded")`. The default style is "compressed." If you are not sure what this means, please refer to the help page `?sass::sass_options` and look for the `output_style` argument.

---

[3]`https://bookdown.org/yihui/rmarkdown-cookbook/eng-sass.html`
[4]`https://twitter.com/andrewheiss/status/1250438044542361600`

16

Managing Projects

When you work on larger projects or reports, you may not want to put all text and code in a single R Markdown document, but organize them in smaller units instead. In this chapter, we introduce tips on how to organize multiple files related to R Markdown.

16.1 Source external R scripts

If your R Markdown document has a large amount of code, you may consider putting some code in external R scripts, and run these scripts via `source()` or `sys.source()`, e.g.,

````
```{r, include=FALSE}
source("your-script.R", local = knitr::knit_global())
# or sys.source("your-script.R", envir = knitr::knit_global())
```
````

We recommend that you use the argument `local` in `source()` or `envir` in `sys.source()` explicitly to make sure the code is evaluated in the correct environment, i.e., `knitr::knit_global()`. The default values for them may not be the appropriate environment: you may end up creating variables in the wrong environment, and being surprised that certain objects are not found in later code chunks.

Next in the R Markdown document, you can use objects created in these scripts (e.g., data objects or functions). This way will not only make your R Markdown document cleaner, but also make it more convenient for you to develop R code (e.g., debugging R code is often easier with pure R scripts than R Markdown).

Note that we used `include` = `FALSE` in the above example because we only want to execute the script without showing any output. If you do want output, you may remove this chunk option, or use the options in Section 11.7 to selectively hide or show different types of output.

16.2   Read external scripts into a chunk

There is a disadvantage of the `source()` method in Section 16.1. That is, you will not be able to see the source code by default. You can use `source(...,  echo = TRUE)`, but the source code will not be properly syntax highlighted. Besides, you need to be careful about the `local` argument of `source()`, as mentioned in Section 16.1. In this section, we introduce an alternative method that does not have these problems.

Basically, when you have one or more external scripts, you may read them and pass the content to the `code` option of a chunk. The `code` option can take a character vector and treat it as the content of the code chunk. Below we show a few examples.

- The `code` option can take a character vector of source code. For example:

  ````
  ```{r, code=c('1 + 1', 'if (TRUE) plot(cars)')}
  ```
  ````

- You can also read an external file:

  ````
  ```{r, code=xfun::read_utf8('your-script.R')}
  ```
  ````

- You can read as many scripts as you want:

  ````
  ```{r, include=FALSE}
  read_files <- function(files) {
    unlist(lapply(files, xfun::read_utf8))
  }
  ```
  ````

  ````
  ```{r, code=read_files(c('one.R', 'two.R'))}
  ```
  ````

You can read scripts of other languages, too. See Chapter 15 for how to use other languages in R Markdown. Here are a few more examples on non-R code.

- Read a Python script:

  ````
  ```{python, code=xfun::read_utf8('script.py')}
  ```
  ````

- Read a C++ file:

  ````
  ```{Rcpp, code=xfun::read_utf8('file.cpp')}
  ```
  ````

With the `code` option, you can develop complicated code in your favorite editor, and read it into a code chunk of an R Markdown document.

16.3   Read multiple code chunks from an external script (*)

In Section 16.2, we introduced a way to read code into a single code chunk. In this section, we introduce one method to read multiple code chunks from an external script. The key is that you need to label the code in the script, and you can use the same labels in the code chunks in your R Markdown document, so the code in the external script can be mapped to the code chunks via the function `knitr::read_chunk()`. To label a block of code in a script, you write the label after `##  ----` (optionally, you can add a series of dashes to the end of this line). One script can contain multiple labeled code blocks, e.g.,

```
## ---- test-a --------
1 + 1

## ---- test-b --------
if (TRUE) {
  plot(cars)
}
```

We assume that the filename of the above script is `test.R`. In the R Markdown document, we can read it via `knitr::read_chunk()`, and use the code in code chunks with the labels, e.g.,

```
Read an external script:

```{r, include=FALSE, cache=FALSE}
knitr::read_chunk('test.R')
```

Now we can use the code, e.g.,

```{r, test-a, echo=FALSE}
```


```{r, test-b, fig.height=4}
```
```

Note that we use `knitr::read_chunk()` mainly for its side effect, so please make sure the code chunk in which you call this function is not cached (see Section 11.4 for the explanation).

Like methods introduced in Section 16.1 and Section 16.2, this method also gives you the flexibility of developing code in a separate environment.

16.4   Child documents (*)

When you feel an R Markdown document is too long, you may consider splitting it into shorter documents, and include them as child documents of the main document via the chunk option `child`. The `child` option takes a character vector of paths to the child documents, e.g.,

```
```{r, child=c('one.Rmd', 'two.Rmd')}
```
```

Since **knitr** chunk options can take values from arbitrary R expressions, one application of the `child` option is the conditional inclusion of a document. For example, if your report has an appendix containing technical details that your boss may not be interested in, you may use a variable to control whether this appendix is included in the report:

```
Change `BOSS_MODE` to `TRUE` if this report is to be read
by the boss:

```{r, include=FALSE}
BOSS_MODE <- FALSE
```

Conditionally include the appendix:

```{r, child=if (!BOSS_MODE) 'appendix.Rmd'}
```
```

Or if you are writing a news report on a football game that has not taken place yet, you may include different child documents depending on the outcome, e.g., child = if (winner == 'brazil') 'brazil.Rmd' else 'germany.Rmd'. Then as soon as the game (between Germany and Brazil) is finished, you can publish your report.

Another way to compile child documents is the function knitr::knit_child(). You can call this function in an R code chunk or an inline R expression, e.g.,

```
```{r, echo=FALSE, results='asis'}
res <- knitr::knit_child('child.Rmd', quiet = TRUE)
cat(res, sep = '\n')
```
```

The function knit_child() returns a character vector of the knitted output, which we can write back to the main document with cat() and the chunk option results = 'asis'.

You can even use a child document as a template, and call knit_child() on it repeatedly with different parameters. In the example below, we run a regression using mpg as the response variable and each of the rest of variables in the mtcars data as the explanatory variable.

```
```{r, echo=FALSE, results='asis'}
res <- lapply(setdiff(names(mtcars), 'mpg'), function(x) {
  knitr::knit_child(text = c(
    '## Regression on "`r x`"',
    '',
    '```{r}',
    'lm(mpg ~ ., data = mtcars[, c("mpg", x)])',
    '```',
    ''
  ), envir = environment(), quiet = TRUE)
})
cat(unlist(res), sep = '\n')
```
```

To make the above example self-contained, we used the `text` argument of
`knit_child()` instead of a file input to pass the R Markdown content to
be knitted. You can certainly write the content to a file, and pass a path to
`knit_child()` instead. For example, you can save the content below to a file
named `template.Rmd`:

```
## Regression on "`r x`"

```{r}
lm(mpg ~ ., data = mtcars[, c("mpg", x)])
```
```

And knit the file instead:

```
res <- lapply(setdiff(names(mtcars), 'mpg'), function(x) {
  knitr::knit_child(
    'template.Rmd', envir = environment(), quiet = TRUE
  )
})
cat(unlist(res), sep = '\n')
```

16.5 Keep the plot files

Most R Markdown output formats use the option `self_contained = TRUE` by default. This causes R plots to be embedded in the output documents, so we do not need the intermediate plot files when viewing the output documents. As a consequence, the plot folder (which typically has a suffix `_files`) will be deleted after the Rmd document is rendered.

Sometimes you may want to keep the plot files. For example, some academic journals require authors to submit figures files separately. For R Markdown, there are three ways to avoid the automatic deletion of these files:

1. Use the option `self_contained = FALSE` if the output format supports this option, e.g.,

    ```
    output:
      html_document:
        self_contained: false
    ```

    However, this means the plot files will not be embedded in the output document. If this is not what you want, you may consider the next two methods.

2. Enable caching for at least one code chunk (see Section 11.4). When caching is enabled, R Markdown will not delete the plot folder.

3. Use the option `keep_md = TRUE` if the output format supports this option, e.g.,

    ```
    output:
      word_document:
        keep_md: true
    ```

    When you ask R Markdown to preserve the intermediate Markdown output file, it will also preserve the plot folder.

16.6   The working directory for R code chunks

By default, the working directory for R code chunks is the directory that contains the Rmd document. For example, if the path of an Rmd file is ~/Downloads/foo.Rmd, the working directory under which R code chunks are evaluated is ~/Downloads/. This means when you refer to external files with relative paths in code chunks, you need to know that these paths are relative to the directory of the Rmd file. With the aforementioned Rmd example file, read.csv("data/iris.csv") in a code chunk means reading the CSV file ~/Downloads/data/iris.csv.

When in doubt, you can add getwd() to a code chunk, compile the document, and check the output from getwd().

Sometimes you may want to use another directory as the working directory. The usual way to change the working directory is setwd(), but please note that setwd() is not persistent in R Markdown (or other types of **knitr** source documents), which means setwd() only works for the current code chunk, and the working directory will be restored after this code chunk has been evaluated.

If you want to change the working directory for all code chunks, you may set it via a setup code chunk in the beginning of your document:

```{r, setup, include=FALSE}
knitr::opts_knit$set(root.dir = '/tmp')
```

This will change the working directory of all subsequent code chunks.

If you use RStudio, you can also choose the working directory from the menu Tools -> Global Options -> R Markdown (see Figure 16.1). The default working directory is the directory of the Rmd file, and there are two other possible choices: you may use the current working directory of your R console (the option "Current"), or the root directory of the project that contains this Rmd file as the working directory (the option "Project").

In RStudio, you may also knit an individual Rmd document with a specific working directory, as shown in Figure 16.2. After you change the "Knit Directory" and click the "Knit" button, **knitr** will use the new working directory to evaluate your code chunks. All these settings boil down to

FIGURE 16.1: Change the default working directory for all R Markdown documents in RStudio.

`knitr::opts_knit$set(root.dir = ...)` as we mentioned earlier, so if you are not satisfied by any of these choices, you can specify a directory by yourself with `knitr::opts_knit$set()`.

There is no absolutely correct choice for the working directory. Each choice has its own pros and cons:

- If you use the Rmd document directory as the working directory for code chunks (**knitr**'s default), you assume that file paths are relative to the Rmd document. This is similar to how web browsers handle relative paths, e.g., for an image `<img src="foo/bar.png" />` on an HTML page `https://www.example.org/path/to/page.html`,

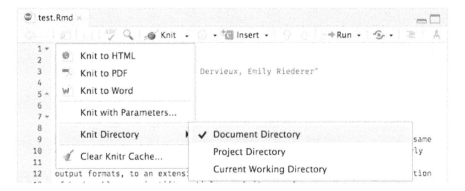

FIGURE 16.2: Knit an Rmd document with other possible working directories in RStudio.

your web browser will try to fetch the image from `https://www.example.org/path/to/foo/bar.png`. In other words, the relative path `foo/bar.png` is relative to the directory of the HTML file, which is `https://www.example.org/path/to/`.

The advantage of this approach is that you can freely move the Rmd file *together with* its referenced files anywhere, as long as their relative locations remain the same. For the HTML page and image example above, the files `page.html` and `foo/bar.png` could be moved together to a different directory, such as `https://www.example.org/another/path/`, and you will not need to update the relative path in the `src` attribute of `<img />`.

Some users like to think of relative paths in Rmd documents as "relative to the working directory of the R console," as opposed to "relative to the Rmd file." Therefore **knitr**'s default working directory feels confusing. The reason that I did not use the working directory of the R console as the default when I designed **knitr** was that users could use `setwd()` to change the working directory at any time. This working directory is not guaranteed to be stable. Each time a user calls `setwd()` in the console, there is a risk that the file paths in the Rmd document may become invalid. It could be surprising that the file paths depend on an external factor (`setwd()`), which is out of the control of the Rmd file. If you treat the Rmd file as "the center of the universe" when thinking of relative paths, the paths inside the Rmd file may be stabler.

Furthermore, if you do not want to think too hard on relative paths, you may enter a path in RStudio using its autocomplete, as shown in Figure 16.3. RStudio will try to autocomplete a path relative to the Rmd file.

- Using the working directory of the R console can be a good choice for knitting documents programmatically or interactively. For example, you may knit a document multiple times in a loop, and use a different working directory each time to read a different data file (with the same filename) in that directory. This type of working directory is advocated by the **ezknitr** package (Attali, 2016), which essentially uses `knitr::opts_knit$set(root.dir)` to change the working directory for code chunks in **knitr**.

- Using the project directory as the working directory requires an obvious assumption: you have to use a project (e.g., an RStudio project or a version control project) in the first place, which could be a disadvantage of this approach. The advantage of this type of working directory is that all relative paths in any Rmd document are relative to the project root directory, so you do not need to think where your Rmd file is located in the project or adjust the relative paths of other files accordingly. This type of working directory is advocated by the **here** package (Müller, 2017), which provides the function `here::here()` to return an absolute path by resolving a relative path passed to it (remember that the relative path is relative to the project root). The disadvantage is that when you move the referenced file together with the Rmd file to another location in the project, you need to update the referenced path in the Rmd document. When you share the Rmd file with other people, you also have to share the whole project.

These types of paths are similar to absolute paths without the protocol or domain in HTML. For example, an image `<img  src="/foo/bar.png" />` on the page `https://www.example.org/path/to/page.html` refers to the image under the root directory of the website, i.e., `https://www.example.org/foo/bar.png`. The leading `/` in the `src` attribute of the image indicates the root directory of the website. If you want to learn more (or further confuse yourself) about absolute and relative paths in HTML, please see Appendix B.1 of the **blogdown** book[1] (Xie et al., 2017).

The working directory pain mainly arises from this question when dealing with relative paths: *relative to what?* As we mentioned earlier, different people have different preferences, and there is not an absolutely right answer.

---

[1] `https://bookdown.org/yihui/blogdown/html.html`

```
24 ▾  ``` {r}
25    read.csv('chars| )
26 ▴  ```
27              [ ]  chars.csv
28              🖼  chars.pdf
                 🌐  chars.Rmd
```

FIGURE 16.3: Autocomplete file paths in an Rmd document in RStudio.

16.7   R package vignettes

If you have experience in developing R packages, or your project requires clear documentation and rigorous tests for custom functions written in the project, you may consider organizing the project as an R package. If you do not know how to create an R package, you can easily get started in the RStudio IDE by clicking the menu File -> New Project, and selecting the project type to be an R package.

There are a lot of benefits of using an R package to manage a project. For example, you can place datasets in the data/ folder, write R code under R/, generate documentation (e.g., using the **roxygen2** package (Wickham et al., 2020b)) to man/, and add unit tests to test/. When it comes to the R Markdown reports, you can write them as package vignettes under vignettes/. In the vignettes, you can load datasets and call functions in the package. When you build the package (via the command R CMD build or RStudio), vignettes will be automatically compiled.

To create a package vignette in R Markdown, the easiest way is through the RStudio menu File -> New File -> R Markdown -> From Template (see Figure 16.4). Then you select "Package Vignette" from the **rmarkdown** package, and you will get a vignette template. After changing the title, author, and other metadata of the template, you can start writing the content of your report.

Alternatively, you can install the package **usethis** (Wickham and Bryan, 2020) and use its function usethis::use_vignette() to create a vignette skeleton. Below is what the YAML frontmatter of a package vignette typically looks like:

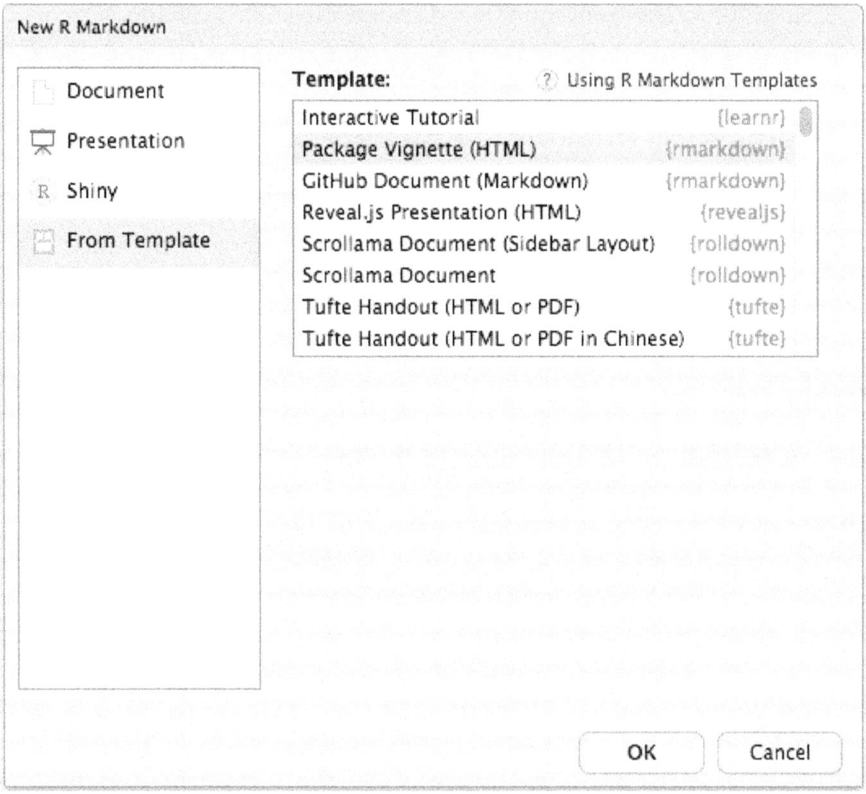

FIGURE 16.4: Create a package vignette in RStudio.

```
---
title: "Vignette Title"
author: "Vignette Author"
output: rmarkdown::html_vignette
vignette: >
  %\VignetteIndexEntry{Vignette Title}
  %\VignetteEngine{knitr::rmarkdown}
  %\VignetteEncoding{UTF-8}
---
```

Note that you need to change the vignette title in both the title field and the
\VignetteIndexEntry{} command. Besides the above information in the vignette, you also need to do two more things in your package DESCRIPTION file:

1. Specify `VignetteBuilder: knitr` in the `DESCRIPTION` file.

2. Add `Suggests: knitr, rmarkdown` in `DESCRIPTION`.

The vignette output format does not have to be HTML. It can also be PDF, so you can use `output: pdf_document`, too. Any other output formats that create HTML or PDF are also okay, such as `beamer_presentation` and `tufte::tufte_html`. However, currently, R only recognizes HTML and PDF vignettes.

16.8   R Markdown templates in R packages

Figure 16.4 of Section 16.7 illustrates the process of retrieving the editable Package Vignette (HTML) template from the **rmarkdown** package. This R Markdown file is pre-populated with the appropriate metadata for an R package vignette.

Similarly, any package may include R Markdown templates that package users can access through the RStudio IDE (as shown in the figure) or across any platform with the `rmarkdown::draft()` function.

16.8.1   Template use-cases

Templates are a useful way to share custom structure, style, and content. There are many excellent examples of this "in the wild."

Many templates add structure and style by pre-populating the YAML metadata. We already saw an example of this with the **rmarkdown** package's Package Vignette (HTML) template. Similarly, the **rmdformats** package (Barnier, 2020) provides a number of templates that pass different custom styling functions to the `output` option.

Other templates demonstrate document structures that the packages require. For example, the **pagedown** package (Xie et al., 2020b) includes numerous templates for posters, resumes, and other page layouts. Similarly, the **xaringan** package's Ninja Presentation template (Xie, 2020f) demonstrates the syntax for many different slide formatting options.

Templates may also demonstrate package features and syntax. For example, both the **flexdashboard** package (Iannone et al., 2020a) and the **learnr** package (Schloerke et al., 2020) include templates with code chunks that call functions from the packages to create a sample dashboard or tutorial, respectively.

Similarly, templates may also include boilerplate content. For example, the **rticles** package (Allaire et al., 2020c) provides many such templates to align R Markdown output to the required style and content guidelines of different academic journals. Boilerplate content is also useful in organizational settings, such as a team generating quarterly reports.

16.8.2   Template setup

The **usethis** package (Wickham and Bryan, 2020) has a helpful function for creating templates. Running `usethis::use_rmarkdown_template("Template Name")` will automatically create the required directory structure and files (you should provide your own Template Name).

If you wish to set up your template manually instead, create a subdirectory of the `inst/rmarkdown/templates` directory. Within this directory, you need to save at least two files:

1. A file named `template.yaml`, which gives the RStudio IDE basic metadata such as a human-readable name for the template. At a minimum, this file should have the `name` and `description` fields, e.g.,

    ```
    name: Example Template
    description: What this template does
    ```

    You may include `create_dir: true` if you want a new directory to be created when the template is selected. This is useful if your template relies upon additional resources. For example, the **learnr** package template[2] sets `create_dir: true`, whereas the **flexdashboard** package template[3] uses the default `create_dir: false`. You

---

[2]https://github.com/rstudio/learnr/blob/master/inst/rmarkdown/templates/tutorial/template.yaml
[3]https://github.com/rstudio/flexdashboard/blob/master/inst/rmarkdown/templates/flex_dashboard/template.yaml

may attempt to open both of these templates in RStudio to notice the different user prompts.

2. An R Markdown document saved under `skeleton/skeleton.Rmd`. This may contain anything you wish to put in an R Markdown document.

Optionally, the `skeleton` folder may also include additional resources like style sheets or images used by your template. These files will be loaded to the user's computer along with the template.

For more details on building custom R Markdown templates, please refer to the RStudio Extensions[4] website and the Document Templates chapter[5] of the *R Markdown Definitive Guide* (Xie et al., 2018).

16.9 Write books and long-form reports with bookdown

The **bookdown** package (Xie, 2020c) is designed for creating long-form documents that are composed of multiple R Markdown documents. For example, if you want to write a book, you can write each chapter in its own Rmd file, and use **bookdown** to compile these Rmd files into a book.

For RStudio users, the easiest way to get started is to create a **bookdown** project with the IDE by selecting `File -> New Project -> New Directory -> Book Project using bookdown`, as you can see from Figure 16.5.

If you do not use RStudio or if you prefer to work from the console, you may produce the same result by calling the function `book-down::bookdown_skeleton('your-book-dir')`.

To demonstrate the usage, we provide a minimal example consisting of three files within the same directory:

```
directory
  |- index.Rmd
  |- 01-intro.Rmd
  |- 02-analysis.Rmd
```

---

[4]https://rstudio.github.io/rstudio-extensions/rmarkdown_templates.html
[5]https://bookdown.org/yihui/rmarkdown/document-templates.html

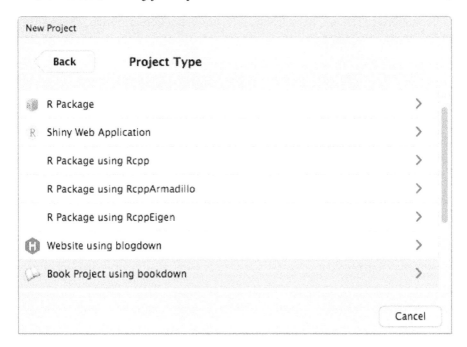

FIGURE 16.5: Create a bookdown project in RStudio.

Below we show the content of each file and explain their roles.

- **index.Rmd**:

```
---
title: "A Minimal bookdown Project"
site: bookdown::bookdown_site
output: bookdown::gitbook
---


# Preface {-}

Some content
```

The first file is typically called `index.Rmd`. It should be the only Rmd file in which you provide the YAML frontmatter. It should also include a special YAML field `site:  bookdown::bookdown_site`, so that **rmarkdown** knows to use **bookdown** to build all Rmd files, instead of rendering a single Rmd file. You can use any **bookdown** output formats, such as bookdown::gitbook, bookdown::pdf_book, bookdown::word_document2, and bookdown::epub_book.

The next two Rmd files are two chapters:

- **01-intro.Rmd:**

  ```
  # Chapter 1

  This is chapter 1.
  ```

- **02-analysis.Rmd:**

  ```
  # Chapter 2

  This is chapter 2.
  ```

To render these Rmd files, you should call book-down::render_book('index.Rmd') instead of rmarkdown::render(). Under the hood, **bookdown** merges all Rmd files into a single Rmd by default and compiles it. Files are merged in alphabetical order. That is why we added numeric prefixes to filenames in the above example.

There are a lot of settings that you can customize for a **bookdown** project. For a more comprehensive overview of **bookdown**, you may see Chapter 18 the **rmarkdown** book (Xie et al., 2018). For the full documentation, see the **bookdown** book (Xie, 2016).

16.10   Build websites with blogdown

If you want build a website based on R Markdown, you may consider using the **blogdown** package (Xie, 2020b). The easiest way to get started is to use the RStudio menu File -> New Project -> New Directory -> Website using blogdown, as you can see from Figure 16.5. If you have never used **blogdown** before, you may use the default settings in the dialog box, otherwise you can customize things like the website theme. If you do not use RStudio, you may call the function blogdown::new_site() under an empty directory to create a new website.

A website project may contain any number of Rmd documents. They could either be normal pages or blog posts. R Markdown makes it easier for you to maintain your website because the results on your website are automatically and dynamically generated.

We recommend that you read Chapter 1[6] of the **blogdown** book (Xie et al., 2017) for an overview of this package as well as the basic workflow of maintaining a website.

---

[6]https://bookdown.org/yihui/blogdown/get-started.html

17

Workflow

In this chapter, we introduce some tips on working with individual R Markdown documents as well as running your R Markdown projects. You may also check out Chapter 30[1] of the book *R for Data Science* (Wickham and Grolemund, 2016), which briefly introduces some tips on using analysis notebooks (including R Markdown documents). Nicholas Tierney also discusses the workflow in the book *R Markdown for Scientists.*[2]

17.1 Use RStudio keyboard shortcuts

The R Markdown format can be used with any editor of your choice, as long as R, the **rmarkdown** package, and Pandoc are installed. However, RStudio is deeply integrated with R Markdown, so you can work with R Markdown smoothly.

Like any IDE (Integrated Development Environment), RStudio has keyboard shortcuts. A full list can be found under the menu Tools -> Keyboard Shortcuts Help. Some of the most useful shortcuts related to R Markdown are summarized in Table 17.1.

Additionally, you can press F7 to spell-check your document. You can also restart the R session by Ctrl + Alt + F10 (or Command + Option + F10 on macOS). Restarting regularly is helpful for reproducibility, because results are more likely to be reproducible if they are computed from a new R session. This can also be done through the drop-down menu Restart R and Run All Chunks behind the Run button on the toolbar.

---

[1]https://r4ds.had.co.nz/r-markdown-workflow.html
[2]https://rmd4sci.njtierney.com/workflow.html

TABLE 17.1: RStudio keyboard shortcuts related to R Markdown.

Task	Windows & Linux	macOS
Insert R chunk	Ctrl+Alt+I	Command+Option+I
Preview HTML	Ctrl+Shift+K	Command+Shift+K
Knitr document (knitr)	Ctrl+Shift+K	Command+Shift+K
Compile Notebook	Ctrl+Shift+K	Command+Shift+K
Compile PDF	Ctrl+Shift+K	Command+Shift+K
Run all chunks above	Ctrl+Alt+P	Command+Option+P
Run current chunk	Ctrl+Alt+C	Command+Option+C
Run current chunk	Ctrl+Shift+Enter	Command+Shift+Enter
Run next chunk	Ctrl+Alt+N	Command+Option+N
Run all chunks	Ctrl+Alt+R	Command+Option+R
Go to next chunk/title	Ctrl+PgDown	Command+PgDown
Go to previous chunk/title	Ctrl+PgUp	Command+PgUp
Show/hide document outline	Ctrl+Shift+O	Command+Shift+O
Build book, website, ...	Ctrl+Shift+B	Command+Shift+B

17.2   Spell-check R Markdown

If you use the RStudio IDE, you can press the F7 key or click the menu Edit
-> Check Spelling to spell-check an Rmd document. Real-time spell checking has become available in RStudio v1.3, so you no longer need to manually
trigger spell checking with this version or a later version of RStudio.

If you do not use RStudio, the **spelling** package (Ooms and Hester, 2019) has
a function spell_check_files(), which can check the spelling of common
document formats, including R Markdown. When spell checking Rmd documents, it will skip code chunks and only check ordinary text.

17.3   Render R Markdown with `rmarkdown::render()`

If you do not use RStudio or any other IDE, you need to know this
fact: R Markdown documents are rendered through the function rmark-

down::render(). This means you can programmatically render an R Markdown document in any R script. For example, you could render a series of reports in a `for`-loop for each state of a country:

```
for (state in state.name) {
  rmarkdown::render(
    'input.Rmd', output_file = paste0(state, '.html')
  )
}
```

The output filename will be different for each state. You can also make use of the `state` variable in the document `input.Rmd`, e.g.,

```
---
title: "A report for `r state`"
output: html_document
---

The area of `r state` is `r state.area[state.name == state]`
square miles.
```

You may read the help page `?rmarkdown::render` to know other possible arguments. Here we just want to mention two of them, i.e., the `clean` and `envir` arguments.

The former (`clean`) is particularly helpful for debugging when anything goes wrong with the Pandoc conversion. If you call `rmarkdown::render(...,` `clean = FALSE)`, all intermediate files will be preserved, including the intermediate `.md` file knitted from the `.Rmd` file. If Pandoc signals an error, you may start debugging from this `.md` file.

The latter (`envir`) offers a way to render a document with the guarantee of an empty new environment when you call `rmarkdown::render(..., envir` `= new.env())`, so objects created in your code chunks will stay inside this environment, without polluting your current global environment. On the other hand, if you prefer rendering the Rmd document in a new R session so that objects in your current R session will not pollute your Rmd document, you may call `rmarkdown::render` in `xfun::Rscript_call()`, e.g.,

```
xfun::Rscript_call(
  rmarkdown::render,
  list(input = 'my-file.Rmd', output_format = 'pdf_document')
)
```

This method is similar to clicking the Knit button in RStudio, which also renders the Rmd document in a new R session. In case you need to render an Rmd document inside another Rmd document, we strongly recommend that you use this method instead of directly calling rmarkdown::render() in a code chunk, because rmarkdown::render() creates and relies on a lot of side effects internally, which may affect rendering other Rmd documents in the same R session.

The second argument of xfun::Rscript_call() takes a list of arguments to be passed to rmarkdown::render(). In fact, xfun::Rscript_call is a general-purpose function to call any R function (with arguments optionally) in a new R session. Please see its help page if you are interested.

17.4   Parameterized reports

In Section 17.3, we mentioned one way to render a series of reports in a for-loop. In fact, rmarkdown::render() has an argument named params specifically designed for this task. You can parameterize your report through this argument. When you specify parameters for a report, you can use the variable params in your report. For example, if you call:

```
for (state in state.name) {
  rmarkdown::render('input.Rmd', params = list(state = state))
}
```

then in input.Rmd, the object params will be a list that contains the state variable:

```
---
title: "A report for `r params$state`"
output: html_document
---
```

```
The area of `r params$state` is
`r state.area[state.name == params$state]`
square miles.
```

Another way to specify parameters for a report is to use the YAML field params, e.g.,

```
---
title: Parameterized reports
output: html_document
params:
  state: Nebraska
  year: 2019
  midwest: true
---
```

Note that you can include as many parameters in the params YAML field or the params argument of rmarkdown::render(). If both the YAML field and the argument are present, the parameter values in the argument will override the corresponding parameters in YAML. For example, when we call rmarkdown::render(..., params = list(state = 'Iowa', year = 2018) on the previous example that has the params field, params$state will become Iowa (instead of Nebraska) and params$year will become 2018 (instead of 2019) in the R Markdown document.

When rendering the same R Markdown document to a series of reports, you need to adjust the output_file argument of rmarkdown::render(), to make sure each report has its unique filename. Otherwise, you will accidentally override certain report files. For example, you can write a function to generate a report for each state and each year:

```
render_one <- function(state, year) {
  # assuming the output format of input.Rmd is PDF
  rmarkdown::render(
    'input.Rmd',
    output_file = paste0(state, '-', year, '.pdf'),
    params = list(state = state, year = year),
    envir = parent.frame()
```

```
  )
}
```

Then you can use nested `for`-loops to generate all reports:

```
for (state in state.name) {
  for (year in 2000:2020) {
    render_one(state, year)
  }
}
```

At the end, you will get a series of report files like `Alabama-2000.pdf`, `Alabama-2001.pdf`, ..., `Wyoming-2019.pdf`, and `Wyoming-2020.pdf`.

For parameterized reports, you can also input parameters interactively through a graphical user interface (GUI) created from Shiny. This requires you to provide a `params` field in YAML, and **rmarkdown** will automatically create the GUI using the appropriate input widgets for each parameter (e.g., a checkbox will be provided for a Boolean parameter).

To start the GUI, you can call `rmarkdown::render()` with `params = 'ask'` if you do not use RStudio:

```
rmarkdown::render("input.Rmd", params = "ask")
```

If you use RStudio, you can click the menu `Knit with Parameters` behind the `Knit` button. Figure 17.1 shows an example GUI for parameters.

For more information on parameterized reports, you may read Chapter 15[3] of the *R Markdown Definitive Guide* (Xie et al., 2018).

17.5   Customize the `Knit` button (*)

When you click the `Knit` button in RStudio, it will call the `rmarkdown::render()` function in a new R session and output a file of the same base name as the input file in the same directory. For example, knitting ex-

---

[3]https://bookdown.org/yihui/rmarkdown/parameterized-reports.html

FIGURE 17.1: Knit an R Markdown document with parameters that you can input from a GUI.

ample.Rmd with the output format html_document will create an output file example.html.

There may be situations in which we want to customize how the document is rendered. For example, perhaps we would like the rendered document to contain the current date, or would like to output the compiled report into a different directory. Although we can achieve these goals by calling rmarkdown::render() (see Section 17.3) with the appropriate output_file argument, it can be inconvenient to have to rely on a custom call to rmarkdown::render() to compile your report.

It is possible to control the behavior of the Knit button by providing the knit field within the YAML frontmatter of your document. The field takes a function with the main argument input (the path to the input Rmd document) and other arguments that are currently ignored. You can either write the source code of the function directly in the knit field, or put the function elsewhere (e.g., in an R package) and call the function in the knit field. If you routinely need the custom knit function, we would recommend that you put it in a package, instead of repeating its source code in every single R Markdown document.

If you store the code directly within YAML, you must wrap the entire function in parentheses. If the source code has multiple lines, you have to indent all lines (except the first line) by at least two spaces. For example, if we want the output filename to include the date on which it is rendered, we could use the following YAML code:

```
---
knit: (function(input, ...) {
    rmarkdown::render(
      input,
      output_file = paste0(
        xfun::sans_ext(inputFile), '-', Sys.Date(), '.html'
      ),
      envir = globalenv()
    )
  })
---
```

For example, if we knit `example.Rmd` on 2019-07-29, the output filename will be `example-2019-07-29.html`.

While the above approach looks simple and straightforward enough, embedding a function directly in your YAML may make it difficult for you to maintain it, unless the function is only to be used once with a single R Markdown document. In general, we would recommend using an R package to maintain such a function, e.g., you may create a function `knit_with_date()` in a package:

```
#' Custom Knit function for RStudio
#'
#' @export
knit_with_date <- function(input, ...) {
  rmarkdown::render(
    input,
    output_file = paste0(
        xfun::sans_ext(inputFile), '-', Sys.Date(), '.',
        xfun::file_ext(inputFile)
    ),
    envir = globalenv()
  )
}
```

If you add the above code to a package named **myPackage**, you will be able to refer to your custom `knit` function using the following YAML setting:

```
---
knit: myPackage::knit_with_date
---
```

You may refer to the help page `?rmarkdown::render` to find out more ideas on how you could customize your `knit` function behind the `Knit` button in RStudio.

17.6 Collaborate on Rmd documents through Google Drive

Based on the **googledrive** package (D'Agostino McGowan and Bryan, 2020), Emily Kothe provided a few wrapper functions in the **rmdrive** package, which is currently available only on GitHub at `https://github.com/ekothe/rmdrive`. At the time of writing, it still lacks rich documentation, so I recommend that you try Janosch Linkersdörfer's fork instead: `https://github.com/januz/rmdrive` (which is based on Ben Marwick's fork—if you still have not learned GIT, you may be motivated by these examples of freely forking and improving other people's GIT repositories).

The workflow with **rmdrive** is outlined below:

1. We assume there is a main author or contributor of the project, who is capable of using version control tools like GIT. The main author writes the initial version of the Rmd document, and uploads it to Google Drive via the `upload_rmd()` function.

2. The Rmd document in Google Drive is shared with other collaborators, who can make or suggest changes in Google Document.

3. The main author can accept suggested changes, and download/preview the Rmd document locally via `render_rmd()`. Other collaborators can also do this by themselves if they have modified code chunks and want to see the new results.

4. If satisfied, the main author can commit changes to the GIT repository.

The collaborative editing can be either synchronous or asynchronous in Google Drive. Multiple people can edit the same document at the same time, or wait for other people to finish their editing first.

There is also a function `udpate_rmd()` in the package, which allows you to edit the Rmd document locally, and upload the local Rmd document to Google Drive. You probably should never want to run this function, because it will completely overwrite the document in Google Drive. The main author may want to warn collaborators about this in advance. Ideally, all collaborators should only edit the document in Google Drive and not locally. It is okay to preview the edited document locally via `render_rmd()`, though (note that `render_rmd()` automatically downloads the document before rendering it).

17.7   Organize an R Markdown project into a research website with workflowr

The **workflowr** package (Blischak et al., 2020, 2019) can help you organize a (data analysis) project with a project template and the version control tool GIT. Every time you make a change to the project, you can log the change, and **workflowr** can build a website corresponding to that particular version of your project. This means that you will be able to view the full history of your analysis results. Although this package uses GIT as the backend for version control, you do not really have to be familiar with GIT. The package provides R functions that do the GIT operations under the hood, and you only need to call these R functions. Furthermore, **workflowr** automates best practices for reproducible code. Each time an R Markdown document is rendered, **workflowr** automatically sets a seed with `set.seed()`, records the session information with `sessionInfo()`, and scans for absolute file paths, etc. Please see the package documentation[4] for how to get started and more information.

The main author of **workflowr**, John Blischak, has also put together a non-exhaustive list of R packages and guides related to the workflow of R projects, which can be found in this GitHub repo: `https://github.com/jdblischak/r-project-workflows`.

---

[4]`https://jdblischak.github.io/workflowr/`

17.8 Send emails based on R Markdown

With the **blastula** package (Iannone and Cheng, 2020), you can render an Rmd document to the email body and send the email. To render an Rmd document to an email, the document needs to use the output format `blastula::blastula_email`, e.g.,

```
---
title: Weekly Report
output: blastula::blastula_email
---


Dear Boss,

Below is an analysis of the `iris` data:

```{r}
summary(iris)
plot(iris[, -5])
```


Please let me know if it is not boring enough.

Sincerely,
John
```

This Rmd document should be rendered via the function `blastula::render_email()`, and the output can be passed to `blastula::smtp_send()`, which will send out the email. Note that `smtp_send()` needs an email server as well as your credentials.

If you use RStudio Connect, you can find more examples at https://solutions.rstudio.com/examples/blastula-overview/, including automated, conditional, and parameterized emails.

A

knitr's Chunk and Package Options

The **knitr** package provides a lot of chunk options for customizing nearly all components of code chunks, such as the source code, text output, plots, and the language of the chunk. It also offers some options at the package level to customize the knitting process. This appendix describes all chunk options and package options available in **knitr**. The default values of these options are in parentheses in the list items.

A.1 Chunk options

Chunk options are written in chunk headers. The syntax for chunk headers depends on the document format, e.g., for .Rnw documents (R + LaTeX), chunk headers are written with << >>=, and for .Rmd documents, chunk headers are written with ``` {r}. The examples below are primarily for .Rmd documents (R Markdown), but in most cases, the chunk options can be used with any document format.

Chunk options are written in the form tag=value like this:

```
```{r, my-chunk, echo=FALSE, fig.height=4, dev='jpeg'}
```
```

A special chunk option is the chunk label (e.g., my-chunk in the above example). Only the chunk label does not need a tag (i.e., you only provide the value). If you prefer the form tag=value, you could also use the chunk option label explicitly, e.g.,

```
```{r, label='my-chunk'}
```
```

The chunk label for each chunk is assumed to be unique within the document. This is especially important for cache and plot filenames, because these filenames are based on chunk labels. Chunks without labels will be assigned labels like unnamed-chunk-i, where i is an incremental number.

You may use knitr::opts_chunk$set() to change the default values of chunk options in a document. For example, you may put this in the first code chunk of your document:

```
```{r, setup, include=FALSE}
knitr::opts_chunk$set(
  comment = '', fig.width = 6, fig.height = 6
)
```
```

Below are a few more tips about chunk options:

1. The chunk header must be written on one line. You must not break the line.

2. Try to avoid spaces, periods (.), and underscores (_) in chunk labels and paths. If you need separators, you are recommended to use hyphens (-) instead. For example, setup-options is a good label, whereas setup.options and chunk 1 are bad; fig.path = 'figures/mcmc-' is a good path for figure output, and fig.path = 'markov chain/monte carlo' is bad.

3. All option values must be *valid R expressions*. You may think of them as values to be passed to function arguments.

    - For example, options that take *character* values must be quoted, e.g., results = 'asis' and out.width = '\\textwidth' (remember that a literal backslash needs double backslashes).
    - In theory, the chunk label should be quoted, too. However, for the sake of convenience, it will be automatically quoted if you did not (e.g., ```{r, 2a} will parsed as ```{r, '2a'}).
    - You can write arbitrarily complicated expressions as long as they are valid R code.

Below is a list of chunk options in **knitr** documented in the format "option: (default value; type of value)".

A.1.1 Code evaluation

- eval: (TRUE; logical or numeric) Whether to evaluate the code chunk. It can also be a numeric vector to choose which R expression(s) to evaluate, e.g., eval = c(1, 3, 4) will evaluate the first, third, and fourth expressions, and eval = -(4:5) will evaluate all expressions except the fourth and fifth.

A.1.2 Text output

- echo: (TRUE; logical or numeric) Whether to display the source code in the output document. Besides TRUE/FALSE, which shows/hides the source code, we can also use a numeric vector to choose which R expression(s) to echo in a chunk, e.g., echo = 2:3 means to echo only the 2nd and 3rd expressions, and echo = -4 means to exclude the 4th expression.

- results: ('markup'; character) Controls how to display the text results. Note that this option only applies to normal text output (not warnings, messages, or errors). The possible values are as follows:

  - markup: Mark up text output with the appropriate environments depending on the output format. For example, for R Markdown, if the text output is a character string "[1] 1 2 3", the actual output that **knitr** produces will be:

    ```
    [1] 1 2 3
    ```

    In this case, results='markup' means to put the text output in fenced code blocks (```).

  - asis: Write text output as-is, i.e., write the raw text results directly into the output document without any markups.

    ````
    ```{r, results='asis'}
    cat("I'm raw **Markdown** content.\n")
    ```
    ````

  - hold: Hold all pieces of text output in a chunk and flush them to the end of the chunk.

  - hide (or FALSE): Hide text output.

- collapse: (FALSE; logical) Whether to, if possible, collapse all the source and output blocks from one code chunk into a single block (by default, they are written to separate blocks). This option only applies to Markdown documents.

- warning: (TRUE; logical) Whether to preserve warnings (produced by warning()) in the output. If FALSE, all warnings will be printed in the console instead of the output document. It can also take numeric values as indices to select a subset of warnings to include in the output. Note that these values reference the indices of the warnings themselves (e.g., 3 means "the third warning thrown from this chunk") and not the indices of which expressions are allowed to emit warnings.

- error: (TRUE; logical) Whether to preserve errors (from stop()). By default, the code evaluation will not stop even in case of errors! If we want to stop on errors, we need to set this option to FALSE. Note that R Markdown has changed this default value to FALSE. When the chunk option include = FALSE, **knitr** will stop on error, because it is easy to overlook potential errors in this case.

- message: (TRUE; logical) Whether to preserve messages emitted by message() (similar to the option warning).

- include: (TRUE; logical) Whether to include the chunk output in the output document. If FALSE, nothing will be written into the output document, but the code is still evaluated and plot files are generated if there are any plots in the chunk, so you can manually insert figures later.

- strip.white: (TRUE; logical) Whether to remove blank lines in the beginning or end of a source code block in the output.

- class.output: (NULL; character) A vector of class names to be added to the text output blocks. This option only works for HTML output formats in R Markdown. For example, with class.output = c('foo', 'bar'), the text output will be placed in <pre class="foo bar"></pre>.

- class.message/class.warning/class.error: (NULL; character) Similar to class.output, but applied to messages, warnings, and errors in R Markdown output. Please see Section A.1.3 for class.source, which applies similarly to source code blocks.

- attr.output/attr.message/attr.warning/attr.error: (NULL; character) Similar to the class.* options above, but for specifying arbitrary fenced code block attributes for Pandoc; class.* is a special application of attr.*, e.g., `class.source = 'numberLines'` is equivalent to `attr.source = '.numberLines'`, but `attr.source` can take arbitrary attribute values, e.g., `attr.source = c('.numberLines', 'startFrom="11"')`.

- `render`: (`knitr::knit_print`; `function(x, options, ...)`) A function to print the visible values in a chunk. The value passed to the first argument of this function (i.e., `x`) is the value evaluated from each expression in the chunk. The list of current chunk options is passed to the argument `options`. This function is expected to return a character string. For more information, check out the package vignette about custom chunk rendering: `vignette('knit_print', package = 'knitr')`.

- `split`: (`FALSE`; logical) Whether to split the output into separate files and include them in LaTeX by `\input{}` or HTML by `<iframe></iframe>`. This option only works for `.Rnw`, `.Rtex`, and `.Rhtml` documents.

A.1.3 Code decoration

- `tidy`: (`FALSE`) Whether to reformat the R code. Other possible values are as follows:

  - `TRUE` (equivalent to `tidy = 'formatR'`): Call the function `formatR::tidy_source()` to reformat the code.
  - `'styler'`: Use `styler::style_text()` to reformat the code.
  - A custom function of the form `function(code, ...) {}` to return the reformatted code.
  - If reformatting fails, the original R code will not be changed (with a warning).

- `tidy.opts`: (`NULL`; list) A list of options to be passed to the function determined by the `tidy` option, e.g., `tidy.opts = list(blank = FALSE, width.cutoff = 60)` for `tidy = 'formatR'` to remove blank lines and try to cut the code lines at 60 characters.

- `prompt`: (`FALSE`; logical) Whether to add the prompt characters in the R code. See `prompt` and `continue` on the help page `?base::options`. Note that adding prompts can make it difficult for readers to copy R code from the output, so `prompt = FALSE` may be a better choice. This option may not work well when the chunk option `engine` is not R (#1274[1]).

- `comment`: (`'##'`; character) The prefix to be added before each line of the

---

[1] `https://github.com/yihui/knitr/issues/1274`

text output. By default, the text output is commented out by ##, so if readers want to copy and run the source code from the output document, they
can select and copy everything from the chunk, since the text output is
masked in comments (and will be ignored when running the copied text).
Set comment = '' remove the default ##.

- highlight: (TRUE; logical) Whether to syntax highlight the source code.

- class.source: (NULL; character) Class names for source code blocks in
  the output document. Similar to the class.* options for output such as
  class.output.

- attr.source: (NULL; character) Attributes for source code blocks. Similar
  to the attr.* options for output such as attr.output.

- size: ('normalsize'; character) Font size of the chunk output from .Rnw
  documents. See this page[2] for possible sizes.

- background: ('#F7F7F7'; character) Background color of the chunk output
  of .Rnw documents.

- indent: (character) A string to be added to each line of the chunk output.
  Typically it consists of white spaces. This option is assumed to be read-only,
  and **knitr** sets its value while parsing the document. For example, for the
  chunk below, indent is a character string of two spaces:

```{r}
rnorm(10)
```

A.1.4 Cache

- cache: (FALSE; logical) Whether to cache a code chunk. When evaluating
  code chunks for the second time, the cached chunks are skipped (unless
  they have been modified), but the objects created in these chunks are
  loaded from previously saved databases (.rdb and .rdx files), and these
  files are saved when a chunk is evaluated for the first time, or when cached
  files are not found (e.g., you may have removed them by hand). Note that
  the filename consists of the chunk label with an MD5 digest of the R code
  and chunk options of the code chunk, which means any changes in the

---

[2]https://www.overleaf.com/learn/latex/Font_sizes,_families,_and_styles

chunk will produce a different MD5 digest, and hence invalidate the cache. See more information on this page.[3]

- `cache.path`: (`'cache/'`; character) A prefix to be used to generate the paths of cache files. For R Markdown, the default value is based on the input file-name, e.g., the cache paths for the chunk with the label FOO in the file IN-PUT.Rmd will be of the form INPUT_cache/FOO_*.*.

- `cache.vars`: (NULL; character) A vector of variable names to be saved in the cache database. By default, all variables created in the current chunks are identified and saved, but you may want to manually specify the variables to be saved, because the automatic detection of variables may not be robust, or you may want to save only a subset of variables.

- `cache.globals`: (NULL; character) A vector of the names of variables that are not created from the current chunk. This option is mainly for autodep = TRUE to work more precisely—a chunk B depends on chunk A when any of B's global variables are A's local variables. In case the automatic detection of global variables in a chunk fails, you may manually specify the names of global variables via this option (see #1403[4] for an example).

- `cache.lazy`: (TRUE; logical) Whether to lazyLoad() or directly load() ob-jects. For very large objects, lazyloading may not work, so cache.lazy = FALSE may be desirable (see #572[5]).

- `cache.comments`: (NULL; logical) If FALSE, changing comments in R code chunks will not invalidate the cache database.

- `cache.rebuild`: (FALSE; logical) If TRUE, reevaluate the chunk even if the cache does not need to be invalidated. This can be useful when you want to conditionally invalidate the cache, e.g., cache.rebuild = !file.exists("some-file") can rebuild the chunk when some-file does not exist (see #238[6]).

- `dependson`: (NULL; character or numeric) A character vector of chunk labels to specify which other chunks this chunk depends on. This option applies to cached chunks only—sometimes the objects in a cached chunk may depend on other cached chunks, so when other chunks are changed, this chunk must be updated accordingly.

---

[3]https://yihui.org/knitr/demo/cache/
[4]https://github.com/yihui/knitr/issues/1403
[5]https://github.com/yihui/knitr/issues/572
[6]https://github.com/yihui/knitr/issues/238

- If dependson is a numeric vector, it means the indices of chunk labels, e.g., dependson = 1 means this chunk depends on the first chunk in the document, and dependson = c(-1, -2) means it depends on the previous two chunks (negative indices stand for numbers of chunks before this chunk, and note they are always relative to the current chunk).
- Please note this option does not work when set as a global chunk option via opts_chunk$set(); it must be set as a local chunk option.

- autodep: (FALSE; logical) Whether to analyze dependencies among chunks automatically by detecting global variables in the code (may not be reliable), so dependson does not need to be set explicitly.

A.1.5 Plots

- fig.path: ('figure/'; character) A prefix to be used to generate figure file paths. fig.path and chunk labels are concatenated to generate the full paths. It may contain a directory like figure/prefix-; the directory will be created if it does not exist.

- fig.keep: ('high'; character) How plots in chunks should be kept. Possible values are as follows:

    - high: Only keep high-level plots (merge low-level changes into high-level plots).
    - none: Discard all plots.
    - all: Keep all plots (low-level plot changes may produce new plots).
    - first: Only keep the first plot.
    - last: Only keep the last plot.
    - If set to a numeric vector, the values are indices of (low-level) plots to keep.

Low-level plotting commands include lines() and points(), etc. To better understand fig.keep, consider the following chunk:

```r
```{r, test-plot}
plot(1)          # high-level plot
abline(0, 1)     # low-level change
plot(rnorm(10))  # high-level plot
# many low-level changes in a loop (a single R expression)
for(i in 1:10) {
    abline(v = i, lty = 2)
```
```

```
}
```

Normally this produces 2 plots in the output (because `fig.keep` = `'high'`). For `fig.keep` = `'none'`, no plots will be saved. For `fig.keep` = `'all'`, 4 plots are saved. For `fig.keep` = `'first'`, the plot produced by `plot(1)` is saved. For `fig.keep` = `'last'`, the last plot with 10 vertical lines is saved.

- `fig.show`: (`'asis'`; character) How to show/arrange the plots. Possible values are as follows:

  - `asis`: Show plots exactly in places where they were generated (as if the code were run in an R terminal).
  - `hold`: Hold all plots and output them at the end of a code chunk.
  - `animate`: Concatenate all plots into an animation if there are multiple plots in a chunk.
  - `hide`: Generate plot files but hide them in the output document.

- `dev`: (`'pdf'` for LaTeX output and `'png'` for HTML/Markdown; character) The graphical device to generate plot files. All graphics devices in base R and those in **Cairo**, **cairoDevice**, **svglite**, **ragg**, and **tikzDevice** are supported, e.g., pdf, png, svg, jpeg, tiff, cairo_pdf, CairoJPEG, CairoPNG, Cairo_pdf, Cairo_png, svglite, ragg_png, tikz, and so on. See `names(knitr:::auto_exts)` for the full list. Besides these devices, you can also provide a character string that is the name of a function of the form `function(filename, width, height)`. The units for the image size are *always* inches (even for bitmap devices, in which DPI is used to convert between pixels and inches).

  The chunk options `dev`, `fig.ext`, `fig.width`, `fig.height`, and `dpi` can be vectors (shorter ones will be recycled), e.g., `dev` = `c('pdf', 'png')` creates a PDF and a PNG file for the same plot.

- `dev.args`: (NULL; list) More arguments to be passed to the device, e.g., `dev.args` = `list(bg = 'yellow', pointsize = 10)` for `dev` = `'png'`. This option depends on the specific device (see the device documentation). When `dev` contains multiple devices, `dev.args` can be a list of lists of arguments, and each list of arguments is passed to each individual device, e.g., `dev` = `c('pdf', 'tiff')`, `dev.args` = `list(pdf = list(colormodel = 'cmyk', useDingats = TRUE), tiff = list(compression = 'lzw'))`.

- `fig.ext`: (NULL; character) File extension of the figure output. If NULL, it will be derived from the graphical device; see `knitr:::auto_exts` for details.

- dpi: (72; numeric) The DPI (dots per inch) for bitmap devices (`dpi` * `inches = pixels`).

- `fig.width`, `fig.height`: (both are 7; numeric) Width and height of the plot (in inches), to be used in the graphics device.

- `fig.asp`: (`NULL`; numeric) The aspect ratio of the plot, i.e., the ratio of height/width. When `fig.asp` is specified, the height of a plot (the chunk option `fig.height`) is calculated from `fig.width` * `fig.asp`.

- `fig.dim`: (`NULL`; numeric) A numeric vector of length 2 to provide `fig.width` and `fig.height`, e.g., `fig.dim = c(5, 7)` is a shorthand of `fig.width = 5`, `fig.height = 7`. If both `fig.asp` and `fig.dim` are provided, `fig.asp` will be ignored (with a warning).

- `out.width`, `out.height`: (`NULL`; character) Width and height of the plot in the output document, which can be different with its physical `fig.width` and `fig.height`, i.e., plots can be scaled in the output document. Depending on the output format, these two options can take special values. For example, for LaTeX output, they can be `.8\\linewidth`, `3in`, or `8cm`; for HTML, they may be `300px`. For `.Rnw` documents, the default value for `out.width` will be changed to `\\maxwidth`, which is defined on this page.[7] It can also be a percentage, e.g., `'40%'` will be translated to `0.4\linewidth` when the output format is LaTeX.

- `out.extra`: (`NULL`; character) Extra options for figures. It can be an arbitrary string, to be inserted in `\includegraphics[]` in LaTeX output (e.g., `out.extra = 'angle=90'` to rotate the figure by 90 degrees), or `<img />` in HTML output (e.g., `out.extra = 'style="border:5px solid orange;"'`).

- `fig.retina`: (1; numeric) This option only applies to HTML output. For Retina displays,[8] setting this option to a ratio (usually 2) will change the chunk option `dpi` to `dpi * fig.retina`, and `out.width` to `fig.width * dpi / fig.retina` internally. For example, the physical size of an image is doubled, and its display size is halved when `fig.retina = 2`.

- `resize.width`, `resize.height`: (`NULL`; character) The width and height to be used in `\resizebox{}{}` in LaTeX output. These two options are not

---

[7]https://yihui.org/knitr/demo/framed/
[8]http://en.wikipedia.org/wiki/Retina_Display

needed unless you want to resize TikZ graphics, because there is no natural way to do it. However, according to the **tikzDevice** authors, TikZ graphics are not meant to be resized, to maintain consistency in style with other text in LaTeX. If only one of them is NULL, ! will be used (read the documentation of **graphicx** if you do not understand this).

- `fig.align`: ('default'; character) Alignment of figures in the output document. Possible values are default, left, right, and center. The default is not to make any alignment adjustments.

- `fig.link`: (NULL; character) A link to be added onto the figure.

- `fig.env`: ('figure'; character) The LaTeX environment for figures, e.g., you may set fig.env = 'marginfigure' to get \begin{marginfigure}. This option requires fig.cap be specified.

- `fig.cap`: (NULL; character) A figure caption.

- `fig.scap`: (NULL; character) A short caption. This option is only meaningful to LaTeX output. A short caption is inserted in \caption[], and usually displayed in the "List of Figures" of a PDF document.

- `fig.lp`: ('fig:'; character) A label prefix for the figure label to be inserted in \label{}. The actual label is made by concatenating this prefix and the chunk label, e.g., the figure label for ```{r, foo-plot} will be fig:foo-plot by default.

- `fig.pos`: (''; character) A character string for the figure position arrangement to be used in \begin{figure}[].

- `fig.subcap`: (NULL) Captions for subfigures. When there are multiple plots in a chunk, and neither fig.subcap nor fig.cap is NULL, \subfloat{} will be used for individual plots (you need to add \usepackage{subfig} in the preamble). See 067-graphics-options.Rnw[9] for an example.

- `fig.ncol`: (NULL; integer) The number of columns of subfigures; see this issue[10] for examples (note that fig.ncol and fig.sep only work for LaTeX output).

- `fig.sep`: (NULL; character) A character vector of separators to be inserted among subfigures. When fig.ncol is specified, fig.sep defaults to a character vector of which every N-th element is \newline (where N is the num-

---

[9]https://github.com/yihui/knitr-examples/blob/master/067-graphics-options.Rnw

[10]https://github.com/yihui/knitr/issues/1327#issuecomment-346242532

ber of columns), e.g., `fig.ncol = 2` means `fig.sep = c('', '', '\\new-line', '', '', '\\newline', '', ...)`.

- `fig.process`: (`NULL`; function) A function to post-process figure files. It should take the path of a figure file, and return the (new) path of the figure to be inserted in the output. If the function contains the `options` argument, the list of chunk options will be passed to this argument.

- `fig.showtext`: (`NULL`; logical) If `TRUE`, call `showtext::showtext_begin()` before drawing plots. See the documentation of the **showtext**[11] package for details.

- `external`: (`TRUE`; logical) Whether to externalize tikz graphics (pre-compile tikz graphics to PDF). It is only used for the `tikz()` device in the **tikzDevice** package (i.e., when `dev='tikz'`), and it can save time for LaTeX compilation.

- `sanitize`: (`FALSE`; character) Whether to sanitize tikz graphics (escape special LaTeX characters). See the documentation of the **tikzDevice** package.

There are two hidden options that are not designed to be set by users: `fig.cur` (the current figure number or index when there are multiple figures), and `fig.num` (the total number of figures in a chunk). The purpose of these two options is to help **knitr** deal with the filenames of multiple figures as well as animations. In some cases, we can make use of them to write animations into the output using plot files that are saved manually (see the graphics manual[12] for examples).

A.1.6   Animation

- `interval`: (1; numeric) Time interval (number of seconds) between animation frames.

- `animation.hook`: (`knitr::hook_ffmpeg_html`; function or character) A hook function to create animations in HTML output; the default hook uses FFmpeg to convert images to a WebM video.

  - Another hook function is `knitr::hook_gifski` based on the **gifski**[13] package to create GIF animations.

  - This option can also take a character string `'ffmpeg'` or `'gifski'` as a

---

[11]http://cran.rstudio.com/package=showtext
[12]https://github.com/yihui/knitr/releases/download/doc/knitr-graphics.pdf
[13]https://cran.r-project.org/package=gifski

shorthand of the corresponding hook function, e.g., `animation.hook = 'gifski'` means `animation.hook = knitr::hook_gifski`.

- – aniopts: (`'controls,loop'`; character) Extra options for animations; see the documentation of the LaTeX **animate** package.[14]

- ffmpeg.bitrate (`1M`; character) To be passed to the `-b:v` argument of FFmpeg to control the quality of WebM videos.

- ffmpeg.format (`webm`; character) The video format of FFmpeg, i.e., the filename extension of the video.

A.1.7 Code chunk

- code: (`NULL`; character) If provided, it will override the code in the current chunk. This allows us to programmatically insert code into the current chunk. For example, `code = readLines('test.R')` will use the content of the file `test.R` as the code for the current chunk.

- ref.label: (`NULL`; character) A character vector of labels of the chunks from which the code of the current chunk is inherited (see the demo for chunk references[15]).

A.1.8 Child documents

- child: (`NULL`; character) A character vector of paths of child documents to be knitted and input into the main document.

A.1.9 Language engines

- engine: (`'R'`; character) The language name of the code chunk. Possible values can be found in `names(knitr::knit_engines$get())`, e.g., `python`, `sql`, `julia`, `bash`, and `c`, etc. The object `knitr::knit_engines` can be used to set up engines for other languages.

- engine.path: (`NULL`; character) The path to the executable of the `engine`. This option makes it possible to use alternative executables in your system, e.g., the default `python` may be at `/usr/bin/python`, and you may set `engine.path = '~/anaconda/bin/python'` to use a different version of Python.

---

engine.path can also be a list of paths, which makes it possible to set different engine paths for different engines, e.g.,

```
knitr::opts_chunk$set(engine.path = list(
  python = '~/anaconda/bin/python',
  ruby = '/usr/local/bin/ruby'
))
```

The names of the list correspond to the names of the engines.

A.1.10   Option templates

- opts.label: (NULL; character) The label of options set in knitr::opts_template (see ?knitr::opts_template). This option can save some typing effort for sets of frequently used chunk options.

A.1.11   Extracting source code

- purl: (TRUE; logical) When running knitr::purl() to extract source code from a source document, whether to include or exclude a certain code chunk.

A.1.12   Other chunk options

- R.options: (NULL; list) Local R options for a code chunk. These options are set temporarily via options() before the code chunk, and restored after the chunk.

A.2   Package options

The package options can be changed using the object knitr::opts_knit[16] (*not to be confused with* knitr::opts_chunk). For example:

```
knitr::opts_knit$set(progress = TRUE, verbose = TRUE)
```

See ?knitr::opts_knit for the alternative approach to setting package options using the R base function options().

---

[16]https://yihui.org/knitr/objects/

Available package options are as follows:

- `aliases`: (NULL; character) A named character vector to specify the aliases of chunk options, e.g., `c(h = 'fig.height', w = 'fig.width')` tells **knitr** that the chunk option `h` really means `fig.height`, and `w` is an alias for `fig.width`. This option can be used to save some typing effort for long option names.

- `base.dir`: (NULL; character) An absolute directory under which the plots are generated.

- `base.url`: (NULL; character) The base URL of images on HTML pages.

- `concordance`: (FALSE; logical) Whether to write a concordance file to map the output line numbers to the input line numbers. This enables one to navigate from the output to the input, and can be helpful especially when a TeX error occurs. This feature is only for `.Rnw` documents, and implemented in RStudio.

- `eval.after`: ('fig.cap'; character) A character vector of option names. These options will be evaluated *after* a chunk has been evaluated, and all other options will be evaluated before a chunk. For example, for `fig.cap = paste('p-value is', t.test(x)$p.value)`, it will be evaluated after the chunk according to the value of `x` if `eval.after = 'fig.cap'`.

- `global.par`: (FALSE; logical) If TRUE, the `par()` settings from the previous code chunk will be preserved and applied to the next code chunk (of course, this only applies to base R graphics). By default, **knitr** opens a new graphical device to record plots and close it after evaluating the code, so `par()` settings will be discarded.

- `header`: (NULL; character) The text to be inserted into the output document before the document begins (e.g., after `\documentclass{article}` in LaTeX, or after `<head>` in HTML). This is useful for defining commands and styles in the LaTeX preamble or HTML header. The beginning of document is found using the pattern defined in `knitr::knit_patterns$get('document.begin')`. This option is only for `.Rnw` and `.Rhtml` documents.

- `latex.options.color`, `latex.options.graphicx` (NULL): Options for the LaTeX packages **color** and **graphicx**, respectively. These options are only for `.Rnw` documents.

- `out.format`: (NULL; character) Possible values are `latex`, `sweave`, `html`, markdown, and `jekyll`. It will be automatically determined based on the input file, and this option will affect the set of hooks to be set (see `?knitr::render_latex` for example). Note this option has to be set *before* `knitr::knit()` runs (it will not work if you set it inside the document).

- `progress`: (TRUE; logical) Whether to display a progress bar when running `knitr::knit()`.

- `root.dir`: (NULL; character) The root directory when evaluating code chunks. If NULL, the directory of the input document will be used.

- `self.contained`: (TRUE; logical) Whether the output document should be self-contained (TeX styles to be written in the `.tex` document, and CSS styles to be written in the `.html` document). This option only applies to `.Rnw` and `.Rhtml` documents.

- `unnamed.chunk.label`: (unnamed-chunk; character) The label prefix for un-named chunks.

- `upload.fun`: (identity; function) A function that takes a file path, pro-cesses the file, and returns a character string when the output format is HTML or Markdown. Typically, it is a function to upload an image and return the link to the image, e.g., `knitr::opts_knit$set(upload.fun = knitr::imgur_upload)` can upload a file to http://imgur.com (see `?knitr::imgur_upload`).

- `verbose`: (FALSE; logical) Whether to show verbose information (e.g., R code in each chunk and message logs), or only show chunk labels and op-tions.

Bibliography

Adler, D. and Murdoch, D. (2020). *rgl: 3D Visualization Using OpenGL*. R package version 0.100.54.

Allaire, J. (2019). *rsconnect: Deployment Interface for R Markdown Documents and Shiny Applications*. R package version 0.8.16.

Allaire, J., Iannone, R., and Xie, Y. (2020a). *distill: R Markdown Format for Scientific and Technical Writing*. R package version 0.8.

Allaire, J., Xie, Y., McPherson, J., Luraschi, J., Ushey, K., Atkins, A., Wickham, H., Cheng, J., Chang, W., and Iannone, R. (2020b). *rmarkdown: Dynamic Documents for R*. R package version 2.3.2.

Allaire, J., Xie, Y., R Foundation, Wickham, H., Journal of Statistical Software, Vaidyanathan, R., Association for Computing Machinery, Boettiger, C., Elsevier, Broman, K., Mueller, K., Quast, B., Pruim, R., Marwick, B., Wickham, C., Keyes, O., Yu, M., Emaasit, D., Onkelinx, T., Gasparini, A., Desautels, M.-A., Leutnant, D., MDPI, Taylor and Francis, Öğreden, O., Hance, D., Nüst, D., Uvesten, P., Campitelli, E., Muschelli, J., Kamvar, Z. N., Ross, N., Cannoodt, R., Luguern, D., and Kaplan, D. M. (2020c). *rticles: Article Formats for R Markdown*. R package version 0.14.

Attali, D. (2016). *ezknitr: Avoid the Typical Working Directory Pain When Using knitr*. R package version 0.6.

Barnier, J. (2020). *rmdformats: HTML Output Formats and Templates for rmarkdown Documents*. R package version 0.3.7.

Barrett, M. (2020). *ggdag: Analyze and Create Elegant Directed Acyclic Graphs*. R package version 0.2.2.

Blischak, J., Carbonetto, P., and Stephens, M. (2020). *workflowr: A Framework for Reproducible and Collaborative Data Science*. R package version 1.6.2.

Blischak, J. D., Carbonetto, P., and Stephens, M. (2019). Creating and sharing reproducible research code the workflowr way [version 1; peer review: 3 approved]. *F1000Research*, 8(1749).

Bodwin, K. and Glanz, H. (2020).   *flair: Highlight, Annotate, and Format Your R Source Code.*   https://github.com/kbodwin/flair, https://kbodwin.github.io/flair/index.html.

Boettiger, C. (2019). *knitcitations: Citations for Knitr Markdown Files.* R package version 1.0.10.

Chang, W. (2019). *webshot: Take Screenshots of Web Pages.* R package version 0.5.2.

Cheng, J., Mastny, T., Iannone, R., Schloerke, B., and Sievert, C. (2020). *sass: Syntactically Awesome Style Sheets (Sass).* R package version 0.2.0.

D'Agostino McGowan, L. and Bryan, J. (2020).   *googledrive: An Interface to Google Drive.* R package version 1.0.1.

Dahl, D. B., Scott, D., Roosen, C., Magnusson, A., and Swinton, J. (2019). *xtable: Export Tables to LaTeX or HTML.* R package version 1.8-4.

Daróczi, G. and Tsegelskyi, R. (2018). *pander: An R Pandoc Writer.* R package version 0.6.3.

El Hattab, H. and Allaire, J. (2017). *revealjs: R Markdown Format for reveal.js Presentations.* R package version 0.9.

Garbett, S. (2020). *tangram: The Grammar of Tables.* R package version 0.7.1.

Garmonsway, D. (2020). *govdown: GOV.UK Style Templates for R Markdown.* R package version 0.9.1.

Gohel, D. (2020a). *flextable: Functions for Tabular Reporting.* R package version 0.5.10.

Gohel, D. (2020b). *officer: Manipulation of Microsoft Word and PowerPoint Documents.* R package version 0.3.12.

Gohel, D. and Ross, N. (2020). *officedown: Enhanced R Markdown Format for Word and PowerPoint.* R package version 0.1.0.

Hlavac, M. (2018). *stargazer: Well-Formatted Regression and Summary Statistics Tables.* R package version 5.2.2.

Hugh-Jones, D. (2020). *huxtable: Easily Create and Style Tables for LaTeX, HTML and Other Formats.* R package version 5.0.0.

Iannone, R. (2020). *DiagrammeR: Graph/Network Visualization*. R package version 1.0.6.1.

Iannone, R., Allaire, J., and Borges, B. (2020a). *flexdashboard: R Markdown Format for Flexible Dashboards*. R package version 0.5.2.

Iannone, R. and Cheng, J. (2020). *blastula: Easily Send HTML Email Messages*. R package version 0.3.2.

Iannone, R., Cheng, J., and Schloerke, B. (2020b). *gt: Easily Create Presentation-Ready Display Tables*. R package version 0.2.1.

Lawrence, M. (2019). *cairoDevice: Embeddable Cairo Graphics Device Driver*. R package version 2.28.

Lin, G. (2020). *reactable: Interactive Data Tables Based on React Table*. R package version 0.2.0.

Luraschi, J. and Allaire, J. (2018). *r2d3: Interface to D3 Visualizations*. R package version 0.2.3.

Luraschi, J., de Vries, A., and Kallin, D. (2020). *nomnoml: Sassy UML Diagrams*. R package version 0.2.0.

Mattioni Maturana, F. (2020). *downloadthis: Implement Download Buttons in rmarkdown*. R package version 0.2.0.

Moon, K.-W. (2018). *ztable: Zebra-Striped Tables in LaTeX and HTML Formats*. R package version 0.2.0.

Murdoch, D. (2020). *tables: Formula-Driven Table Generation*. R package version 0.9.3.

Müller, K. (2017). *here: A Simpler Way to Find Your Files*. R package version 0.1.

Müller, K. and Walthert, L. (2020). *styler: Non-Invasive Pretty Printing of R Code*. R package version 1.3.2.

Nutter, B. (2020). *pixiedust: Tables so Beautifully Fine-Tuned You Will Believe It's Magic*. R package version 0.9.0.

Oller Moreno, S. (2020). *condformat: Conditional Formatting in Data Frames*. R package version 0.9.0.

Ooms, J. (2018). *gifski: Highest Quality GIF Encoder*. R package version 0.8.6.

Ooms, J. (2020). *magick: Advanced Graphics and Image-Processing in R*. R package version 2.4.0.

Ooms, J. and Hester, J. (2019). *spelling: Tools for Spell Checking in R*. R package version 2.1.

Owen, J. (2018). *rhandsontable: Interface to the Handsontable.js Library*. R package version 0.3.7.

Pedersen, T. L. and Robinson, D. (2020). *gganimate: A Grammar of Animated Graphics*. R package version 1.0.6.

R Core Team (2020). *R: A Language and Environment for Statistical Computing*. R Foundation for Statistical Computing, Vienna, Austria.

Ren, K. and Russell, K. (2016). *formattable: Create Formattable Data Structures*. R package version 0.2.0.1.

Robinson, D., Hayes, A., and Couch, S. (2020). *broom: Convert Statistical Objects into Tidy Tibbles*. R package version 0.7.0.

Schloerke, B., Allaire, J., and Borges, B. (2020). *learnr: Interactive Tutorials for R*. R package version 0.10.1.

Sharpsteen, C. and Bracken, C. (2020). *tikzDevice: R Graphics Output in LaTeX Format*. R package version 0.12.3.1.

Sjoberg, D. D., Hannum, M., Whiting, K., and Zabor, E. C. (2020). *gtsummary: Presentation-Ready Data Summary and Analytic Result Tables*. R package version 1.3.2.

Soetaert, K. (2017). *diagram: Functions for Visualising Simple Graphs (Networks), Plotting Flow Diagrams*. R package version 1.6.4.

Stephens, J., Simonov, K., Xie, Y., Dong, Z., Wickham, H., Horner, J., reikoch, Beasley, W., O'Connor, B., and Warnes, G. R. (2020). *yaml: Methods to Convert R Data to YAML and Back*. R package version 2.2.1.

Textor, J. and van der Zander, B. (2016). *dagitty: Graphical Analysis of Structural Causal Models*. R package version 0.2-2.

Urbanek, S. and Horner, J. (2020). *Cairo: R Graphics Device using Cairo Graphics Library for Creating High-Quality Bitmap (PNG, JPEG, TIFF), Vector (PDF, SVG, PostScript) and Display (X11 and Win32) Output*. R package version 1.5-12.2.

Ushey, K., Allaire, J., and Tang, Y. (2020). *reticulate: Interface to Python*. R package version 1.16.

Wickham, H. and Bryan, J. (2020). *usethis: Automate Package and Project Setup*. R package version 1.6.1.

Wickham, H., Chang, W., Henry, L., Pedersen, T. L., Takahashi, K., Wilke, C., Woo, K., Yutani, H., and Dunnington, D. (2020a). *ggplot2: Create Elegant Data Visualisations Using the Grammar of Graphics*. R package version 3.3.2.

Wickham, H., Danenberg, P., Csárdi, G., and Eugster, M. (2020b). *roxygen2: In-Line Documentation for R*. R package version 7.1.1.

Wickham, H. and Grolemund, G. (2016). *R for Data Science*. O'Reilly Media, Inc.

Wickham, H., Henry, L., Pedersen, T. L., Luciani, T. J., Decorde, M., and Lise, V. (2020c). *svglite: An SVG Graphics Device*. R package version 1.2.3.2.

Wickham, H. and Hesselberth, J. (2020). *pkgdown: Make Static HTML Documentation for a Package*. R package version 1.5.1.

Xie, Y. (2015). *Dynamic Documents with R and knitr*. Chapman and Hall/CRC, Boca Raton, Florida, 2nd edition. ISBN 978-1498716963.

Xie, Y. (2016). *bookdown: Authoring Books and Technical Documents with R Markdown*. Chapman and Hall/CRC, Boca Raton, Florida. ISBN 978-1138700109.

Xie, Y. (2017). *printr: Automatically Print R Objects to Appropriate Formats According to the knitr Output Format*. R package version 0.1.

Xie, Y. (2019a). *formatR: Format R Code Automatically*. R package version 1.7.

Xie, Y. (2019b). Tinytex: A lightweight, cross-platform, and easy-to-maintain latex distribution based on tex live. *TUGboat*, (1):30–32.

Xie, Y. (2020a). *animation: A Gallery of Animations in Statistics and Utilities to Create Animations*. R package version 2.6.1.

Xie, Y. (2020b). *blogdown: Create Blogs and Websites with R Markdown*. R package version 0.20.

Xie, Y. (2020c). *bookdown: Authoring Books and Technical Documents with R Markdown*. R package version 0.20.2.

Xie, Y. (2020d). *knitr: A General-Purpose Package for Dynamic Report Generation in R*. R package version 1.29.4.

Xie, Y. (2020e). *tinytex: Helper Functions to Install and Maintain TeX Live, and Compile LaTeX Documents*. R package version 0.25.

Xie, Y. (2020f). *xaringan: Presentation Ninja*. R package version 0.16.1.

Xie, Y. (2020g). *xfun: Miscellaneous Functions by Yihui Xie*. R package version 0.16.1.

Xie, Y., Allaire, J., and Grolemund, G. (2018). *R Markdown: The Definitive Guide*. Chapman and Hall/CRC, Boca Raton, Florida. ISBN 9781138359338.

Xie, Y., Cheng, J., and Tan, X. (2020a). *DT: A Wrapper of the JavaScript Library DataTables*. R package version 0.14.

Xie, Y., Hill, A. P., and Thomas, A. (2017). *blogdown: Creating Websites with R Markdown*. Chapman and Hall/CRC, Boca Raton, Florida. ISBN 978-0815363729.

Xie, Y., Lesur, R., and Thorne, B. (2020b). *pagedown: Paginate the HTML Output of R Markdown with CSS for Print*. R package version 0.10.

Zhu, H. (2019). *kableExtra: Construct Complex Table with kable and Pipe Syntax*. R package version 1.1.0.

Index

Milton Keynes UK
Ingram Content Group UK Ltd.
UKHW031533071024
449327UK00005B/84